Marcel's Letters

Marcel's Letters

A FONT AND THE SEARCH
FOR ONE MAN'S FATE

CAROLYN PORTER

Skyhorse Publishing

Skyhorse Publishing books may be purchased in bulk at special discounts for sales promotion, corporate gifts, fund-raising, or educational purposes. Special editions can also be created to specifications. For details, contact the Special Sales Department, Skyhorse Publishing, 307 West 36th Street, 11th Floor, New York, NY 10018 or info@ skyhorsepublishing.com.

Skyhorse® and Skyhorse Publishing® are registered trademarks of Skyhorse Publishing, Inc.®, a Delaware corporation.

Visit our website at www.skyhorsepublishing.com.

10 9 8 7 6 5 4 3 2 1

Library of Congress Cataloging in Publication Control Number: 2017001221.

Cover design by Erin Seaward-Hiatt

Print ISBN: 978-1-5107-1933-0
Ebook ISBN: 978-1-5107-1934-7

Printed in the United States of America

To Aaron, *Mon Chéri*

"Maybe it was on a list somewhere, the name,
where I come from and so on.
But in the camp no names were used."

—STEPAN SAIKA, SURVIVOR

Chapter One

White Bear Lake, Minnesota

July 2011

As I lifted the nearly weightless pages off my desk, I was surprised to realize I had forgotten so many things. The decades-old paper felt simultaneously soft and brittle. The ink had faded to a brackish gray. Tiny tears and wrinkles created a feather-like ruff along the edges. Translucent blue grid lines filled the background of one yellowed page. A papermaker's watermark was embedded into the fibers of another. It seemed impossible I could have forgotten how the handwriting went to the very edge of some pages, and that watery blue and red stripes had been brushed across the background of others.

My eyebrows arched. *How could I have forgotten about the postage stamps bearing Hitler's profile?*

Yet I intimately knew the alphabet of letters that filled these five pages. The roundness of each curve, the width and angle of each straight letterstroke: every nick and loop of this writing was as familiar as my own.

No. I corrected myself. *I knew this handwriting better.*

I turned the top letter over and skimmed past paragraphs I could not read, until my eye landed on the flourished signature in the bottom corner: Marcel. The *l* looped backward to form a proud, angled line underneath his name. I tried to recall how long these letters had been pressed flat inside the sketchbook in my office closet. *Had it been two years? Four? More?*

I carefully set the letter down and looked at the next piece of paper. The small postcard had been mailed from Berlin to a place called Berchères-la-Maingot. The blotchy cancellation mark read 1944. "*Sprache Französische*" had been scrawled in tiny cursive along the top edge. Armed with a single year of high school German, I guessed that said "written in French."

As I set the postcard down, I focused on the letter that had seized my attention all those years ago. It wasn't even the entire letter, actually. It was *one* letter: the *M*. The left stem of the *M* in the greeting "*Mes chères petites*" swept far to the side and ended with a sweet little loop.

The affection infused into that greeting was undeniable, yet I did not know precisely what that meant. *My dear? My little darling?*

The thought was fleeting, but definitive: *I should translate one letter.* After all this time, it would be interesting to find out what "*Mes chères petites*" actually meant. And even if the letter didn't say anything interesting, I might learn who Marcel was, and why his letters had been mailed from Berlin to France during the depths of World War II.

Aaron and I ate dinner in the living room as we watched the evening news. He sat on the couch; I sat on the chair, as if we had assigned seats. The tsunami in Japan had been four months earlier, but the story still made headlines because of the leaking radiation. Protests in Egypt and Libya were gaining attention as stories about bin Laden, who had been killed two months earlier, had started to fade.

"What's your plan for the evening?" I asked.

Aaron looked gray and spent from long shifts at the hospital, so I did not expect he would do anything other than watch television. He nestled deeper into the couch, confirming my guess. "You?"

I nodded in the direction of my office. I had been freelancing out of a home office for nearly ten years. Tidying up the day's loose ends had become a familiar after-dinner activity.

"I'll take Hoover out later," I promised, hoping the day's blistering temperature would dip low enough to safely take our old black-furred retriever out for a walk.

An hour or so later, after wrapping up client work, I slid Marcel's five letters to the center of my desk. Spending time on personal projects was my reward for a long day; a creative respite from routine tasks. And working on personal projects only after paying work was done allowed me to keep the promise I made to Aaron long ago.

That morning, I had decided not to return the letters to their home, pressed flat under the cover of the sketchbook in my office closet. All day, the five handwritten letters lay on my desk, intermittently covered and uncovered as I cycled through project paperwork.

Instead of opening the font file, I decided to pursue that morning's curiosity and find out what Marcel's letter said. I moved the letter with the beautiful swash *M* in front of me, and typed the first sentence into a website that provided free French-to-English translation. *C'est aujour cl'hui, le printemps, et il fait un temps superbe, cet apris midi, Moutardier cloit venir me voir, en l'attendant, je reponds a votre gentille petite lettre qui m a fait beaucoup plaiser.* The translation read: "It is cl today, the spring, and the weather is beautiful, this learned midi, successive dentals end must come to see me, in the meantime, I am responding to your sweet little letter which m has done much plaiser."

My shoulders sank. I had purchased the letters because I knew Marcel's cursive handwriting would make a beautiful font, but deciphering his writing as *words* rather than individual letters was a challenge. Lowercase *s*'s looked similar to *i*'s; *e*'s looked like *o*'s. And since I did not know French, I could not tell whether I was interpreting the words correctly.

The next sentence resulted in an equally garbled, worthless translation. I shook my head, stood up, and returned the letters to the sketchbook in the closet.

I settled back into my chair and rolled to face the two large side-by-side computer monitors. As the font file opened, a familiar grid of tiny black letters appeared. I opened the Preview Panel—the window that allowed me to view and test strings of letters or whole words—and stared at the blank screen. I positioned my hands over the keyboard and slowly typed the only words that came to mind: *Mes chères petites.*

As I scrutinized the grave over the *è* and the sweeping lead-in stroke of the *p,* I decided to have one letter professionally translated. Throwing away hard-earned money on a translation I did not *need* to read just to satiate a curiosity was folly, an impractical waste of money. I understood the translation might not serve any purpose other than providing a momentary diversion from the seemingly endless rounds of tweaks and revisions. But after being reminded of the letters' raw beauty—full of color and texture and history—my curiosity had been piqued.

The next day I began to search for a translator. Most of the translation service providers I found seemed to be brokers who sent documents *who knew where* to be translated by *who knew whom.* I preferred to find someone local. It even crossed my mind to hire a college student who might work for a case of beer, though—as I envisioned the Hitler stamps—I decided it would be prudent to find someone who would provide a bit more discretion.

"I am a local graphic designer," I wrote to names on a list of potential translation vendors provided by a French language school in Minneapolis. "I have a handwritten letter from World War II that I would like to have translated. It is two pages long. I can pick out a few words, including Paris and cinema, and a reference to 1,300 kilometers."

Responses trickled in. One person's curt email just listed a per-word translation rate. Another person expressed interest, but the error-filled email did not bolster confidence in the quality of his work.

The email that caught my attention was from a man named Tom. "A personal letter will be a nice break from the birth certificates and academic records that are the bulk of my translation work," he wrote. "I will need to see the letter to give you an accurate quote. Price depends on word count and vocabulary. Please scan and email the letter to this address. I will, of course, treat it confidentially." I appreciated Tom's fair approach to pricing, and took comfort in his proactive promise of confidentiality.

I retrieved the sketchbook from the closet and withdrew the letter with the big, beautiful *M.* The surface of the tissue-thin yellowed paper had a faint ribbed texture. One corner was dog-eared. The ink had probably once been black, though it was now a faded gray-brown. The sheet of paper had a distinct horizontal crease across the center; I assumed that meant it had been folded in half before being placed inside some long-lost envelope. Watery, parallel blue and red stripes—proud colors of the French flag—extended down the entire page. At least, I guessed the stripe had once been red; it had faded to a rosy pink. The numbers 4220 were jotted in pencil near the top. I tried to recall whether that had been some inventory number scribbled by the antique shop where I purchased the letters.

The handwriting in this letter was neater and larger than the writing on any of the other letters. It was as if Marcel had written slowly and taken the utmost care. Some lines had as few as five words; other lines had seven or eight.

After scanning the front and back, I emailed the files to Tom. He outlined his price, sixty dollars, and an estimated turnaround time before summarizing the content: "It is a sweet, loving letter from a lonely father to his daughters."

My head snapped back. *It's to children?*

All these years I assumed the letters had been from a man to a woman. *I had hoped for romance!* I had imagined the flourished greeting was followed by confessions of affection from a heartsick soldier to a faraway girlfriend. Or that the page had been filled by a husband, resting between military maneuvers, lavishing his wife with words of love. It had never once crossed my mind it might be a letter from a father to children, though the large, careful writing now made sense.

Despite the twang of disappointment, I approved Tom's estimate. I confirmed his suggested turnaround time of a couple of weeks was fine, and assured him a check would go out in the next day's mail. If nothing else, I figured, I would learn a thing or two about the man whose handwriting I knew so well.

Marienfelde le dimanche

21 mars à trois heures

Vous direz à maman, qu'aujourd'hui se mange
les derniers haricots, qu'elle fait en envoyer
d'autres. Bons baisers de Papa à tous

Mes chères petites

C'est aujourd'hui, le printemps, et
il fait un temps superbe, cet
après midi, Moutardier doit venir
me voir, en l'attendant, je réponds
à votre gentille petite lettre, qui
m'a fait beaucoup plaisir. Avant
de vous écrire, j'ai fait ma lessive,
une fois qu'elle sera sèche, j'aurai
pas mal de travail, pour la
raccommoder. Il faudrait bien que
j'ai l'une de vous deux avec moi.
Comme je vois au mardi gras, vous
avez dû bien vous amuser, je pense
que vous n'avez pas fait peur à
Lily ou à la petite Jacqueline.
De ce temps là vous devez aller
cueillir des violettes au bois Billé

Marienfelde, Germany

March 21

Sunday at three o'clock

You can tell Mom that today I'm eating the last of the beans and that she can send some more. Love and kisses from Papa to everyone.

My dear little girls,

Today it's springtime and the weather is excellent. This afternoon Moutardier should come to see me, so while waiting for him I'll reply to your very kind letter, which pleased me very much. Before writing to you I did my laundry. Once it's dry I will have quite a bit of mending to do. It would be great to have one of you two with me.

So I see that you had a good time at Mardi Gras. I hope that you didn't scare Lily or little Jacqueline. In the meantime you should go pick violets in the Billé woods.

This morning I had some bad luck. While combing my hair, my comb broke in my hand. You can tell Mom that she can send me another one.

Denise, I would like to receive a letter from you, so you can tell me what you did in Montreuil. Did you go to the movies with Mom? Did you go shopping by yourself?

And what about you, Suzanne? Were you the one getting the milk and bread while Mom was in Paris? As for Lily, I'm glad that she's no longer sucking her thumb. I recommend that she doesn't pick the blossoms from the cherry tree or the pear trees. She should wait until the fruit is ripe.

My dear little ones I don't have much else to tell you today. I recommend that you be on your best behavior.

Please give my love to your mother, hug her a lot, and the same for Grandma too. Your Papa who sends his love from 1,300 kilometers away. Your Papa who thinks about you all the time.

Papa

Chapter Two

White Bear Lake, Minnesota

August 2011

"It's heartbreaking to hear how much he missed his girls," I wrote to Tom. I could not tell his daughters' ages. Lily and Jacqueline sounded quite young. Denise and Suzanne sounded older, though I could not determine who was oldest. *How old would someone be to fetch milk on her own? Twelve? Thirteen?* "It makes me even more curious to know why he was so far away from his family," I wrote.

Marcel did not sound like a soldier; a soldier should not have to buy his own beans. He did not sound like a businessman either; a businessman would have been able to buy a comb. And it seemed unlikely a businessman would be wearing clothes that needed so much mending. *But if he hadn't been a soldier or a businessman, why had he been in Berlin?*

Tom messaged back immediately. He had only seen the March 21 date, not a year, and wondered whether Marcel might have worked in Berlin's French sector after the war.

I retrieved the other letters from the sketchbook and examined them for dates and clues. The other letters had been written in 1943 and 1944, so I reviewed an online calendar for springtime Sundays that were the 21st. March 21, 1943, had been a Sunday—the only March 21 that fell on a Sunday between 1937 and 1948, so 1943 seemed to be a safe bet. But that meant Marcel had written the letter two years *before* the war's end.

Could he have been a prisoner of war? The thought made me gasp.

I typed "Marienfelde" into a search engine. The first article to appear outlined Marienfelde's history as the site of a refugee center for East Germans escaping to the west. *Had Marcel been a refugee?* But, then I read the refugee camp did not open until 1953, a full decade after he had written the letter.

The days that followed were busy with client work, but questions swirled in the back of my mind: *Why had Marcel been in Berlin? How long had he been there? How did his letters end up in an antique store in Stillwater, Minnesota?*

It would take years to understand why Marcel's letters secured a place inside of me as they did. The connection had been immediate. Unequivocal. Marcel's words to his daughters were like fishing hooks that curled into muscle and skin. Men writing tender expressions of love did not exist in my world, and the affection Marcel showed his family was undeniably enchanting. Intoxicating, even.

When Tom agreed to translate a second letter, I reviewed the remaining pages to determine which one to send next. I chose the longest letter, figuring the volume meant it would be most likely to hold answers. The letter was a single piece of paper folded in half vertically to create four pages. I presumed Tom would want to see a scan to quote a price, so I carefully straightened the corners and scanned the front, then the interior left, then the interior right, then the back.

Some aspects were similar to the first letter. The page was the same size—about 5.5" by 8". Stripes of blue and red had been brushed across the page, though instead of running vertically, these were at an angle, and in places the thick paint made Marcel's writing nearly indecipherable. A second, horizontal crease indicated this letter had been folded in half, too.

Differences existed: this paper was thicker, whiter, and a papermaker's watermark made it feel like official stationery. The ink was blue, not gray-brown, and the writing was considerably smaller. In places, three or four words fit in an inch of space. And each line of text went to the very edge, as though Marcel wanted to make use of every precious fragment of space.

I was about to email the scans to Tom, but stopped and let out a long sigh.

Then I deleted the first scan from the email.

I opened the original scan in Photoshop and magnified the upper left-hand corner. Using one of Photoshop's retouching tools, I carefully eliminated every trace of a small, hand-drawn swastika.

On the day I had bought the letters, the handwriting's loops and curves were all that mattered. The odd little swastika had not been important. Not that it wasn't *important*, but it didn't factor as a reason to buy, or not buy, the letter it was on. To me, the wobbly, intertwined lines were a relic of the era, no different than the Hitler stamps or the cancellation mark from Berlin. But after reading Marcel's loving words, the swastika now made me confused and uncomfortable—especially since it appeared to be in his handwriting. Marcel no longer felt like just a name—he was a man whose daughters picked violets and went to Mardi Gras. A man who sent love and kisses from afar. It was as if Marcel were on a piece of photographic paper slowly being swished back and forth in a bath of developing chemicals. The image had not yet started to appear, but I did not want the swastika to be the only thing to become visible.

After Tom received the email with the retouched scan, he provided an estimate of $320. I was displeased about the expense, but I approved it. I had been unable to get Marcel out of my mind, and I hoped this letter would answer all my questions. I wanted to put this folly—put Marcel—aside and get back to client work. Practical, paying client work.

Ten days later, Tom sent an email asking whether anything had been cut off of the scans. My heart lurched. *How could he have known about the swastika?* But, it turned out, he was referring to something else. He wondered whether I mixed up the page order or if I might have cut off a line when I scanned the pages. The sentences spanning the page breaks did not make sense; he had even tried switching the page order. With the exception of the swastika—which I still did not mention—I was confident the scan showed everything. *Might another piece of paper have been folded in the middle?* That scenario did not make sense either because the writing on the front page should have continued on to the backside of the same piece of paper.

I told Tom I did not have an answer.

Z pour la classe et à la volonté
de dieu. Bons baisers à tous de
Papa qui pense beaucoup à vous. 18/17

Papa

Ma petite chérie.

Aujourd'hui, dimanche, il est une heure et demie
et je suis dans la baraque, avec Marcel, mimile et Bernard
on ne sais pas quoi faire, aussi avec Marcel, on se
décide à écrire. Il fait un sale temps, par moment un
beau soleil, qui serait bien engageant pour nous
inciter à aller se ballader, mais quelques minutes après
il tombe de la neige. J'avais envie d'aller au cinéma,
et puis, comme on n'est pas sur d'avoir un billet, je
suis resté là. Mimile est au coin du feu, comme un vieux
grand père, il nous chante la chanson du maçon de
Maurice Chevalier. Tout à l'heure il y a un match de
foot ball, derrière le camp, si le temps se maintient, j'irai
y faire un petit tour. Hier je t'ai écris une carte,
seulement la postière n'était pas disposée à travailler, et
quand je suis allé à la poste pour mettre les lettres, elle
était déjà partie. comme cela le courrier ne partira que
lundi après midi. Il y a quelques permissionnaires de
rentrés, ils disent qu'à Paris ils ont su que les
permissions étaient supprimées, je suis bien content comme

Marienfelde, Germany

Sunday the 12th

Ł for the class and by the will of God. Hugs and kisses from Papa who thinks about you a lot. Papa

My darling,

Today, Sunday, it is one-thirty and I am in the barracks with Marcel, Mimile and Bernard. We don't know what to do, so with Marcel we decide to write. The weather is terrible, one minute some beautiful sun that invites us to go for a walk, but a few minutes later it starts snowing. I wanted to go to the movies but then, because we're not sure we can get tickets, I stayed here. Mimile is in the corner by the fire, like an old grandfather, and he sings to us, the Song of the Mason by Maurice Chevalier. In a little while there will be a soccer game behind the camp. If the weather holds I'll go for a walk over there. Yesterday I sent you a card but the mail lady didn't feel like working, and when I went to the post office to mail the letters, she was already gone. So the mail won't go out until Monday afternoon. Some guys who were on leave have come back, and they said that in Paris they learned that their leaves were canceled. I'm quite happy

[1–2 page break]

at the same place, too bad for those who are lower on the list. The last one happened Wednesday, they demolished a bar about four kilometers from camp, a funny piece of work. Since then we sleep nice and quiet. Besides that, there's not much news. Oh yes, today is the twelfth, exactly 14 months since I started working at Daimler, and today they were supposed to give us some tobacco, but they stuck their tongues out at us, another exercise to lighten our pocketbooks. Too bad that will be for next Sunday. Yesterday I received a letter from the boss, that's depressing, all the letters I get say that they are waiting impatiently for me. That gets me down, growing two weeks older, but I shouldn't think about that too much anymore. Okay enough with all the drama. Spring is here, and this year the gardens are in early. Will you be able to easily find a hired man, and did you get the trees put back in the garden? And what about the little plum trees that we put in at the beginning, will I maybe have the honor of eating some plums this year? I also received a letter from Dad. He says the peaches are still waiting for me. When I go there the weather will be nicer than it is now, and I will be able to tease the little fish a bit in the ferns and also in the pond at Gommier. As for me, you see, they thought that by this time there wouldn't be much in the gardens and we wouldn't be able to easily find food. I'll stop here because I can't think of anything else to tell you. I'll leave my letter here but will return to it tonight. Today it's me who is

[2–3 page break]

this you can see that I'm not making this up. For the past week we've been living the good life. I should explain a little bit. In the square there's a guy from Amiens who has some tricks to get food. You can imagine how we are three big mouths, Mimile, Marcel, and me, we are served. It's the wallet that finds this the funniest, because a one thousand bill only represents a little more than one kilo of bread. Yesterday we ate one kilo of cake, which was worth much more than one simple crêpe with blackberry jam. Actually that fills the stomach all the same. Speaking of crêpes, I decided to make some, since a friend gave me some flour. There you go just a little flour and water, with nothing to cook them with, funny looking crêpes. I also have to tell you about how I got a work suit yesterday. The work office gave them to us, but you should see me with, just imagine, the heavy fabric to wash like what we had before the war, and the same color, it's made in Poland. All the French here will be wearing the same thing, just like the Russians who got them, so that now we won't be able to tell each other apart. Let's talk a little about the alerts. Our paper, the brave Écho de Nancy, talks about that, like a nice little tall tale, what a funny farce. Certainly they mistook the planes for crows. At the factory they told us that when the sirens go off, we can do as we please. Also you will see how we act like crazy little kids in the country because now they drop a whole bunch

[3–4 page break]

I will tell you what I did to them. I forgot to tell you that this is the first Sunday I'm spending in the square, because up until now I was working on Sundays. So this morning I took advantage of it, I got up at 9 o'clock. I started to read a nice book, but it got me dizzy because it was only talking about eating and beautiful women, all the things that are not allowed. I'll write more tonight, because if I continue now I'll run out of room. I sorted through my mail. I tossed all my letters because when we leave here, I'll have to leave them at the border. Here's a big kiss while waiting for tonight. We're going to the game. Mimile says he's going to send you the holes in his socks, so what can I say. I think the censor guy will have some work to do. Okay now I'm writing again after having eaten. I made them a blanquette of veal with the veal bones that a friend gave me, and a small piece of lard, we stuffed ourselves, with potatoes, not with meat. Mimile acted like a dog, going after the bones. At the moment he's doing the dishes but not like Tommy. The sun was shining bright when we were leaving for the soccer game so I made a crease in my pants. That didn't last long, not the crease, the sun, so Marcel and I came back at halftime because we were cold.

    I don't have much else to tell you for today. I'm going to go to bed and continue reading my book. You see I am reasonable, it is ten minutes before eight. I'll bet my daughters are not yet in bed. Are they still arguing with you about their bedtime? When I come back they will have a hard time with that.

Meanwhile we can talk a bit to try to get the compensation for the accident, because I think that after 14 months they should think about paying us. For the moment I would really like if it were already tomorrow evening at the mailbox. I don't get much news these days. Please give a big hello to Mr. and Mrs. Gommier and the little Jacqueline, she's walking by herself now. Do they have any good news from Daniel? Today I thought about Mrs. Jumentier and Mrs. Leduc, I don't know why. Please tell them hello from me also. My little treasure, I will end my letter due to lack of space. Kiss my little daughters for me, as well as our dear mother. Your big guy who loves you with all his heart, and sends you his best love and kisses.

Marcel

Chapter Three

White Bear Lake, Minnesota

September 2011

I read the translated text, then read it again. Then I printed it out, walked into the living room, and read it to Aaron.

"Not what you were expecting, huh?" he said.

I tried to make sense of the information. Marcel used the words "barracks" and "camp." He had been there fourteen months. Russians were there. Sirens went off. A guy had tricks to get food. He cooked veal bones. He had been given a uniform.

Yet, despite all that, his letter ended with tenderness. I sighed as I realized this was, in fact, a love letter. It was not the kind of love letter I expected, but it was a love letter. I did not know anything about his wife, but I hoped for Marcel's sake she loved him as much as he loved her.

I took a deep breath and thought of that hand-drawn swastika. *Why would Marcel, who was living in a barrack and mailing letters from Berlin, have drawn a swastika and written, "for the class and by the will of God"? Why would he have written "Hugs and kisses"? The words seemed inappropriately cheerful to be next to a swastika. Could he have been forced to draw it? Would it have helped the letter get past the censor he mentioned?*

I tried imagining a scenario where Marcel might have been sincere, but it seemed impossible. More correctly: I did not *want* it to be possible.

I returned to my office and emailed Tom a note of thanks. He replied immediately, noting how touching he found Marcel's words.

I felt oddly conflicted. Reading Marcel's intimate words felt like an inappropriate violation of privacy. It made me feel like some kind of voyeur. Yet the letter piqued my curiosity, and I yearned to know more.

I typed "Daimler Marienfelde World War II" into a search engine. The first article to appear was on the *Panzerkampfwagen V*—the Panther tank. The Panther, the article stated, was a medium-size German tank known for its combination of firepower and mobility. I skimmed past paragraphs on armor, production counts, ammunition, and transmission and suspension specifications—details I did not care about—until these words caught my eye: "Demand for this tank was so high that manufacturing was soon expanded to include the Daimler-Benz Berlin-Marienfelde plant."

My head snapped back. *Marcel was making tanks? But Marcel was French—not German. Why would he make German tanks?* I stared at my computer monitor, stunned.

I never imagined it could matter to me *where* a tank had been made. But the sentence on Marienfelde was like an invisible string pulling me to Marcel, and I wanted to grab hold and pull until I had answers.

"You coming to bed?" I jumped when I heard Aaron's voice. I had been consumed by the article on Panther tanks and had not noticed he was leaning on the frame of my office door. I shook my head. It would be hours before I would be able to fall asleep.

"Don't stay up *all* night." He stepped into the office and kissed the top of my head.

I brought a copy of the translation and my laptop into the living room, sat on the couch, and read his letter again. And again. Each time, something different caught my attention: singing in the barrack, reading a book, planes being passed off as crows, an accident that happened fourteen months earlier.

Some passages would not make sense for many months, such as Marcel's reference to "Écho de Nancy." Later, I would learn *L'Écho de Nancy* was a French-language propaganda newspaper published during the war.

Berchères-la-Maingot, the place where his wife and daughters were, filled my imagination. Sometimes I envisioned the older girls, Suzanne and Denise, reading Marcel's letter aloud to Lily and Jacqueline. Other times, I imagined his wife gently whispering his words as the girls slipped into a deep sleep. I envisioned the peach and plum trees, the neighbors who were friends, but not familiar enough to call by their first names.

I pulled up the online calendar again, thinking of Marcel's proclamation, "spring is here." The only springtime Sunday that was also the twelfth was March 12, 1944. Marcel noted he had been there for fourteen months. That fit the timeline if the first letter had, in fact, been from March 1943.

There were so many unknowns, so many questions. I took inventory of what I knew: Marcel's first and last name, the names of his daughters, the address in Berchères-la-Maingot, and that he worked at a Daimler factory in Berlin. I realized I did not even know his wife's name, since he only called her "my darling."

There was only one place to start.

I pulled my laptop close, opened a search engine, and typed his name: M-a-r-c-e-l H-e-u-z-é.

Aaron lay on the couch, watching baseball on television. I sat in the armchair, legs propped on the coffee table, my laptop balanced on my knees. Hoover slept on the floor between us, snoring. It was as exciting as evenings got in our home, with two introverts and an old dog.

I had assumed answers to the basic questions—*Who was Marcel? Did he survive? How long had he been there?*—would be easy to find. But I had searched for weeks and was still seeking the first breadcrumb that would create a trail to Marcel. The only thing I had discovered so far was that "Heuzé" was an uncommon name.

"What's wrong?" Aaron asked.

"What do you mean?" I looked up in surprise.

Without glancing away from the television, he dramatically mimicked the long, slow sigh I had released. I promised to try to contain other loud sighs as I continued scouring search results.

"I think I found something," I eventually whispered.

Aaron did not respond, so I typed "Ravensbrück" into a search engine and read for another fifteen or twenty minutes. When I learned where Ravensbrück had been located, a lump began to form in my throat. It grew so big it felt impossible to swallow.

"I found him." My voice crackled as the words came out.

"Found who?" Aaron still did not turn away from the television.

I looked up over the top of my glasses and almost asked who else he thought I was searching for. "Marcel."

Aaron swiveled his head to look at me. I shook my head and outlined what I found: a French citizen named Marcel Heuzé had been killed April 26, 1945, at the Ravensbrück concentration camp. "April 26 was four days before the camp was liberated. Ravensbrück was only fifty miles from Berlin," I explained. Moments earlier, when I looked at the map and saw how close it was to Berlin, I had the sickening realization that *close* would have also meant *conveniently located*.

"It says Marcel was a pastor." I had been surprised to see that profession listed, but then recalled he had scribbled, "by the will of God," next to the swastika.

"His wife's name was Simone." Simone's death had been listed as "sometime between 1979 and 1993," which meant she had outlived him by at least thirty-four years. I stopped and took a slow, deep breath as a wave of sadness washed over me.

After a long silence, Aaron offered his condolence. He turned back to the television, but a few minutes later he added, "You knew that was probably going to be the outcome, right?"

"I hoped it wasn't."

Ravensbrück had been the Reich's largest concentration camp for women. The 130,000 women who cycled through Ravensbrück represented every country Germany occupied. Beatings, starvation, medical experiments, back-breaking labor, and forced prostitution made Ravens-brück a "special kind of hell."

Yet, nothing I read had explained why Marcel would have been at a women's camp.

A small camp for men had been built adjacent to Ravensbrück's main camp, I eventually learned. For four months in 1945, men gassed the women, then burned their bodies in Ravensbrück's crematorium. Con-sidering the tender words Marcel had written to his wife and daughters, the thought that he might have been responsible for burning the bodies of women and children made my heart feel as if it had been cleaved in two. *How could anyone—especially a pastor—have done that?*

How could he have lived with that?

He didn't, I reminded myself. *Marcel didn't live.* As the reality of the situation soaked in, a thick cloud of grief seemed to settle over me.

The record did not show when Marcel had been transferred to Ravensbrück. I hoped he had only been there minutes, or hours, or days. I hoped he had not been there long enough to work the crematorium, or to witness the murder of thousands of women and children.

Aaron turned my way. "If the Germans hadn't killed him, it's likely we would have, you know."

"Why's that?" My eyebrows soared.

"You told me the factory where he worked made tanks, right? What would be a higher-value military target than a factory making German tanks? We probably bombed the shit out of it," he said with a shrug. "Collateral damage."

I did not say anything, and he turned back to the television. After a few minutes, he added more. "A worst-case scenario would have been if he was still there when the Russians took Berlin. They were ruthless motherfuckers."

I knew he was trying to help me understand, but I wanted him to stop. I did not want to hear another word, yet I felt compelled to ask what he meant. "The Russians suffered under the Germans, right? So, when they took Berlin, they were merciless. If the Russians got him, he might have spent the rest of his miserable life in a coal mine in Siberia." After a few moments, he quietly added, "Ravensbrück could have been a small mercy over the Russians."

I read what some Russians had done when they liberated Ravensbrück. Only three thousand women—those who were too weak to take part in the evacuation march—were still alive when the Russians entered the camp. Many women were raped, even if they were pregnant or were Russian themselves.

"You're not making me feel any better, you know," I said.

Aaron turned back to the television. The game and Hoover's snoring filled the void with sound.

"Can you imagine?" I tried wrapping my head around the situation. "You're working at a factory a thousand miles from the people you love. That factory is making tanks for the Nazis. Those tanks are killing the people who are trying to liberate your country. If the Allies are going to succeed, they need to destroy the factory where you're working."

It was a desperate, no-win situation every way I looked at it.

The next evening, after cleaning up dinner dishes, I headed to my office, and Aaron retreated to the garage to tinker on one of his projects.

After wrapping up the day's unfinished business, I opened the font file and stared at a grid of nearly four hundred rectangles, each one filled with a number, an upper or lowercase letter, or two-letter ligatures such as *Of,* or *Fr,* or *bb.* The font represented so many hours of work. Years of work.

How could I not have known?

Guilt surged through me. After scrutinizing Marcel's handwriting for so many years, it felt as if some *how*—some *way*—I should have known Marcel died. It was as if I expected the fibers in the paper would have transferred that information to the muscle fibers in my fingers when I first held his letters.

I should have known.

I opened the Preview Panel and slowly typed the only word that came to mind: R-a-v-e-n-s-b-r-ü-c-k. The letters looked correct: the *a* looked like an *a,* the *s* looked like an *s.* Yet every curve felt backward, every arc inverted. Seeing that word—the place where Marcel had been killed—written in a font based on his handwriting sent a shiver down my spine.

I rolled my chair backward, rested my elbows on my knees, and knitted my fingers together as the word "Ravensbrück" glowed above me on the screen. Thoughts battled inside my head. *How could I finish the font knowing it was based on the handwriting of someone killed in a concentration camp? But, after all these years, could I abandon the project? Could the font be a testament to Marcel? Was that even appropriate? Could I finish the font and not identify the source?*

I stood up, closed the file, and walked out of the office.

Hoover lay on the living room floor; I stretched out beside him. His tail began to drum the floor as I stroked his silken ears. He was still big and strong, though he rarely chased squirrels or rabbits out of our yard anymore. Instead, he offered dramatic sighs when we disrupted his naps, and grumped disapproval when treats or walks were delayed. But our sweet boy still gave us more love than we could measure.

"Let's go see Daddy," I whispered. Hoover jerked to his feet and trotted to the kitchen door. I slipped on shoes and grabbed one of Aaron's old plaid flannel shirts off a hook on the wall.

The scratchy play-by-play of a baseball game radiated from a radio perched above Aaron's garage workbench. When he saw us walking toward him, he turned the volume down and pushed a metal stool my way. I sat down, wrapping his shirt tight around me.

We chatted for a few minutes, then he turned his attention back to his project. Occasionally, an excited outburst by the announcer filled the void, though to me, his words were like static. I did not tell Aaron about the battle that waged inside my head. The font was my project—my problem—to sort out. Not his.

A numbed sadness filled me for days, though the sadness was confusing. Marcel wasn't family. And intellectually, whenever I bought old handwritten letters, I understood, if not assumed, the person who had written them had long since passed. Perhaps it was because of *where* he died, but the unexpected, complicated grief that was unleashed after learning his fate felt like a lead weight slowing down the beating of my heart. *Fifty million people died in World War II; why did I think Marcel would not have been part of that statistic?*

I needed to see the listing of Marcel's death again to convince myself it was true in the way someone might need to read a medical diagnosis over and over before accepting the result. I returned to the website, which was a registry of Protestants persecuted for their faith. After staring at Marcel's record, I scrolled through page after page of other names. The registry contained exhaustive detail, and once I better understood how the document was organized, I was surprised to realize no children had been listed for Marcel and Simone. It seemed like a significant oversight that Suzanne, Denise, and Lily were not included. (After rereading both letters, I had begun to doubt whether Jacqueline was one of Marcel's daughters; it seemed more likely she was a member of the Gommier family.)

The registry listed Marcel's birth year as 1897, which meant he had been forty-eight when he died—years older than what I had expected. I ran a quick calculation: knowing people often got married younger decades ago, if Marcel had been twenty or twenty-one when he got married, then if they had children right away, and if the girls were twelve or thirteen—old enough to fetch milk on their own—Marcel might have only been thirty-four.

Maybe—*just maybe*—between the age difference and the fact daughters were not listed, this was a different Frenchman named Marcel Heuzé. My heart soared at the possibility.

My Marcel might have lived!

My Marcel. The corners of my mouth curled into a smile when I realized I had thought of him as *my* Marcel.

I smiled even more as I realized this was a second chance to search for—to hope for—a happy ending for *my* Marcel.

Chapter Four

Wisconsin—Texas—Minnesota

1980 to 2011

When I was just ten or eleven, one of my uncles made this suggestion: "When you grow up," he said, "you should get a job at a museum inking tiny inventory numbers onto dinosaur bones." I gazed up at him in wonder. I had never seen a dinosaur bone before, but I liked the idea if that meant people would notice my tidy handwriting.

I had always been fastidious about my handwriting. Posters and class projects would be carefully penciled before I ever dared trace over the words with a marker. In math class, columns of numbers were always precisely aligned. Sometimes I copied English assignments over and over until my longhand looked *just so.*

For my twelfth birthday, my parents gave me a Ken Brown Method Calligraphy Kit. The kit included eight chisel-tip markers filled with a variety of colored inks, practice pages with angled guidelines, and thick sheets of gold and white parchment. The instruction booklet outlined the fourteen individual pen strokes required to master proper Chancery Cursive lettering: vertical and horizontal strokes, top curves used on letters such as *a* or *o*, bottom curves used on letters *u* or *c*.

The words ELEGANT WRITER were screen-printed onto the barrel of each marker in Ken Brown's masterful scrolled lettering. To me, those plastic markers were like magic wands, and holding them in my still-growing hands made me feel ennobled with the gift of beautiful writing. Evenings, after schoolwork was done, and after the ducks and geese and our three sheep were fed and penned for the night, I would sit at our plastic-covered dining room table and compose words using the fourteen pen strokes combined with "swift uplifting movements" for the flared finishing details.

Despite diligent practice, the curves and lines of my letters were never perfect. Or never perfect enough. The felt tips of Ken Brown's markers lacked precise edges, which could result in rough curves and wobbly lines. Often I would write a letter or two, maybe a word, then furiously scribble through the flaws. Other times, I completed a few lines before crumpling the paper and starting over on a fresh sheet. Even at that young age, an unforgiving drive for perfection could rear its ugly head.

For my thirteenth birthday, I received a set of Schaeffer pens with interchangeable metal nibs and disposable ink cartridges. The pens came with an entirely different instruction book, so for months I studied Schaeffer-style lettering. I expected the metal nibs would allow my letters to be smooth and perfect. But they weren't. Imprecision always haunted my curves and lines, and every flaw felt like an amplified reflection of my own imperfections.

The summer before my fourteenth birthday, we butchered the ducks and geese and sold our sheep. My parents traded our home in rural southern Wisconsin—an idyllic place surrounded by vast cornfields and rolling pastures dotted with thick groves of oak trees—for a split-level home in a sprawling suburb of St. Paul, Minnesota. The impossibly cool things in my huge new school—designer jeans and big hair—trumped hand lettering. The Ken Brown Method Calligraphy Kit, gold parchment paper, and the Schaeffer pens remained inside a box tucked underneath my twin bed in the room I shared with my older sister.

Lettering did not cross my mind again until college.

"Letterform" was a fundamental course for graphic design majors. It was the equivalent of a pre-med student studying anatomy, a science major studying calculus. If Letterform students did not show interest in, or sensitivity to, proportion or scale, or could not be bothered with crafts-manship, it was a warning sign they might not be cut out for the graphic design program.

We began by studying typefaces designed by the fifteenth to eigh-teenth-century masters: Claude Garamond, William Caslon, John Bask-erville, Giambattista Bodoni. We learned to identify the surprisingly anatomic-like parts of letters: arms, legs, ears, eyes, tails, shoulders, feet, spines, hairlines. Perhaps that was no coincidence; to a person who loved typography, every nuance in a letter's shape could be as beautiful and as individual as a human body.

After studying classes of typefaces—sans serif, slab serif, Didone, Humanist, Blackletter—our professor sought to reinforce lessons on shape and proportion by having us replicate letters in that style. We would begin each assignment by penciling a grid onto an oversized sheet of thick white paper. Then, we constructed letters, paying exacting atten-tion to the subtleties of curves, the thickness of stems, the lengths of serifs, the vertical placement of crossbars.

The tiniest wobble in a curve, the slightest mismeasurement in the width of a serif, or any inconsistency in the width of a stem were flaws that would incur demerits from Professor DeHoff. He was not being cap-tious—he wanted to share his passion for letterforms. He wrote detailed notes on assignments to help us understand the imperfections: "This is a hair too flat; push the curve a tiny bit more," "Hairlines should be a bit thinner," or "Slim down the stresses." He encouraged keen observation by noting, "Do you see how this *O* looks in comparison to the *C*?" or "The spine angle in the *S* is a bit off—look again." He ensured we respected the personality of each typeface with notes such as, "This is an elegant face, keep that feeling as you work." And he gently reinforced class lessons with notations such as, "Remember, swells should be a little heavier than normal stems."

As the semester progressed, grades were based not only on the shape of individual letters, but on the placement of letters in relation to other letters. Letters that were too close together or too far apart would disrupt the rhythm of the letters and destroy the visual harmony of a word. To revise the spaces, every letter had to be reconstructed and redrawn. Assignments were tedious, time consuming, and maddening.

Even though I earned an *A* in Professor DeHoff's class, it never crossed my mind to design a font. That seemed to be the purview of long-dead European masters and foundries who cast type from molten metal, not nineteen-year-olds attending college in Menomonie, Wisconsin. Besides, my focus was on advancing through the graphic design coursework so I could enter the emerging world of desktop publishing.

The first years of my career were spent at a prestigious graphic design firm in downtown Minneapolis. My boss, Tim, had a reputation for exacting craftsmanship, and as we designed annual reports, marketing brochures, and corporate identity systems, we researched and tested typefaces, then spent hours detailing type to ensure aesthetic harmony. A dog-eared, sticky-note-filled copy of Robert Bringhurst's *The Elements of Typographic Style* became my bible.

One of my favorite projects from those years was the design of an annual report for an environmental organization preserving vast swaths of Northern Tallgrass Prairie. Spectacular photos of bushy magenta wildflowers, wild grasses bending in the breeze, and yellow coneflowers reaching skyward accompanied pages of carefully set type.

To help tell the story of what the prairie looked like one hundred and fifty years earlier, the annual report's cover featured a journal entry from June 1840, written by a pioneer named Eliza Steele. "We passed whole acres of blossoms all bearing one hue, as purple, perhaps, or masses of yellow or rose; or narrow bands, as if a rainbow had fallen upon the verdant slopes. When the sun flooded this Mosaic floor with light and the summer breeze stirred among their leaves, the iridescent glow was beautiful and wondrous beyond anything I have ever conceived." Eliza's journal had been written with indigo ink on mottled, off-white parchment paper. A flourished signature decorated the bottom of the page, and splotches and stains seemed to prove the rugged conditions of her cross-continental journey.

The scratchy old handwriting, lyrical words, and expressive longhand seemed to throw open a window to Eliza's soul, and it brought her to life to such a degree people were thoroughly convinced she had been a real pioneer writing by lantern-light in the back of a covered wagon. But she wasn't. Tim and I conjured Eliza from our imaginations. Her name had been invented. Her words had been carefully copy-written. And the lettering had been completed by a man in Florida named Jack.

But what Eliza—what the project—did was this: the handwriting's expressive individuality reawakened the thirteen-year-old inside of me who had had a passion for handwriting. And for the first time in a decade, I took out my Schaeffer metal-nib pens and began to play.

Aaron did not say a word as he slid the heavy envelope across the table. He did not have to tell me what was inside; the thickness revealed the answer. He had been accepted. Months earlier, he had traveled from Minneapolis to Dallas to interview for a trauma nurse fellowship at Parkland Hospital. The fellowship was a career-altering opportunity for him, and after working for Tim for four years, I was ready for a change. We packed a U-Haul with hand-me-down furniture, clothes, books, and the television we purchased with the money we were given at our wedding eleven months earlier.

"It will be an adventure," Aaron promised as we drove nine hundred miles south.

I took a job as an art director at an advertising agency. I developed concepts and layouts, then production artists completed the work. After a project was passed to the production department, I rarely saw it again. A handful of times, the final product made my heart sink: type had been horizontally scaled to accommodate a last-minute addition, or the space between lines had been reduced to squeeze in an extra line of text. I offered to detail the type, but was told it was not my job. It felt as though every skill I honed while working for Tim was roundly dismissed.

In less than a year, our grand adventure felt like a failure. Our bicycles were stolen. Our apartment became infested with rats, then with fleas. Aaron and I squabbled about money, and I was furious he had not disclosed the enormity of his student loans—loans that came due shortly after our move. For a while we shared one car, which meant as soon as I got home from work he left for the hospital. We struggled to communicate, and I did not know how to tell him I felt abandoned.

I grew up in a family that kept emotions and opinions strictly in check. We did not yell or fight. Confrontation was avoided. We were loved, though love was not openly demonstrated. We were typical farm-background Midwesterners: proudly stoic, practical, industrious. Never too excited, never too sad. In contrast, Aaron grew up in a family that could hurl insults with the force of baseballs. So when Aaron and I argued about money, the car, yet another rat, or one of the hundred other things we had to figure out those first years, he yelled. I hid in the bathroom.

Aaron was contractually obligated to remain at Parkland Hospital, but I did not think I could stay. One lonely evening I walked through the apartment and made a mental list of how we might divide our belongings. I would take my books and clothes. He could keep the new television.

Yet my need to stay was greater than the compulsion to leave. Aaron made me laugh. He coaxed me out of my shell. His irreverence was oxygen to my suffocating sense of decorum. And Aaron claimed my calm demeanor helped him realize he did not have to react to everything with anger. It was the first time he had ever felt that way. We were good together.

We killed the rats and fogged the fleas. We chipped away at the loans. We learned how to talk to each other and tried to embrace all that Texas had to offer. I cooked tortilla soup and baked pecan pie. We drove meandering rural roads seeking explosions of wild bluebonnet or Indian blanket. We went to a rodeo and to a dance hall with a saddle-shaped disco ball.

It was during those months of trying to embrace Texas that I learned about Thomas Jefferson Rusk. One hundred fifty years earlier, the stern-looking Rusk had been a major general in the Republic of Texas militia. He was an advocate for annexation, and after Texas became the twenty-eighth state, Rusk was elected one of Texas's first US Senators.

Some of Rusk's original letters, which were archived at the University of Texas at Austin, caught the eye of graphic designer Brian Willson. Brian used photocopies of those handwritten letters to design a computer font that captured the varying thicks, thins, and rough irregularities of Rusk's nineteenth-century ink-on-paper handwriting. I was awed at the font's rustic beauty and enamored with the way the letterforms seemed to scratch and dance across the page. The font, named Texas Hero, seemed to bring Rusk's words to life.

Prior to seeing Texas Hero, I had never made the association between handwriting, type design, and what could be made with the new font design software. My reaction was immediate. Unequivocal. *I'm going to do that someday! I'm going to design a font based on old handwriting!* The proclamation was similar to someone gazing at a far-off mountain and, without owning a map or hiking boots, knowing with absolute certainty they would someday climb it.

But I did not equate the effort required to design a font with the effort required to climb a mountain. I thought designing a font would be a quick side project. In fact, I assumed a font based on handwriting would be the perfect first project because irregularities in writing would provide a certain amount of wiggle room for imprecision. *How hard could it be to scan someone's writing and trace the letters?*

Years later, I read an interview with Brian Willson where he admitted he underestimated how difficult it would be to design a font based on connected cursive handwriting. The biggest challenge, he explained, was ensuring that individual letters flowed together.

If I had read that interview the day I saw Texas Hero, I might not have started designing a font at all. But by the time I read the interview, I had been working on my font for years. And often, designing a font felt less like hiking a mountain and more like scaling a cliff wall, knowing that at any second an avalanche of technicality might sweep me off my feet.

Dallas never felt like home. Once Aaron completed his fellowship, we packed another U-Haul and returned to Minnesota. Aaron took a job as an emergency room nurse, and I joined the in-house creative team at a large financial services company. I was not enamored with the job, but I accepted the offer because of the ebullient woman who would be my boss, Kathy. She radiated positivity. I wanted to work for *her*.

Aaron and I bought a small house in White Bear Lake, a suburb north of St. Paul. The house was one of thousands of nearly identical single-level ranch homes built in the early 1950s for booming postwar families. The house's interior was pink when we bought it: pink scalloped shades, pink blinds, pink paint, pink wallpaper. Aaron said it was like moving into a bottle of Pepto-Bismol. In the first week, we covered nearly every surface with paint. The house was reborn in tones of caramel, sage, and denim blue.

The following summer we adopted Hoover, though he was nameless on the day we carried him home. He was a nine-week-old roly-poly ball of floppy ears, pleading eyes, and massive retriever paws. We were smitten. As he raced across our deck, nose down, sucking up everything in his path, our neighbor commented, "He's a vacuum cleaner." Hoover was the perfect name.

The first years in our little house were bliss. After moving six times during the first five years of our marriage, we felt settled. We nested. We talked about having children, but as it turned out, our family never grew beyond our tight little trio.

During those years, I always—though sometimes lazily—kept an eye out for the perfect reference specimen for my font. I looked at museums, in antique stores, on eBay. I hoped to find a specimen with the scratchy character of Thomas Jefferson Rusk's writing, yet it had to be different somehow. I did not know precisely what it would look like, but I trusted I would know it once I saw it.

I assumed my specimen would be from the late 1800s. I had a particular weakness for handwriting from that era. The combination of graceful restraint and wild flourish appealed to me in the same way someone can be unstoppably drawn to a certain piece of music, a certain flower, a certain shade of blue.

Along the way, I acquired other typographic gems. Many were a dollar or two, and *something* about them caught my eye: an 1853 Valentine's Day poem written with a meticulous, rolling cursive; an 1857 legal filing with a tornado-shaped swirl below the lawyer's signature; an 1863 bank receipt with a spectacular dollar sign; a wedding invitation from 1900 that featured a hand-drawn nesting dove. The specimens had no value to anyone other than a typography lover. In fact, the bank clerk might have had a good laugh at the notion that one hundred and fifty years down the road, someone would buy a scrap of paper that held his flourished scribble.

As much as I treasured those specimens, none were right for a font. The samples were not comprehensive enough. I needed to find a specimen that included numbers, along with a near-complete set of upper and lowercase letters. So I continued to look.

The financial services company where Kathy and I worked eliminated our entire department in one unceremonious snip. Forty-one of us were trimmed off as though we were corporate hangnails. Kathy and I had become good friends and we entertained the notion of starting a business together. Timing was not right, though, so she took a job at a medical device company, and I took a job at a design firm in Minneapolis. We remained in frequent contact, and two years later, when I decided to freelance, Kathy became my first official client.

The first morning as my own boss, a Monday, I could barely contain the swell of excitement. Options and opportunities seemed limitless. I envisioned renting an office in a hip warehouse with soaring windows, a shiny espresso machine, and sleek leather chairs. Bookcases would be artfully arranged with design annuals and type-related knickknacks.

Enormous metal letters salvaged from some old factory would hang on exposed-brick walls.

That was the long-term plan, anyway. In the short term, I set up my computer on a desk in a spare bedroom. Books and supplies were stacked in the closet.

That first evening, Aaron took me out to dinner and we toasted to all the possibilities in my exciting new venture. The next morning, the two of us sat on the couch, glued to the live news feed of the 9/11 attacks. Fireballs consumed every shred of optimism. Petty, materialistic wishes for a shiny espresso machine and sleek leather chairs were replaced by disbelief, helplessness, rage. It was unclear how any of us would move forward in this scary new world.

Stillwater is a city of eighteen thousand people twelve miles east of our home. It is nestled along the picturesque St. Croix River, which feeds into the Mississippi twenty or so miles downstream. In the town's earliest days, trappers, lumbermen, and fearless pioneers scratched out a living along the river, and as the area was settled, sawmills, mercantiles, and inns went up along Stillwater's bustling main street.

Those historic brick and stone buildings now housed restaurants; shops selling designer kitchen tools, gourmet olive oils, or high-end paper goods; and antique shops peddling a typical mix of dishes, furniture, and books.

In the months after 9/11, Aaron and I went to Stillwater often. We did not understand at the time, but those trips were driven by a yearning to be surrounded by simplicity and nostalgia. For a couple of hours, Stillwater allowed us to trade the reality of the still-smoldering Ground Zero and threats from al-Qaeda for billowing American flags and a communal sense of kindness.

Antiquing with Aaron was always a game. I would hold up some worn-down, obscure item and he would identify what it was: a cigar press, a sugar mold, a hand-held cranberry harvester. If he did not know, he would invent some fantastical use: a nineteenth-century pen warmer, a chicken sorter, a lime peeler. Sometimes I was gullible enough to believe him.

It was during one of those trips that I found Marcel's letters. What immediately caught my eye was the flourished endearment, "*Mes chères petites.*" The left leg of the *M* swooped far to the side and ended with a little loop that made my heart swell. The scratchy, old, ink-on-paper writing was *exactly* what I had hoped to find. As I stood in the store, I knew with certainty that this handwriting would be the basis for my font.

The handwritten letters were a variety of shapes and sizes. Many were single sheets with writing on the front and back, others were four pages, folded. Some papers were a light butter-colored yellow, other papers were dark like marigold. Some letters had been written with blue ink, others with brown or black. One had been written in pencil. But the signature at the bottom of each letter showed they had all been written by the same man, a man named Marcel.

Aaron looked over my shoulder to see what had so thoroughly seized my attention. I held up one letter, smiling ear to ear.

"For my font," I whispered. The store was nearly empty. Secrecy was unnecessary.

"Ahhh, the font." He had heard me mention the project many times, though this was the first time it was more than an abstract, distant idea. "What are they in, French?"

I nodded. That was my guess, anyway.

"Um, honey, you can't read French," he whispered, as though he wanted to remind me of something obvious I had forgotten.

"Yes, I can, look: Lily, Jacqueline," I said as I pointed to names on the front of the letter. I did not recognize anything else, so I flipped the page over and pointed out a few more words: Paris, Denise, 1,300 kilometers. I pointed to another phrase, and in a sultry voice whispered, "*Beaucoup de caresses.*" I swiveled to look at Aaron and gloat over the words I recognized.

Aaron dropped his chin and rolled his eyes.

It did not matter to me what the original letters said or what language they had been written in. For the purpose of the font, I only needed to reference the *shape* of the letters. An *a* in French looked the same as an *a* in English, after all. The curves, lines, and loops were what mattered. And these curves, lines, and loops were beautiful.

The letters were not expensive, but I had not been freelancing long and economic uncertainty was on everyone's mind. I decided I could afford to buy four letters without feeling guilty.

The dates on the letters ranged from early 1943 to mid-1944. I was surprised they were that modern; from the style of the handwriting, I assumed they were older.

Some letters were embellished with watery blue and red stripes. Perhaps it was because of the abundant post-9/11 displays of US patriotism—American flags flew everywhere—but the blue and red stripes struck me as a lovely gesture of Marcel's French national pride.

As I shuffled through the letters, culling out favorites, I noticed a swastika, then green and brown postage stamps with Hitler's profile. I did not give much weight to those things. They were artifacts from the era, disconnected from Marcel's beautiful writing. Or perhaps I dismissed those things because I wanted them to be disconnected.

A bored saleswoman leaned against the wall behind the register. I inquired where the letters had come from. She shrugged.

I shuffled through the letters a second time. No question existed I was going to buy the first letter that caught my eye. In addition to the swash *M* in the flourished greeting, it had large, clear, careful writing. It was simply more beautiful than any other, and it seemed undeniable the page had been written with affection. Other pages made the cut if I noted particularly interesting swashes or letters. One letter included lots of numbers, and I knew I needed numbers.

I shuffled through the stack a third time. Then a fourth. Settling on four letters was impossible, but I narrowed it down to five: four letters and a postcard.

The handwriting on the postcard was not particularly beautiful, but the card included Marcel's last name, a return address in Berlin, and an address in France. As I shuffled through Marcel's letters, I thought about the font based on Thomas Jefferson Rusk's writing and realized it might be worthwhile to have basic information about the man who had written *these* letters.

Later, as Aaron and I strolled down the sidewalk, I cradled the paper bag holding my newly purchased treasures. "Do you even know how to design a font?" he asked.

"No," I admitted as Aaron's eyebrows shot up. "I'll figure it out." Creating the font seemed like a technicality now that I had the perfect specimen.

"How long is it going to take?"

I shrugged. "A couple months?" I promised Aaron I would work on my silly side project only after all paying client work was done.

After making high-resolution scans of Marcel's letters, I pressed the five sheets of paper inside the front cover of a sketchbook for safekeeping. I printed oversize black-and-white copies of each scanned page, then with a yellow highlighter and a pencil marked individual letters I wanted to incorporate into the font: a favorite *a*, an interesting *t*, a *p* that swooped high before angling low. Many were the same individual letters I noticed in the store, but other favorites emerged only after I scrutinized each and every line of handwriting. I did not know if this was how other font designers began projects—I did not know any other font designers—but it was the only starting point I could think of.

I enlarged scans of favorite individual letters so each was as large as a hand. I set the scans over a light table and fastidiously traced each letter, carefully replicating every minuscule nick and every place where the ink feathered to nothingness. The work seemed to transport me fifteen years back in time to Letterform class, when I labored over Professor DeHoff's assignments.

Once I assembled a complete alphabet of traced letters. I scanned each pencil outline, then over the course of months—evenings and weekends as I could carve out time—I recreated the same detailed nicks and feathered edges in Adobe Illustrator, a vector-based software program I often used with client projects. Each letter was composed of a thousand or more tiny line segments, but every detail seemed critical if I was going to faithfully replicate Marcel's handwriting. I still did not know how the individual letters would become a font, but I read somewhere I would be able to import Illustrator outlines into font design software.

Initial tracing and final glyph

Years later, I learned those two time-consuming steps—tracing by hand, then outlining in Illustrator—could have been accomplished in hours with a few clicks of a mouse. I was unsurprised when I learned that. Throughout the project, if two ways existed to accomplish the same thing, I inevitably chose the slower, more labor-intensive process. I did not do it on purpose. I just seemed destined to choose the least efficient option.

If I had automated those steps, though, I would have missed gaining an intimate familiarity with Marcel's handwriting. The loop at the bottom of the *z*, the break in ink on the upstroke of the *q*, the hint of squareness in the bowl of the *g*: those were the details I might have overlooked if I had automated tracing and outlining. Because I had done the work by hand, I knew each letter's idiosyncrasies. I knew the rhythm of the writing. I could replicate the sweep of Marcel's hand. For those reasons, every hour spent tracing and outlining felt eminently worthwhile.

Since individual letters were in Illustrator—not in a font program—I could not type an *a* on my keyboard and make an *a* appear anywhere. The only way to preview complete words was to manually assemble one letter at a time within Illustrator. It was akin to moving individual jigsaw puzzle pieces around a table filled with hundreds of other puzzle pieces. It was inefficient and impractical, and some of the first words I tested were "bullshit" and "waste of time."

Those first words revealed surprising—and fundamental—flaws. Varying angles, heights, and inconsistent thicknesses resulted in a hodgepodge of styles. It made sense once I realized the root cause: I had selected favorite individual letters from five separate pages. On some pages, Marcel's handwriting had been small and condensed. On others, it had been loopy and loose. In some places Marcel's handwriting had a sharp-angled slope. In others, his handwriting had been nearly vertical.

I needed a standard to hold every individual letter to. I decided my favorite letter—the one with the large handwriting and the beautiful *M*—would be the archetype. Months disappeared coaxing angles, heights, and thicknesses into compliance. Some letters were maddening in their deception. I would make them the proper mathematic angle, height, or thickness, but additional optical adjustments would be needed.

"For you," I said as I slid a small box across the table. It was one of those brick-size cardboard boxes for schoolchildren chock-full of pens and pencils, tape, and pointy pencil erasers. It was a silly back-to-school gift, but it made Aaron smile.

After eight years working as an emergency room nurse, Aaron was on the verge of burning out. He decided to go back to school. It was impossible for Aaron to work during the two and a half-year master's program, so I took every freelance project I could get my hands on.

Most were projects I enjoyed: brochures and marketing materials for high-tech and medical clients. But to make ends meet, I worked on projects I despised: forms, banner ads, business cards. My evenings and weekends were consumed by client work; Aaron's were spent studying pharmacology. At times, months elapsed without working on the font. But it was always in the back of my mind, patiently waiting for time and attention.

After Aaron graduated, I scaled my workload down to a more sustainable level and decided it was time to finally purchase the font design software, FontLab Studio.

I flipped through the 923-page user guide, attempting to decipher instructions on auto-hinting alignment zones, editing axis graphs, building anchor composites. The user guide made as much sense to me in English as it would have had it been written in French, and each attempt to transfer the Illustrator outlines into a font file was a spectacular failure. I would only get so far before trashing the file in frustration. Other times, the software would crash or freeze, and the decision to restart would be made for me.

In late 2008, I stumbled across an ad for an introductory FontLab class. It was exactly what I needed. "This class will introduce you to the basic skills necessary for the wild journey into the mysterious world of type design," the ad read. "You will expand lettering to a full-functioning font, scan type specimens of your own handwriting, and learn the basics of designing and generating a typeface with FontLab."

The one-day class was sponsored by the New York Type Director's Club. I asked Aaron if he would want to travel with me. Aaron had been at his new job less than three months; he could not even ask for the time off.

"You should go," he insisted. Within an hour, I had reserved my spot in class and purchased a plane ticket to New York.

Nine of us attended the class. The instructor, James, asked each of us to introduce ourselves, so we went around the small room and stated our name and where we were from. One of the students expressed surprise I had traveled so far just for the class. I explained I had never seen anything of the sort offered in the Midwest.

James began by showing us how to establish a new file, and how each letter—called a glyph—was structured. Left and right side bearings defined the width; baseline, x-height, ascender, and descender measurements defined the height. James demonstrated several techniques to construct glyphs, then showed us how to preview and test glyphs using the Preview Panel. I carefully replicated every one of James's movements as if I were a dancer learning intricate choreography.

Addressing every tool and tip was impossible in a one-day class. James did not even mention kerning, which was the programming of incremental spaces between problematic letter combinations such as *VA* or *LI*. Years later, kerning would almost bring my project to an excruciating end, but in that moment, sitting in that room, I remained blissfully unaware of the hurdles that awaited.

In the late afternoon, James gave us time to play with the software and put our new skills to work. By 5:00, my font included seven wonky glyphs. They lacked elegance and symmetry, but I did not care. I now knew how to get started, and those seven glyphs seemed as precious as seven nuggets of gold.

That night, I propped my twelfth-floor hotel window open an inch, which was enough to keep out the December chill, but enough to let in sounds of taxis accelerating, far-off sirens echoing through concrete canyons, and the endless *thunk-thunk* of vehicles driving over a manhole cover on the street below. Dreams of glyphs, side bearings, and serifs swirled together with the sounds of the city.

Aaron had encouraged me to spend Saturday in the city. I felt a sliver of guilt about the extra night's hotel expense, but after the previous two and a half years, I needed an infusion of inspiration. As I wandered Manhattan's streets, I let my eyes and ears fill with the city's treasures: a brassy Salvation Army band playing familiar Christmas tunes, festive window displays, constellations on Grand Central Terminal's ceiling, ice skaters spinning on the rink at Rockefeller Plaza, stately galleries at the Metropolitan Museum of Art.

At the end of the day, I hailed a cab to take me back to my hotel. I asked the driver if he would take me through Times Square. I wanted to see the lights and frenzy. The request would have only created a slight detour, and I told him I was willing to pay for any inconvenience it might cause.

"No, hon," the driver said with a brusque, condescending laugh that made me feel like I had asked for a detour through Maine.

That night, as I drifted to sleep listening again to the *thunk-thunk* of vehicles driving over the manhole cover on the street below, I would never have been able to guess it would be the font based on Marcel's writing that would bring me back to New York City.

Or that Aaron and I would stay at a hotel one block off of Times Square.

Hours after Aaron picked me up at the airport, I began slowly and methodically transferring individual outlines from Illustrator into my new font file. I carefully aligned each glyph to the baseline, then positioned the left and right side bearings as James had taught us. The first time I typed a letter on the keyboard and watched the same letter appear in the Preview Panel, I nearly jumped out of my chair with joy.

Once most letters had been transferred into FontLab, I yelled for Aaron.

"Look! Look!" I said, pointing at my monitor.

I pecked out Aaron's name, looking to confirm each letter appeared when it was supposed to.

"Gimme a word!" I commanded after clearing the Preview Panel. I held my fingers above the keyboard like a pianist waiting to strike an opening chord. "Gimme a word," I repeated.

"Yippee." Aaron's voice dripped with sarcasm.

I typed Y-i-p-p-e-e. I hadn't created the uppercase *Y* yet, so it appeared as "ippee."

I swiveled to Aaron. He seemed to be trying to figure out how to gently break the news the font was not working. I stole a glance back at the monitor, then looked at Aaron.

"I haven't done the *Y* yet," I explained as I jumped up, wiggled my shoulders, and swiveled my hips. Aaron rolled his eyes. He hated my Happy Dance.

Within weeks, every bit of buoyant enthusiasm drained away. FontLab had an audit feature that checked each glyph for problems such as incorrect line intersections, almost-but-not-quite-straight lines, overly complex lines, and myriad shape errors. When I toggled the audit feature on, I was sickened to realize the software did not allow all the tiny details I had meticulously labored over. Each and every glyph was hidden under a multi-layer cloud of red error flags. Some errors could be fixed with the click of a mouse, but most required careful revision. If I did not pay attention, gentle curves might bulge or flatten; converging lines might become parallel. As I watched hundreds, then thousands, of details disappear, I berated myself for all the wasted time and for having naïvely believed I would be able to effortlessly transfer the outlines from Illustrator to Font-Lab and be done.

Other issues arose, too: incorrect PostScript path directions, reversed and open contours, ghost points. Had I been aware of all the issues and problems, I would have tackled them with a methodical plan, but problems revealed themselves one at a time, which resulted in a frustrating merry-go-round of revisions that devoured evenings and weekends.

"Think of letters like bricks in a building," design professor and type designer Craig Eliason explained once at a typography lecture. "Every brick needs to fit perfectly with every other brick. It's the same thing with letters; they have to be designed so no matter what word you type, no matter what letters are *in* that word, every letter fits with every other letter."

I had always remembered that comparison because it was such a beautifully simple way to explain the complexity of type design.

As I began testing the font, it did not take long to see that the lead-in and lead-out strokes—the tiny sweeping lines in a script font that connect one glyph with the next—needed additional refinement. More months elapsed standardizing the angle, size, and position of each sweeping line. I did not understand this then, but those lead-in and lead-out strokes were the trickiest thing about designing a connected script font. In fact, those tiny strokes were the difference between success and failure. And in true form, it would be years before I learned a trick to make it easy.

The first official test prints included an alphabetical list of animals: "Aardvark," "Armadillo," "Baboon," "Butterfly," "Chimpanzee," "Chickadee" . . . After animals, I moved on to lists of food, then names of famous people, then cities and states. Other times I tested random words: "Rumpelstiltskin," "Gerrymandering," "Jabberwocky," "Scrumpdillyicious." After generating each new test print, I covered each page with red-pen notes on curves that required smoothing, strokes that needed narrowing or fattening, or lead-in or lead-out strokes that needed additional adjustment.

By that time, Marcel's handwritten letters had been pressed flat inside the front cover of the sketchbook for years. All of those tiny revisions to shape, proportion, and angle meant the font still retained the essential character of Marcel's handwriting, but it had evolved into something that existed on its own. The custom mix included a thousand parts Marcel's writing, and a thousand other tweaks and revisions.

As maddening as it could be to make round after round of revisions, there was also something wickedly addictive about the work. Sometimes I would completely lose track of time and work until the wee morning hours. Designing type, I ultimately found, was more satisfying than calligraphy ever had been. Designing type turned out to be the ideal solution for the girl who lamented her Ken Brown chisel-tip markers did not have precise edges, because I could revise and refine each line and curve until it looked exactly the way I wanted it to look.

Time spent designing type also provided a bewitching liberation from client work. During business hours, a client's lawyer might dictate the type size of a disclaimer. Clients might debate whether a statistic should include one or two numbers after a decimal point. Engineers might revise a product schematic over and over. With the font, I made every decision: not a lawyer, not an engineer. My opinion was the only one that mattered.

Individual glyphs remained true to the character of Marcel's writing—albeit with less textural detail and a thousand other revisions—but when I scrutinized long passages of text, something was off. I printed page after page before identifying what was wrong with the font: all the letters were incrementally too close to each other.

Unlike serif or sans serif fonts where individual glyphs do not touch, changing the width of a connected script font meant every single glyph had to be adjusted twice. First I had to adjust the lead-in stroke on the left. Then I had to adjust the lead-out stroke on the right. The amount of work required to fix the problem felt insurmountable, and I contemplated giving up on the project altogether.

The test prints taped to my office wall were taken down.

I did not work on the font for months.

But the loops and swirls of Marcel's writing were never out of mind.

Every couple of months Kathy and I met for lunch. Sometimes it would be an official business lunch where we discussed a project she hired me to design. Other times we met to chat about design industry issues, books, or world events. She adored Aaron and always inquired about his latest culinary creations. Inevitably, we would talk about whatever grand adventure Kathy was planning next: kayaking around the Dalmatian Islands or bicycling across southern France.

"Can I show you something?" I had presented enough design concepts to Kathy over the decade I had known her to be able to read her reaction. I drew in a long breath before handing over a page with letters *a* through *z* and line after line of animal names. I proffered an apology: "It's a work in progress."

It had taken months to fix the issue of the font looking too condensed, but in the end, I was glad I had not given up.

"This is gorgeous!" Kathy said as her eyes widened. She drew circles in the air above glyphs she particularly liked. "How do you know how to do this?"

"I don't." When she looked at me, I shrugged and added, "I'm figuring it out as I go."

Fewer than twenty people knew about the font. Aaron, and now Kathy, were the only ones who had seen it. I had stopped telling non-type people about the project because I usually received one of these questions: "You're designing a *what*?" "Doesn't Word already come with the fonts I need?" "People buy fonts?" "What do you *mean* you've been working on the font for five/seven/nine years?" And my favorite: a blank look, followed by someone's head slowly tilting to the side, their eyebrows crunching together, followed by one word: "Why?"

Type people—*my people*—understood what I was doing. Most were fellow graphic designers who took pride in matching the right typeface to the project at hand. They might use a scrolled font with extreme thicks and thins on an article on peonies, a hand-drawn font on packaging for artisan chocolates, a modern sans serif on a state-of-the-art medical device brochure. Type people understood the allure of a beautiful typeface. They never asked *why*.

I showed Kathy alternate versions of glyphs. The *M*, *A*, and *H* existed both as fancy swash versions and as space-saving alternates. *J*'s and *7*'s existed with and without crossbars. A decorative *St.* abbreviation existed for Saint. A *zz* ligature existed for when anyone might type the word "pizza," "blizzard," or "dizzy." A European-style *1* existed where the lead-in stroke swept upward from the baseline.

As the months went by, Kathy turned into the font's biggest cheerleader. She always inquired how it was progressing. Each time I confidently told her it was almost complete.

The reality was I did not have any concept of how much work remained.

I had been trying to perfect the upper left-hand corner of the *J* for days. The shape of the *J* was similar to the *J* in John Hancock's famous signature, though instead of having an inward bow on the stroke that hung below the horizontal arm, my *J*—Marcel's *J*—bowed outward. The bow did not look correct, though I had been unable to figure out why.

I had tried dozens of tweaks and revisions: adding weight to the left, straightening the curve on the right, deepening the bend at the top, straightening the left side, rounding the end. But the shape still was not right. The minuscule refinements would be imperceptible if someone used the font at a small size. But at a large size, flaws would be unbearable, so I *had* to solve the *J*.

I tried a few more adjustments: shortening the bar along the top, increasing the angle, thinning out the arm. I glanced at the clock; hours had elapsed. Aaron had gone to bed long ago. It was time to put it away and try again tomorrow.

When I stepped into the bedroom, I bent down to rub the crest of Hoover's head.

"Sweet boy," I whispered. Hoover opened his eyes, but he did not move. His frosted jowls remained puddled on the floor. For a decade, Hoover had slept on the bed with us. Aaron slept on the left, Hoover slept on the right, and I nestled into the channel of warmth between their two bodies. But Hoover had not slept with us for months. The jump, we guessed, hurt his aging back or legs.

The following evening, I printed out the *J*, put tracing paper over it, and drew shapes freehand as we had in Professor DeHoff's class. Even though I had been working in FontLab for two and a half years, I still struggled to get the results I wanted. I hoped sketching freehand would help me figure out what was wrong.

The hand-drawn shapes were better, but they still were not right. I was frustrated and tired. I let out a long sigh.

It occurred to me to look at Marcel's original handwritten letters. *Maybe the originals will show me where one—or one hundred—of the thousand revisions led me astray.*

It took a moment to find the sketchbook among the business books, design annuals, color reference guides, and supplies that filled the closet shelves. I flipped open the sketchbook's front cover, and there they were— the four letters and the postcard—pressed flat alongside the Valentine's Day poem, the legal filing, the bank receipt, the wedding invitation with the nesting dove.

I removed Marcel's letters, and as I returned to my desk, I skimmed the handwriting for a *J*. When I found one, the answer was clear: the out-ward bow needed to be higher up. I set the letters on the desk, slumped into my chair, and swiveled to my computer, filled with hope that in another hour or so the *J* would finally be solved.

Marcel's letters lay on the desk, silent and infinitely patient. The next morning, I would pick them up, and as the bright morning sunlight flooded through my office window, I would be reminded of the paper's beauty, the brackish ink, the blue and red stripes, the Hitler stamps, the odd little swastika.

In less than a day, I would decide to have the first letter translated.

Chapter Five

White Bear Lake, Minnesota

October 2011

"What do you know about World War II history?" The evening news droned on in the background as Aaron and I ate dinner. "*French* World War II history," I clarified.

Aaron's blank expression changed to a smirk and he rattled off one of his favorite jokes: "You can buy French rifles cheap; only been dropped once."

"Not nice," I said with an eye roll.

After a few moments of silence, his bearing turned somber. "I know some of the bloodiest battles were in France."

Aaron outlined what he recalled about the political and economic conditions that gave rise to the Third Reich, then he listed some of World War II's major military campaigns. I had not had a history class since high school, and for the most part, his recollections overlapped with what I had been able to shake loose from my memory. Beyond the D-Day landings in Normandy, and France's division into occupied and unoccupied zones, neither of us could recall much about *French* World War II history.

During the previous weeks—after realizing *my* Marcel might not have perished at Ravensbrück—I resumed a search for answers. But as I stumbled over locations, names, and terms, the need for a history refresher became painfully apparent. My goal was not to become an expert in French World War II history. I only wanted to learn enough to know where to look for information on Marcel.

After washing dinner dishes, I curled into the couch, cocooning myself in an afghan my grandmother crocheted for me when I was a teen. The bold zigzag pattern and bright rainbow-colored yarn clashed with our forest green couch and the muted colors in our home. Still, it was my favorite. I pulled my laptop close and began to read.

In early 1938, Germany annexed Austria. The following year they annexed Czechoslovakia, then invaded Poland. In May 1940, Germany launched a full-scale invasion of the Netherlands and Belgium, then of France. French and British forces fought back, but were overwhelmed by the Germans' tactical superiority. Many soldiers retreated; others tenaciously dug in. In mid-June, just days before France's surrender, vicious battles raged in the countryside southwest of Paris. Two French Senegalese regiments were decimated in the fields and forests surrounding Berchères-la-Maingot.

After the armistice was signed, France was divided. The eastern region of Alsace-Lorraine was annexed by Germany, and the far northern departments of Nord and Pas-de-Calais fell under Brussels-based German military rule. A new French government—the Vichy regime— governed France's southern "unoccupied" zone. The northern and western "occupied" zones were also governed by the Vichy regime, though in those regions officials and citizens were subject to strict military rules, and Germany exercised all rights of an occupying power.

French resources were plundered. Horses and machines were loaded onto trains and sent to Germany. Thousands of pigs and cows, tons of wheat, twelve million bottles of Champagne, and the entire 1940 Bordeaux grape harvest were sent east, too. Meanwhile, French civilians faced dire rationing of food and fuel. The amount of food civilians could procure with government-provided vouchers was "barely enough to support life," and people were forced to the black market to acquire staples such as milk, butter, and cooking oil. Other items—cheese, chicken, soap—were simply unavailable.

By mid-1942—six months before Marcel wrote the letter to his daughters—twenty thousand Jews had been transported from France to Germany. My heart lurched. *Had Marcel been deported because he was Jewish?* As the war raged on, Jews in France were "hunted down" by Vichy's paramilitary force. By the end of the war, more than seventy thousand Jews would be deported. Only a couple of thousand would survive.

As I continued to read about resistance, deportation, deprivation, and the complexity of survival under German and Vichy rule, my head began to pound. *The French fought against the Germans—then against each other.* The situation seemed impossibly tangled, and I understood why neither of us had been able to recall our history lessons. One of the few things I thought I knew—that France had been cleaved into occupied and unoccupied zones—was only partially true. By late 1942, Germany occupied the entire country.

Hours later, I slid my laptop onto the coffee table, stood, and stretched. I walked into our kitchen, and as I filled a glass with cool tap water, I peered out the window to our dark, peaceful street.

Had Marcel been one of the 1.8 million French soldiers taken prisoner of war? Was that why he had been in Berlin? Most of those soldiers were transferred to camps in Germany. And many were forced to work to support Germany's war industry despite that being a violation of the 1929 Geneva Conventions.

Had Marcel, his wife, and his daughters been among the millions of Parisians who fled once they realized German troops were about to sweep into the city? Many Parisians evacuated to country homes or family farms, or stayed with distant relatives. Was that why they had been in Berchères-la-Maingot?

Had Marcel mailed his letters from a concentration camp? Was that even possible? If he was Jewish, wouldn't a postcard with an address on it lead authorities directly to his family?

I began second-guessing every precious fact I thought I knew. Perhaps Marcel was not even French. Maybe he was from Belgium or Luxembourg. Those were French-speaking countries too, and thousands of civilians fled from Belgium and Luxembourg into France.

But why would Marcel have painted blue and red stripes on his letters if he wasn't French?

I looked up the flags of Belgium and Luxembourg. Luxembourg's flag was blue, white, and red, too. The thought of not even knowing one thing for certain—Marcel's nationality—made my head ache even more. So for the moment, I clung to the assumption Marcel had been French.

A few nights later, I stumbled over a three-letter acronym that changed everything: STO. As soon as I understood what those letters represented I *knew* that was why Marcel had been in Berlin.

Within Germany, approximately twenty million working-age men had been transferred to military units on the eastern or western fronts. Initially, German women filled jobs left behind in factories, mines, and farms. But when women could not fill the need for manual labor, Hitler empowered his Commissioner-General for Manpower, Fritz Sauckel, to acquire new workers "at whatever cost." Some of the first workers were brought by cattle car from Ukraine to work on German farms. Other workers were swept up in raids, or abducted, then deported en masse. Some were as young as ten years old.

By the end of the war, more than five million workers would be brought into Germany. By the Germans' own admission, fewer than 200,000 were there voluntarily.

In mid-1942—two years after Germany invaded France—Sauckel demanded 250,000 French workers. To fill the quota, the Vichy government announced the *Relève*, a campaign that encouraged French citizens to volunteer for the German war effort. Radio broadcasts promised favorable wages, comfortable living conditions, and assured prospective workers that the Germans respected everybody, "be he a manual or intellectual worker." As extra incentive, the Germans agreed to release one French prisoner of war for every three volunteers.

One Relève propaganda poster showed a hand thrusting a key skyward with a headline that proclaimed, "You have the keys to the camp;

you release prisoners by working in Germany." Another included an illustration of a burly, broad-shouldered man in overalls, a gear and the Eiffel Tower in the background. It promised, "You will be the ambassador of French quality." Another showed German and French workers shaking hands while standing on a curved-Earth illustration of Europe. "Come to us!" it read. "You will be well received, you will make money." Small text at the bottom promised the Germans would "take care of you after your departure." Another poster featured an illustration of a canary-haired German with an enormous smile and a sledgehammer balanced on one shoulder. "German workers invite you to join them," the text proclaimed. The German looked so carefree—so downright giddy—that if the sledgehammer had been a golf club, it would have been a perfect advertisement for a country club.

Many of the first French "volunteers" were from the fringes of society: petty criminals who chose Germany over prison; the "idle" who had been rounded up at cinemas, cafés, and racetracks; foreigners living in France; and women who were pregnant by German soldiers, or who had no other way to support their children. Reports even swirled of the Vichy government deporting children on public assistance.

When the number of volunteers filled less than half of the quota, the Vichy government needed a different strategy. The pretense of voluntary recruitment was abandoned, and *Service du Travail Obligatoire*—STO— was implemented.

A chill shot through me as I realized what that meant: working for the Germans was no longer optional.

The first STO provisions were published as the "Law of 4 September, 1942, on the Use and Orientation of the Workforce." "Among the French and French nationals residing in France," the law stated, "and whose fitness has been medically certified, any male person over the age of eighteen years and less than fifty years, and any female person, single, over twenty-one and under thirty-five years, may be subject to carry out all work that the Government deems appropriate in the best interests of the nation." My heart sank as I realized "in the best interests of the nation" did not refer to France—but to Germany.

Thirteen articles outlined technicalities of implementation. The formal terminology, official-sounding department titles, and references to employment contracts provided an "air of legality"—despite the fact that making "conquered peoples . . . work for their conqueror's war effort" was prohibited by international law. In a letter Sauckel wrote to Hitler, he explained, "I have ordered the introduction of labor employment commissions . . . this way makes a complete control and intensive utilization of the French working potential possible."

Five months after the September STO law was published, after Sauckel demanded even more French workers, a second law subjected men who were in their early twenties—those who had been born in 1920, 1921, or 1922—to work in Germany for two years in lieu of fulfilling traditional military service. The second law, published in February 1943, also outlined increased penalties for evasion and non-compliance. In a later letter to Hitler, Sauckel explained, "I left no doubt . . . if the demands for furnishing necessary manpower are not fulfilled, further stronger measures will be taken."

I did not have a single shred of proof, but deep in my bones I *knew* that was what had happened to Marcel. STO was the first thing that made any sense. It explained why, four months after the first law passed, Marcel might have been in Berlin. It explained why he sounded like neither a soldier nor a businessman, why he referenced barracks and his status as a prisoner, why he might ask for beans and a comb. And it seemed to be the only explanation for why he had been so far from the people he loved.

Yet, it seemed impossible to make sense of the situation, and I had to take a few minutes to process the information. STO meant almost anyone—regardless of religion or political affiliation—could be forced to work for the Nazis. *To work for the enemy.*

By the end of the war, 650,000 French civilian workers would be deported.

Tens of thousands would not return.

I began scouring the Internet for any STO record that might confirm my suspicion and reveal what happened to Marcel, but the only record that seemed to exist was the first one: the reference to Marcel Heuzé, pastor, aged forty-eight, with a wife named Simone, who died at Ravensbrück four days before the camp was liberated.

"Press check tonight?" Aromas of cinnamon and vanilla filled the kitchen as Aaron pulled a sheet of thick oatmeal cookies out of the oven.

"Type Tuesday," I said as I hung my coat.

"Ahhh, right. Geeks' night out."

Craig Eliason, the design professor and type designer who equated letters with bricks, had organized the group. Similar groups of typography lovers quietly met in cities across the country.

At the first Type Tuesday gathering, I was astonished to learn a small but vibrant community of type designers existed in the Minneapolis/St. Paul metropolitan area. Their fonts filled magazines and adorned packaging. The designers had shelves of awards and had been featured on television. They possessed an encyclopedic knowledge of typographic history and had a command of the font design software that filled me with jealous admiration. One designer's font was even the basis of Facebook's iconic *f*. I was awed to be in their presence.

At that first gathering, when someone asked if I designed type too, I shrugged and offered an unconvincing nod. *Type meddler* felt like a more appropriate claim, but I acknowledged I had a font in the works. When they asked how long I had been working on it, I confessed it had been years. They did not seem surprised. In fact, their shrug seemed to say *well, that's how long they take sometimes.*

We gathered the third Tuesday of most months. Some evenings, members gave presentations on work in progress. Other times we attended lectures, or screened typography-related films. One month we watched an early twentieth-century Ludlow typesetting machine change molten metal into type. Another month we looked at slides of sixteenth-century ornamented capitals. As the group ooh'd and aah'd at letters embellished with cherubs, spiraling vines, or mischievous animals—one particularly delightful *C* included an illustration of a pig playing the bagpipes—I had to confess Aaron's nickname for the group was spot-on. But I wore the geek label with pride. I speculated that everyone in the group would. And no matter what the evening's topic was, one thing was certain: I would return home inspired. Often I worked on my font until the early morning hours.

"The pressure! A room of people fretting over their name tags," Aaron said. With the quilted oven mitt still covering his hand, he pointed to the rectangle adhered to my lapel. I looked down and slowly peeled it off. The letters of my first name included carefully drawn serifs.

"You're an asshole," I said as he chuckled. "Everyone's nice," I added defensively.

"I'm sure they are. I'm sure it's a *great* time—if you think it's fun to debate how much you love or hate Helvetica."

Despite professing apathy for typography, Aaron had picked up enough over the years to know good type from bad. He occasionally called out horrible kerning, or questioned a typeface selection. For years he had playfully threatened to engrave my tombstone with a font I despised, saying it was the single best way to ensure I would outlive him.

"What was tonight's compelling topic?" Aaron did not even try to disguise his sarcasm. I opened my mouth to answer, then closed it, opting not to provide more ammunition.

"We've been invited to a party," I eventually said.

"One of the type people?" His tone implied we belonged in a category of curious odd fellows: people who bred exotic orchids, or people who built replica cathedrals out of toothpicks, or people who cut intricate patterns into eggshells.

A long silence filled the room. "Why don't you want to go?"

"I don't . . ." he fumbled. After another long silence, he confessed: "I'm scared of the type people." A laugh burst out of my lungs. "You're too intense," he explained. "You get excited about serifs and upset about kerning. You can spend a half hour talking about the dot on an *i*."

"It's a . . ." My shoulders caved in as I let out a long sigh. "The thing over an *i* is a tittle, not a dot."

"You're making my argument for me, you know," he said with a chuckle. I gave him a playful scowl as he pulled another batch of cookies out of the oven. I got up and poured two glasses of milk.

A faded navy blue T-shirt with holes worn through the seams hung from his shoulders. Crackled fragments of the silk-screened words "White Bear Lake Fire" sat over his heart. He was no longer in the department, though he had been a volunteer firefighter for seven years.

"How fucked up is that?" I asked as I stared at the degraded white letters. "You'd rather run into a burning building with the guys than go to a party with my friends?"

He offered a hint of a smile. "Truth hurts, babe."

As 2011 drew to a close, evenings and weekends were devoured by end-of-year deadlines, work on the font, and the search for Marcel. Before I knew it, Christmas had arrived. I had not set up a tree or hung a single decoration. Gifts had been purchased online and wrapped in haste.

As Aaron and I gathered first with his family, then with mine, a nagging guilt consumed me, though *guilt* did not entirely make sense. Guilt implied I had done something wrong, and from the best I could figure, the guilt was for what I had not done: I had not found whether Marcel survived. It was as if the answer's absence left him locked inside the camp, lost in time, never returning home, never growing old. Marienfelde seemed to be a Neverland of unknowns.

Maybe the guilt was because Aaron and I were surrounded by bowls of chocolates and candy. Carols played on the stereo. Shiny bows decorated boxes. The aroma of fresh bread permeated the air, and tables were filled with more food than we could eat. Every one of those things felt unnecessary. The abundance seemed shameful.

Or maybe the guilt stemmed from the fact that neither Aaron nor I were consumed by the deep yearning for family Marcel expressed. I would have loved gatherings to be filled with embraces so long and tight I could not breathe, laughter that made my belly hurt, expressions of love that would echo in my memory for decades. But that was not the reality of either of our families. Weeks, sometimes months, elapsed between phone calls. A quick hug good-bye after wrapping ourselves in thick winter coats would be the extent of physical contact.

No one asked if I was working on anything interesting, and I did not offer a word about Marcel's letters or my search for answers. School for our nieces and nephews, and the weather; those were the safe, neutral topics discussed.

As we went around the room, opening practical gifts of kitchen tools, socks, or cash pressed flat inside a card, my mind wandered to Marcel. *How had he spent Christmas Day 1943? Did he even celebrate Christmas? Had Marcel been able to eat something that reminded him of home? Did his girls send him a card? A small gift?*

I hoped for Marcel that he made it home by Christmas 1944. But a sinking feeling washed through me, and I realized I did not even know if he was alive for Christmas 1944.

Chapter Six

White Bear Lake, Minnesota

January 2012

I knew about the cattle cars, the trays of gold fillings and wedding rings, the mountains of shoes and hair, the gas chamber selections. I could rattle off the camps' death-filled names: Auschwitz-Birkenau, Bergen-Belsen, Buchenwald, Dachau, Treblinka.

But it did not take long to realize how little I actually knew.

Some camps had functions other than extermination, though those were the only ones I remembered learning about in school. Some functioned as transit hubs, or were specifically for Communists, Roma, or Spanish refugees. Or, as with Ravensbrück, were for women. Others were true labor camps with *some* incentive to keep workers alive.

I was surprised to learn that camps in Germany had opened as early as 1933, camps existed in Norway and Finland, nearly eighty camps existed inside France, and 170 camps were located in Berlin. I was surprised to learn an organized hierarchy of camps and subcamps existed, that some were outposts with a "handful of prisoners," while others had been built to serve specific factories. In total, more than forty thousand camps, ghettos, and detention sites existed. The number felt too enormous to wrap my head around.

I was also surprised to learn a hierarchy existed among prisoners: Western European prisoners, political prisoners, and criminals received better treatment than Russians, Poles, and Jews—groups considered "subhuman" by the Germans. Western European workers received higher wages for their work and, in some cases, additional food. Some groups, including STO workers, had privileges even prisoners of war did not have, such as the right to unlimited correspondence.

Most online directories of concentration and labor camps—even ones with lists so shockingly long I had to scroll and scroll to get through them—did not include Berlin-Marienfelde. I was dumbfounded by its absence; I had not expected it would be as difficult to find information on Marienfelde as it was to find Marcel.

But I kept digging, and eventually found a description within a massive encyclopedia of camps.

"Berlin-Marienfelde was established as a subcamp of Sachsenhausen in late 1942 or early 1943," the book said. Marienfelde was described as a collection of "six or seven wooden barracks surrounded by barbed wire." The SS—the brutal Nazi paramilitary force—guarded the perimeter from watchtowers. An underground bunker was located near the entrance.

The five to six hundred prisoners in Marienfelde were from all across Europe and the Soviet Union. German political prisoners were even interred in camp. Prisoners cleared Berlin's streets, repaired and retiled roofs after bombings, and built air-raid shelters. Some were tasked with removing unexploded bombs.

Prisoners in Marienfelde subsisted on starvation rations of bread and beet soup and had to withstand long roll calls. Beatings were frequent, and one particularly cruel SS officer was known for pistol-whipping prisoners.

In August 1943, the book noted, most of the camp was destroyed in a bombing and subsequent fire. The prisoners who survived were transferred to other camps.

The description ended with an unsurprising caveat: sources describing Marienfelde were scarce.

It felt as though I had been holding my breath for weeks. This article was a breath of air—though it felt as if the air was choked with soot and blood.

Whenever I learned something new, I searched with increasingly specific terms such as "Marcel Heuzé Sachsenhausen," or "Marcel Heuzé *fremdarbeiter*" (the German term for foreign worker). One website would lead to another. Hours would disappear in a labyrinth of databases and documents. Whenever I found something promising, I pasted the text into a website to convert French or German into English. It was not difficult; it just added time. *Listes nominatives des registres.* Lists of names of registers. *Ressources biographiques et généalogiques.* Biographical and genealogical resources. *Inventaires d'archives.* Archive inventories.

But I still could not find any trace of Marcel. It began to feel as if he had been intentionally erased from history.

"You okay?" Aaron looked at me, then scanned the kitchen for clues to my anger. Scrubbing the stove at midnight was not something he expected to see when he came home after a long shift at the hospital. "Did a client piss you off?"

"Nope."

"Did *I* piss you off?"

"Nope." I tucked long, loose hairs behind my ear. We learned long ago when to leave each other alone; this was one of those times. I heard the armchair in the living room creak, followed by muffled sounds from the television.

Forty-five minutes later, I joined him.

"This evening I was reading about the corporations that used forced labor: Daimler, Bayer, Krupp . . ." I peeled the rubber gloves off my hands. "I didn't see a statistic for Daimler, but in other places the average life span of forced laborer was three and a half months. The Germans worked them to death, then . . ." The words felt sharp as they caught in my throat. "Then they would order more workers."

Aaron's expression mixed sorrow and pity with something I could not make sense of. *Should I have known that information already?*

The most backbreaking work was often completed by Russians, Poles, or Jews; those groups were considered more disposable than Western European laborers. *Disposable.* Treating people as a resource to be used, then tossed like garbage, was what enraged me. And it wasn't just Daimler and Bayer and Krupp. It was BMW, Siemens, Volkswagen, Porsche, Audi, and Kodak. It was Hugo Boss, who used forced labor to sew German uniforms. It even included Ford's German division, Fordwerke.

Hundreds of individuals were put on trial after the war, I had read, including Hitler's Commissioner-General for Manpower, Fritz Sauckel—the man who had been in charge of recruiting and distributing laborers. Sauckel was hanged for crimes against humanity, though any justice in his execution was too late for the thousands of forced laborers who died working for I.G. Farben, or for the starving Siemens workers returned to labor camps once they became too weak to be useful, or for Daimler workers executed after they "hesitated to obey a work command."

I did not tell Aaron the specific calculation that ran through my mind while I unleashed anger on the stove's black enamel: by the time Marcel had written the second letter, he had already survived fourteen months—four times longer than the average laborer. He had beaten the odds. But I did not expect he could be lucky indefinitely.

Lucky. As soon as that word formed inside my brain, a flood of shame washed through me. Surviving fourteen months in a camp where people were starved, beaten, and forced to build tanks for Nazis did not represent any shade of luck.

Lucky was definitely not the right word.

I sensed Aaron's growing frustration with the time and emotional energy I had been devoting to the search. To make time for the three of us—Hoover, Aaron, and me—he scheduled a long get-away weekend. Aaron had not said so explicitly, but I knew Marcel was not invited. So, despite the thoughts that swirled inside my head during the five-hour drive north, I was careful not to utter Marcel's name.

Our destination was a family-owned resort on a lake that straddled the Minnesota–Ontario border. The property included twenty or so cabins nestled along a frozen shore, a boathouse, and a sprawling main lodge. Thick wooden beams crisscrossed the lodge's high ceiling, and a moose head crowned with enormous antlers stared down from one wall.

On Friday morning, as we ate breakfast in our cabin, several white-tailed deer sauntered past our large picture window. Hoover looked at the deer, then swiveled to look at us with wide eyes, as if he were asking, *what the hell kind of giant dog is that?*

"Shake the bag, they'll come running," the man behind the front desk said later that morning as I filled a paper bag with scoops of dried corn kernels.

"If you're lucky they'll eat out of your hands," a guest standing nearby added. I carried the corn back to our cabin and tried to lure the deer in, though none would come closer than ten or fifteen feet.

For hours that afternoon, the three of us trekked the lodge's maze of snow-dusted trails. I kept a hopeful eye out for timber wolves or moose, though the only wildlife I saw was a snowshoe hare with back feet so out of proportion to its body, it reminded me of a child trying to walk in their parent's shoes.

Back in our cabin, we curled into the couch as logs in the fireplace crackled and roared. A week earlier, I had begun reading a new book on Vichy France, but I left it at home and brought a work of fiction that did not have anything to do with war. That night, I slept better than I had in months.

On Saturday morning, I pulled on my boots and parka and headed to the lodge for another bag of corn. The small herd was gathered in a thicket at the end of the property, and after offering exaggerated shakes to prove I had what they wanted, a few deer wandered my way. I held a cupped hand mounded full. It took a long while, but one deer eventually ate out of my hand. As she nibbled away, Aaron stood behind the cabin's picture window, making a silent clapping gesture. Hoover seemed frantic with jealousy I was giving treats to someone else.

That afternoon, we went on another hike deep in the forest. "Don't you dare," I warned as we walked through an enchanted grove where snow balanced on evergreen branches like thick swirls of frosting.

"What?" Aaron said in a *who-me?-I'm-perfectly-innocent* voice as he tucked his arm behind his back to hide a snowball. He tossed it to Hoover, who tried to catch it mid-air.

By the time we returned to our cabin, we were tired and cold but filled with peaceful wonder. Aaron started another fire, and as we wrapped ourselves in blankets and curled into the couch, all three of us succumbed to naps. Six months had elapsed since I had the first letter translated, and for the day, I was happy to let World War II retreat into history. Every new thing I learned pulled me deeper into an abyss of hate and horror. Spending the weekend free from visions of labor camps was what I needed. Here with my two brown-eyed boys was the only place I wanted to be.

On Sunday morning, as soon as we stepped outside with Hoover, we felt a precipitous drop in temperature. Our cabin did not have Internet access or television, so the change caught us off guard. Aaron marched to the lodge. The woman behind the front desk warned a storm would hit hard by midday and continue for twenty-four hours or more. As quickly as we could, we packed everything into Aaron's truck. We hoped to get ahead of the storm for the long drive home.

After an hour on an ice-rutted, two-lane road, we made it to Highway 61. Aaron released a long sigh as he merged onto the better-maintained, wider highway.

Highway 61 runs along the western shore of Lake Superior, extending from the Canadian border to Duluth. Some stretches of the road tower high above the lake; other places run low along the water's edge. The highway runs through tunnels carved from granite and past waterfalls, vertical rock walls, and the one-hundred-year-old yellow-and-white Splitrock Lighthouse.

A staccato plink of sleet hitting the windshield began just as we got caught behind a slow-moving sedan. We followed it for a mile or so, but Aaron could not contain his impatience. He accelerated to pass. As he pulled into the oncoming lane, he hit ice, and his truck skidded to the left. He corrected. We swung to the right and he corrected again. As we swung back to the left, his big truck lilted as if we were a boat going sideways over a wave. Despite this more-severe swing, he corrected again and we swung back to the right. But this time we kept going. As we spun in a full 360 going more than fifty miles per hour, I looked to confirm we were not on one of the stretches where cables attached to knee-high wooden posts were the only thing between us and a 150-foot plummet to the lake. I lifted my hand to confirm my seatbelt was on.

As I listened to the zipper-like whir of tires spinning on ice, I tried to assess what would fly around when the truck flipped: my purse, snow boots, hats, gloves. I glanced to the truck's back seat. Hoover was on the floor, out of view. I could not do a thing to secure him.

We went off the road. *Sideways.* My stomach lurched and jerked as we dipped into a ditch, angled up a small bank, then stuttered sideways like a stone skipping across a lake. Branches snapped. Limbs cracked. We careened into trees. Finally, we stopped so hard it felt as if we had hit a cement wall.

Aaron and I looked at each other in silence. Words had not yet caught up with us, it seemed. I glanced to the back seat and watched Hoover lift his blocky head to peer out the window to see what had disturbed his nap.

"You're okay," I said as I reached to rub his ear. "You're okay," I repeated.

Aaron's side of the truck was wedged against a tree, making it impossible to open his door. I kicked my door open to dislodge branches and step halfway out.

A semi rolled to a stop on the highway. The driver leaned out his window and hollered into the wind: "Should I call 911?"

I asked Aaron if he was okay. After what felt like an eternity, he nodded. He was okay. I was okay. Hoover was okay. I waved to the semi driver.

He yelled another question. I cupped my hand to my ear and he yelled again: "Do you have a cell phone?" I gave an affirming wave before I realized I had no idea where the phone was or if its battery was charged. I looked up to see the trucker begin a slow acceleration.

I squeezed out of the truck and told Aaron what I saw: a boulder in front of the bumper, a collection of scattered limbs and ripped branches.

"Why didn't the airbags go off?" I whispered. Aaron did not answer, and I realized he had not yet uttered a word. I fixed my gaze on him to confirm he really was uninjured.

After several tries, Aaron's truck roared back to life. Using every bit of horsepower the truck had, he extricated the truck from the trees, and with careful maneuvering, he got around the boulder and back on the highway.

The entrance to a state park was a few miles down the highway. I implored Aaron to pull into the parking lot. After rolling to a stop, he let out a long breath and peeled his fingers off the steering wheel. When I stepped onto the pavement, my knees buckled.

There were a hundred ways that could have ended badly, and only a couple of ways that could have ended well.

"You must have a guardian angel," I said.

If the ditch had been deeper, if we had crashed into a cliff, if we had careened into the water below, if a tree branch had entered the cab, if we had hit an oncoming car. *If, if, if.* None of those scenarios ended with us walking away.

"I was sure we were going to flip," Aaron mumbled again and again as we picked branches out of the bumpers. He seemed to be repeating it to convince himself we had not, in fact, flipped over. I attached Hoover's leash to his collar and had him jump out to confirm he was uninjured. He still seemed irritated his nap had been interrupted.

The drive home was calm and silent other than the occasional question. *Did we swerve three times or four? Did we spin clockwise?* Piecing together the sequence of events felt like splicing together snippets of film. The swerve-swerve-swerve-spin-fly-land sequence looped in my mind. I told Aaron it was beginning to feel like one of those highly scrutinized, super slow-motion, sports-commentator-accompanied videos of an ice skater preparing for, then completing, a triple toe loop jump.

"Well, in that case," Aaron said, "I'd get deductions for leaving the road and landing in trees. But you've gotta admit, I'd get high marks for the landing."

I twisted to look at him, unsure of what he meant.

"I landed on all four wheels. I *totally* stuck that landing," he said with a nod and a smirk.

"Yes," I conceded as I cracked a smile, "you stuck the landing."

That evening we sat on the couch and watched television, though the reality of what could have happened continued to consume our thoughts. At one point, Aaron pulled me close and held me tight.

Hours later, as we crawled into bed, I asked Aaron what he had thought about as the truck slid sideways. "Did you see your life flash before your eyes?"

"No," he said in a tone so deep and somber I had only heard it a few times in the sixteen years we had been married. "I just hoped the end would be fast and that I wouldn't feel it." He drew in a long breath. "How about you?"

I told him I did not remember, but that was not true.

In the second before impact, my final thought had been clear and definitive. And surprising. It should have been about Aaron or Hoover, friends or family. But it wasn't.

It was about Marcel.

My final thought was this: *I can't die before finding out if Marcel lived.*

Chapter Seven

White Bear Lake, Minnesota

January 2012

After the accident, Marcel's fate was no longer a curiosity. I *had* to know what happened to him.

Until that point, I had alternated between working on the font and searching for answers. To give the search all of my time and energy, I decided to stop working on the font. After years of starting, stopping, then starting again, this was different. This was a stop as definitive as Aaron's truck slamming into trees. This was putting down years of work until I had an answer. And, depending on what I learned, it was unclear whether I would—if I could—ever finish the font.

I retrieved the caramel-colored postcard from the sketchbook. Familiar stripes of blue and red angled across the card. Several small numbers had been penciled near the bottom: 5265, 4087. A large crimson "Ae" had been stamped over the address.

A mossy green stamp with Hitler's profile was preprinted in the corner; an adhesive-backed brown stamp with the same engraved illustration was adhered to its left. The illustration's detail and the formal pose—the portrait's veneer of respectability—surprised me. And sickened me.

I attempted to decipher Marcel's writing. The postcard appeared to be addressed to Madame Marcel Heuzé, Route de Sr Prest, Berchères-la-Maingot, jar Chartres, Eure-et-Lou. Despite what clearly appeared to be a dot over a *j* in *jar*, the letter was actually a *p*. It read *par Chartres*, by Chartres. And the *u* of *Lou* was actually an *i* next to an *r*. It read *Eure-et-Loir*.

A satellite map confirmed Berchères-la-Maingot was indeed a village near Chartres in the department of Eure-et-Loir. Vast farm fields and pockets of thick woods surrounded the small village. During the war, four hundred people lived in Berchères-la-Maingot. Seven hundred now called it home.

I scoured the map for Route de Sr Prest. I found a Rue Albert, Rue du Docteur, Rue aux Fleurs, Rue Gabriel, Rue du Moulin, Rue Panama, Rue Saint-Rémy. There was even a Rue de Préau, so I checked the postcard again to see if I might have misread that too, but the word Prest seemed clear. *Could the village have been bombed and rebuilt? Could streets have been renamed or rerouted?*

With a quick online search, I found a handful of charming images— old sepia postcards—with photos of Berchères-la-Maingot. On the first, which had been mailed in 1903, brick and stone barns enclosed a courtyard blanketed with a layer of hay. A man, a dog, and a young boy guarded a flock of fifty or so sheep huddled in a pinwheel of thick woolly bodies. Farmers stood in the background, tending to horses hitched to wagons with wheels as tall as a man.

The second postcard showed a dirt road running between brick and stucco buildings. One building had ornate diamond- and herringbone-patterned brickwork and rows of dark and light brick that looked like Morse code. Wide shutters flanked ground-floor windows. Some buildings in the distance had thatched roofs. A dozen people stood on the road. A woman in a shin-length skirt had a hand set high on her hip. Two boys wore tunics and knee socks with boots. A half dozen men wore newsboy caps; worn shirts draped from their shoulders. Their confounded stares made me wonder if that had been the first camera they had ever seen.

A third postcard showed a large pond surrounded by a swaybacked barn and tall stone walls. The heads and necks of two white geese poked above a fringe of grass. A woman sat near the water's edge; two young children sat nearby. I imagined the woman was drawing water. Maybe she had been doing laundry.

Life in Berchères-la-Maingot did not appear easy, in the way rural life can often be consumed by a never-ending cycle of chores. But I hoped its rural location and small size provided a safe haven for Marcel's family.

I would have written a letter to the current homeowner if I had a valid address. With luck, someone in the family would still live there. But I only had the name of a street—a street that did not seem to exist—so the only option seemed to be to send a letter to the city office. In a village that small, it was hard to believe someone wouldn't know something.

My letter included a request for information about the property's current ownership and, more boldly, asked if someone might know the postwar status of the Heuzé family. I used an online service to translate the short letter into French and added the note: "*Je m'excuse pour les erreurs dans la traduction; Je ne parle pas Français.*" I apologize for errors in the translation; I do not speak French.

I was confident I would receive a response in a week or two. Three weeks at the most.

But that letter to Berchères-la-Maingot was the first in what would become a long list of letters mailed to France. It was also the first in a long list of letters that would go unanswered.

I assumed a small farming village would be safer than Paris, but I came to understand that was not necessarily true. In June 1944, the Germans received word that the Résistance in Oradour-sur-Glane—a farming village slightly larger than Berchères-la-Maingot—had captured a German officer. The intelligence was actually about a village called Oradour-sur-Vayres, but the Germans did not seem to care about the mistake. Every resident of Oradour-sur-Glane was rounded up. The men were shot. Women and children were locked inside a church, then burned alive. If the women attempted to escape, they were shot, too. One hundred and ninety men, 247 women, and 205 children were murdered. One baby was crucified. Only one woman survived.

A thought entered my mind that made thick tears pool in my eyes. Maybe the letters had been in Stillwater because Marcel's wife and daughters did not survive.

Maybe *no one* in the family survived to treasure his letters.

"Here is the latest from our dear friend Marcel," Tom's email read.

Weeks earlier, when I scanned the third letter for Tom, I had to take the utmost care to prevent the fragile center crease from dissolving in two. The letter had been written in opaque black ink on a single piece of wheat-colored paper preprinted with light blue grid lines, then folded in half vertically to create four pages. Dark smudges ran along one of the front edges, though those were the only marks. Tiny numbers had not been scribbled in pencil. Blue and red stripes had not been painted across the page.

I had bought this letter because it included several lovely characters: a sweeping *R*, a curlicue *E*, a looping *z*. But I had failed to anticipate that the nearly vertical writing would make those specific letters a nightmare to incorporate into the angled font.

At the bottom of the last page, Marcel signed his name with a backward loop that formed a long, bold underline. He had been in Marienfelde nearly ten months, and the signature seemed defiant, as if he were proclaiming: *I'm still here. I'm still strong. I haven't given in. I haven't given up.*

Tom noted he had spent time searching for information on Marcel, too, but had not found a thing. "Marcel doesn't give up his secrets easily," he wrote.

I slowly nodded. *No, no he did not.*

Marienfelde le 3 Novembre

Ma petite Chérie

Aujourd'hui, mercredi, il fait un temps triste,
comme, je ne suis pas descendu, à la cantine, j'en
profite pour te faire une petite lettre. D'abord il
faut que je te souhaite une bonne fête, car ma
lettre te parviendra, sans doute un peu avant le
11 novembre. C'est la première fois que je ne
serai pas avec toi pour te souhaiter ta fête.
Rassure-toi, je ne serai peut être pas long
a arrivé quand tu auras reçue cette lettre, car
on parle beaucoup, d'un départ, pour le 22
ou le 23 novembre, mais c'est toujours la même
chose, rien d'Officiel. Des chuchotements, dans les
carrées et dans les bureaux. Et pour finir on
attend toujours. Ce qu'il y a de certain, c'est
qu'on a relevé les noms de tous ceux qui étaient-

Marienfelde, Germany

November 3 (1943)

My little darling,

Today, Wednesday, the weather is dreary. So I didn't go down to the canteen but decided to write you a little letter instead. First I need to wish you a happy Name Day because my letter will probably get to you a bit before November 11th. This is the first time I won't be with you to celebrate your Name Day. Rest assured that it won't be long before I return when you will have received this letter, because they're talking a lot about a departure on November 22nd or 23rd, but it's always the same thing, nothing official. Whispering in the squares and in the offices. And we're still waiting. What is certain is that they revealed the names of those who might get leave and that's all.

Today I'm going to the office to send you money, maybe I'll learn something new. Last night I went to the station to get information about the train schedule for my Saturday trip to see Pierrot. I have to leave at 6:30 in the morning to arrive in Eisenach at 12:30. As usual I ran into some cops and they had me show them my papers for 15 minutes. My job isn't very hard right now, so I can think about writing to you peacefully. My poor dear, this year you won't have the pain of asking for something for your Name Day. I wanted to buy you something in Berlin, but I couldn't find anything there. I will make it up to you when I'm in Paris.

It has been a while since I've received a letter. That seems strange to me because when I write to you I like to reread the last letter that I received from you. And the last was from October 15, I know it by heart. The day before yesterday I received a letter from Moutardier. His house has started the process to release him as a father of four children. I would really like to have news from my daughters also, now that they've gone back to school, they should really write to their father. And Lily, does she go with her sisters? I have some good news from Uncle Joseph who says his children are misbehaving more and more and he doesn't have the means to control them. It's probably because winter has started. Here we haven't yet gone below zero and now it looks more like rain. Unfortunately again at noon someone got sick on my ladle. It took some work to find another, luckily I still have two in stock. The first one that shines too much, watch out for that one. I just went to send 100 marks and to look for my permission to go see Pierre. It's 3:30, now I will work a little. Since I last heard from you I think Grandma must have gone to Berchères, I was thinking I could go see them there. I can't wait for 7 o'clock to see if I have a letter or a little package. My buddy Maurice says hi to you and also asks you to think about the chicken. He's asking how that is progressing.

Here we are at the final page of my letter, and this morning I didn't really know what to write. I have a friend who is supposed to get his permission the same time as mine, he's the former client of the Boss. One strange guy here is the Sports Director. He already has plans to find work in the countryside. So if he is forced to come back he will come back with me, but not where we are now.

My little wolf, I will finish this letter for tonight. If I have news, I will write you again tomorrow. Give my little girls big kisses from me, and to Mother too. Your big boy who sends you, for your Name Day, the most tender kisses, always looking forward to be able to hold you in his arms. Your Marcel who loves you always and who says maybe see you soon. In one hour it's supper. Your big boy, Marcel

Chapter Eight

White Bear Lake, Minnesota

February 2012

I immediately emailed a message back to Tom: "What's a Name Day?"

In France and other European nations, Tom replied, it is a special day, kind of like a birthday, but it is celebrated on the day of the saint for whom a person is named. Tom, for example, celebrated his Name Day on July 3, the day designated for Saint Thomas. People often give friends and family small gifts or flowers, he noted, and in some places, Name Days are celebrated more widely than actual birthdays.

I nearly leapt out of my chair when I realized what that meant. So far, I had only known Marcel's wife as "my little darling" or "Madame Marcel Heuzé"—but I could determine her name by looking up her Name Day!

Within moments, I was reviewing a French Name Day list. November 11 was the day for Saint Vérane.

I had never heard the name Vérane before. I turned it over in my mind and tried saying it out loud: first with an emphasis on the *é*, then with an emphasis on the *n*.

She finally had a name!

And I had another name to search for.

Once the jubilation subsided, I read Tom's translation again. Then again. I scrutinized each line for clues.

I considered the way Marcel referred to Berchères-la-Maingot, and had a renewed sense it was not home. I let out a sigh. *If that was true, where was he from?*

The passages about traveling to Eisenach and shopping in Berlin were surprising. *Was he really able to leave the camp?*

The reference to the ladle was unusual. I read the line over and over. Coded messages were sometimes hidden in benign-sounding phrases such as "the dice are on the mat," "It's hot in Suez," or "John has a long mustache." I could only guess whether "the first one that shines too much, watch out for that one" actually referred to a ladle—or if it alluded to something else entirely. In the days that followed, I searched for ladle-related coded messages, but did not find a thing.

I thought of Pierrot, Maurice, and Moutardier, along with the men Marcel mentioned in the second letter: Marcel, Mimile, and Bernard. I did not know anything about them other than their first names, but I was grateful for their presence. It was reassuring to read that Marcel was surrounded by men he considered friends. There had to be benefit in having people watch out for each other, having people to provide camaraderie and moral support.

Finally, I thought of Marcel's confident hopefulness. It warmed me to my core. I admired the fact he told Vérane he would buy her something "*when* I'm in Paris," not "*if* I come home." *Did Marcel truly believe he was going home in a few weeks?* My heart ached because I knew it was untrue; from the date on the postcard, he would be there at least five more months.

The next morning, I sent Tom scans of the fourth letter and the postcard. I did not care how much it would cost to translate them. I had to know if the letters held answers to Marcel's fate.

After scanning the letters for Tom, I shuffled through office supplies until I found clear plastic sheet protectors. One by one, I slid Marcel's letters between the pieces of plastic, then carefully pressed the sleeves flat under the sketchbook cover. It was the least I could do to protect them.

When Aaron and I lived in Dallas, I bought a charming pear-shaped teapot at a neighborhood antique store. The handwritten tag claimed the teapot was decades old, which made its fifteen-dollar price seem like a bargain. A chip marred the handle, but I did not mind. The flaw seemed to provide proof of years of cozy gatherings. After bringing it home, I placed the teapot in the center of our small kitchen table.

Weeks later, when I was in a megastore and saw the exact same teapot, new and unchipped, on clearance for a few dollars, I was furious at myself for being so gullible. I got rid of the teapot soon after. I could not bear to keep a reminder of how easily I could be deceived.

I am aware of my gullible nature. I vigilantly avoid people who break promises, and I try to guard myself from people who do not have good intentions. I try to keep foolish optimism in check, yet every once in a while I fall for something.

When the thought materialized that Marcel's letters might not be real—a question whispered, I assumed, by my inner, self-protective skeptic—the familiar knot began twisting in my core, and I berated my foolishness. *Who the hell finds handwritten letters from a World War II labor camp at an antique store in Minnesota? Why hadn't it occurred to me before now these letters might be forgeries written on artificially discolored paper, or that twenty variations might have been sold in antique stores across the Midwest?* Instead of being written to Suzanne, Denise, and Lily, maybe other versions had been written to Sarah, Diane, and Rose from a man named Martin. Or to Simone, Danielle, and Iris from a man named Michel.

The pit in my stomach grew as I realized how *convenient* it was that Marcel had only called his wife "my darling." And that Route de Sr Prest did not exist. The more I thought about it, the more enraged I became. *No wonder I had been unable to find him!* I had wasted money on translations, then wasted months trying to find a person that did not exist. Someone, it seemed, had made Marcel up with as much ingenuity as Tim and I had used to invent Eliza Steele fifteen years earlier. And I fell for it.

I had believed Marcel was real in the exact same way people had believed Eliza had been a pioneer writing in a lantern-lit journal. *Who signs letters, "your big boy who sends you the most tender kisses, always looking forward to be able to hold you in his arms"? Or writes about someone singing in a barrack? Far-off bombings? The odd-looking swastika? Painted blue and red stripes?* As the list of suspicious elements grew, I berated myself mercilessly. No one can be more cruel than I am to myself in moments like that.

I wanted to rip up the letters and destroy every shred of evidence of my gullibility in the same way I had to get rid of the pear-shaped teapot. *Idiot! How could I have been such an idiot?*

At least I had not gone public with my search, which, mercifully, meant I would not have to go public with a humiliating retraction. I could try to forget about the time and money wasted, the nights I shorted myself on sleep. I could finish the font and never mention where the inspiration came from. Kathy, Tom, and Aaron were the only ones who knew about the translations. When the time was right, I would confess to Kathy and Tom what I had learned. Aaron knew how gullible I could be; I knew he would not shame me.

That night, as I lay in the blackness, listening to Aaron's slow and steady snore, I churned through every detail. Every piece of evidence was reexamined.

Could I put a drop of water on the paper to see if it had been age-stained with tea?

Could an expert authenticate the Hitler stamps? The papermaker's watermark? The cancellation mark made by the post office?

I tried to recall how much I paid for the letters. I knew it had not been much. If they were fake, it seemed like a whole lot of work went into creating something that did not sell for much money. But a devil of doubt whispered a reminder in my ear: the pear-shaped teapot had not been expensive, either.

Ultimately, I decided if a grain-of-sand chance existed these letters were real, I *had* to keep looking. I had to find out if Marcel was reunited with his wife and daughters. I decided to continue searching for him— but with heightened skepticism. I vowed not to say a word to anyone else about what I was doing until I could determine with certainty whether Marcel and his letters were real.

I unceremoniously dumped the contents of the font's job jacket onto my desk. Every project was assigned a job jacket; it was a way to organize records of budgets and approvals, copies of preliminary and final layouts, and detailed time and expense records. Even though the font was not an *official* client project, I had assigned the project a job jacket so I could keep the tracings and the progression of test prints in one place.

I shuffled through the papers looking for the expense record; it would have an annotation with the name of the store and how much I paid. I knew from other visits to Stillwater that the store was no longer open, but if I had the name of the store, I might be able to track the antique dealer down. It seemed possible they might still live in the area. If so, I could ask what, if anything, they remembered about where they got the letters.

The expense record was blank. There was not a single word or number written on the page. "Fucking figures," I muttered.

I went through every piece of paper again, hoping the original receipt might be stuck between the tracings and test prints, but it was not there. I retrieved the sketchbook from the closet and flipped through every page, looking for any scrap of paper that might be a receipt. It was not there, either.

Had I paid for the letters out of our personal checking account? It seemed possible since "font design" was not yet something I felt comfortable claiming as a business expense. I tried conjuring any memory of the payment transaction, but came up blank. For all I knew, I could have paid in cash and told the saleswoman I did not need a receipt.

Did I find the letters the summer before I started freelancing? The summer after? Had it been winter? The first entry on the time sheet was May 2004. By then, I was digitizing individual glyphs, which meant none of the time tracing the handwriting had been recorded.

I had not assigned the font a job number right away since I thought it would be a quick and easy little project. I rolled my head back and stared at a cobweb draping from the ceiling fan as I let out a long sigh. This meant I had neither a record of where, nor of when, I bought the letters. And no clear record of when I started the project.

Aaron got home from work at midnight. I was in bed; the reading lamp created a cone of light over my head. Aaron peeked into the room. When he saw I was still awake, he crawled into bed next to me.

"Now what are you reading?"

I snapped the book shut so he could see the cover. Below the title, the famous Mercedes star was positioned above a swastika. Then, as now, Daimler-Benz built Mercedes cars.

"That's a book"—Aaron paused as he chose his words—"I never want to read."

I suspected he knew I did not really care about Daimler-Benz; I only hoped to learn something that would shed light on Marcel.

"It's about management strategy more than anything." I looked at Aaron and shrugged. "It's like reading a textbook."

"No other motor company did so much for the Third Reich," the book claimed. In the 1930s, Daimler factories roared to life manufacturing airplane motors and armored vehicles, then tanks, trucks, and rocket parts. As Germany's military buildup continued, Berlin-Marienfelde management received guarantees they "would be provided with sufficient business with army contracts from the War Ministry for . . . years."

"It has tables on month-by-month factory output," I growled.

Aaron rolled his eyes. "I suppose they couldn't say 'no' to what Hitler demanded."

"That doesn't excuse how they achieved it."

"No, certainly not." After a moment of silence, he asked whether the book said anything about Marienfelde.

I nodded and shrugged; Marienfelde had been mentioned a few times. Pockets of resistance had been found within Marienfelde's workforce. At least five workers had been executed.

"Daimler would order a thousand workers at a time," I said. They could order workers as easily as we ordered pizza, it seemed.

"At Marienfelde?" Aaron clarified.

"That was a different factory. Gens-something." One thousand workers had been ordered from the Ravensbrück and Sachsenhausen camps to work at Daimler's Genshagen factory. *Ravensbrück, Sachsenhausen*: the names made a shiver run down my spine.

"Marcel was lucky to be in Germany." I paused, catching the repeat of my unfortunate word choice. "The worst human rights violations happened in Poland."

In 1942, Daimler requested workers for their aircraft engine factory in Reichshof, Poland. Workers were initially unavailable, so German authorities invited factory officials to participate in the next "combing out." Daimler brought trucks to Debica, where five thousand Jews from the city's ghetto had been "herded together by the SS." The Daimler representative handpicked the workers he wanted. Anyone not selected was sent to the Bełzec extermination camp.

It was quiet for a few minutes.

"I'm getting you new books," Aaron said.

"Why?" I asked with a little laugh.

"You need to start reading chick lit like a normal girl."

Daimler's World War II activities were not hidden on their website, but the information was not easily found without searching for it.

I searched for it.

"Armament production accounted for an ever-growing proportion of the company's revenues up to the start of the war," their website stated. "Spare parts production and the repair of military vehicles and engines were also growing in importance. New staff were needed to handle the increased armament production because many workers were fighting on the front line.

"Initially, the company recruited women in order to cope with the required unit volumes. However, as staff numbers were still too low, Daimler-Benz also used forced laborers. These prisoners of war, abducted civilians and detainees from concentration camps were housed close to the plants. Forced labourers from western Europe lived in guest houses, private accommodation or schools.

"Workers from eastern Europe and prisoners of war were interned in barrack camps with poor, prison-like conditions. Concentration camp detainees were monitored by the SS under inhumane conditions. They were 'loaned out' to companies in exchange for money. In 1944, almost half of Daimler-Benz's 63,610 Daimler Benz employees were civilian forced labourers, prisoners of war or concentration camp detainees."

A handful of black-and-white photos accompanied the text. One image showed rows of aircraft engines propped on frames inside the Marienfelde factory. Another showed a line of spare, single-level wooden barracks along a barren road. The image was of the Riedmühle labor camp, not Marienfelde, and it was as if the photo had been taken after construction was complete to show how clean and tidy Daimler's accommodations were.

I submitted a brief inquiry on Marcel to Daimler's US Corporate Communications department using a form on the website. I hoped to hear back, but I did not expect I would. I had not received replies to any of the other letters or emails I had sent to various organizations.

When an email arrived two days later, in English, from a Daimler archivist in Stuttgart, Germany, my heart began to race. "In order to make further investigations," the email read, "I want to ask you: What is the reason of your question? Have you any relations or references to Mr. Heuzé? I have to ask because your question is about confidential personal information."

I felt like jumping up and dancing around my office. *They know something! They've got to know something!* But I sat in my chair, frozen, staring into my monitor, processing an unanticipated problem: if I acknowledged I was not related to Marcel, Daimler might not be able to tell me anything. They might be *prohibited* from sharing information with anyone other than family. It felt as if the answers I sought were hidden behind some kind of trapdoor.

I knew I should not lie. I knew I should not claim to be family. But dishonesty was a tempting path if it led to answers.

For a week, I held a fierce debate with myself.

After drafting my response to the Daimler employee, I read it to Aaron:

"Regarding my inquiry about Marcel Heuzé, no, I am not a relative, but I do have a deep personal connection to him. Please allow me to explain.

"I am a graphic designer and a type designer. Years ago I purchased a small collection of handwritten letters. I have no information about how these letters ended up in Minnesota. The letters are written in French, and although I could not read anything more than the occasional word, I purchased them because the extraordinary handwriting provided the inspiration for a computer font I have been designing.

"I began to wonder about the letters' contents. Six months ago, I commissioned the translation of the first letter. Marcel wrote the letters to his wife and three daughters in France. The letters are written with tremendous affection—it's heartbreaking to read how much he misses them. He states he thinks about them all the time.

"The letters include detail about his life working at the Daimler-Marienfelde factory, and I believe he was one of the many conscripted French civilians. He writes about many things. Food is a common topic. Mr. Heuzé talks about letters being censored, having to show his papers when traveling, mending clothes, the weather, and enjoying a soccer game despite the cold. The first letter was written February 1, 1943, and the last letter is postmarked April 4, 1944.

"I hope to find out he returned home and was reunited with his wife and his daughters. I realize not many World War II stories end happily, but I hope this is one story that does. I understand, though, the possibility of being injured at the factory, falling ill, or being killed in one of the bombings is a real potential outcome. So, too, is the possibility he was taken by the Russians when they gained control of Berlin. I have attempted to search for answers online, but I have not been able to find anything, which is why I contacted you."

I outlined what I knew:

Name: Marcel Heuzé

Hometown: Berchères-la-Maingot, France

Dates at factory: Start date of January 12, 1943–April 1944 (or later)

His return address: Lager D4 West, Chambre 21/3, Berlin Marienfelde, Deutschland

"If you are able to share only one bit of information," my email continued, "I am interested in finding out whether he was released to return home, or if you have a record of his death. If you are able to share any other information, I am also interested in learning what work he did at the Daimler factory because that may provide context for passages in his letters."

I looked up at Aaron and shrugged. He asked me to repeat the name of the Daimler employee.

"Wolfgang," I said.

"*Volfgaaang. Offf course, hisss name ist Volfgaaang.*" I rolled my eyes at Aaron's comically thick, deep, mock-German accent.

"Where did you find the start date?" The specificity of Aaron's question surprised me since he had not shown much interest in my search.

"In one letter Marcel said 'today is the twelfth, exactly fourteen months since I started working at Daimler.' I just did the math."

After a few moments he nodded and said, "It's good. Send it."

In the end, I could not lie. I understood my decision might have consequences. I understood telling the truth might mean Wolfgang might not be able to give me information even if he wanted to. But it would have felt as if I was lying to Marcel, and I could not do that. If Wolfgang took anything from my email, I hoped he would see it was an earnest inquiry. And since I still did not have proof Marcel's letters were real, I also hoped the information I outlined was true.

Yet, after sending the email, I could not shake a feeling of dread. I felt certain I had made the wrong choice by revealing everything. I felt certain I should have lied.

I had gotten into the habit of checking email every morning immediately after waking up. A couple of mornings later, an email from Wolfgang awaited. I did not yet have my glasses on, so I squinted and leaned close to my computer monitor. "Indeed," Wolfgang wrote, "we have a handwritten record, in which Mr. Heuzé is mentioned as a worker in the Daimler-Benz plant Berlin-Marienfelde."

Wolfgang outlined what their records showed:

Name: Marcel Heuzé

Born: January 26, 1912

Hometown: Boissy-le-Châtel

Family: Married. Wolfgang noted a numeral 3 had been written on the record, which he assumed meant three children.

Date of entrance: January 13, 1943

Date of leaving the factory: November 11, 1943

Working for: Department 210 as a turner

Home: Berlin-Marienfelde, Daimlerstraße

"There are some differences to your information, concerning the hometown and the period Mr. Heuzé was engaged in the plant. But I am convinced that Marcel Heuzé in our records matches with your Marcel Heuzé." Wolfgang added, "We are sorry, we haven't any additional information about the destiny of Marcel Heuzé."

Wolfgang went on to note Marcel's letters were of "high interest for our archives, as he describes the situation in the plant."

Finally, Wolfgang explained that a book titled *Forced Labor with Daimler-Benz* included a chapter on Berlin-Marienfelde. He offered to send a PDF of the chapter, though he noted it was only available in German.

The room seemed to spin as I tried to make sense of everything: *Was Boissy-le-Châtel home? Wolfgang's start date was one day different than what I had figured—could that have been an issue of when paperwork was processed? Department 210 turner: what did that mean?*

My mind returned to the words "date of leaving the factory: November 11." My heart nearly burst in half from happiness. *He went home! Marcel went home! Or he might have gone home; at least Wolfgang's record had not included a record of his death.*

I pushed back from the desk, and with an enormous smile, I geared up to take Hoover out for our morning walk. If any of our neighbors saw us, they might have been surprised to see how cheery I looked that cold winter morning. I trudged along in my boots and parka, but it felt as though I were one of those inflatable parade balloons floating fifty feet in the air, tethered to the ground by Hoover's thin leash. *He went home! Marcel went home!*

Another thought materialized, and it felt as though a ton of bricks had just been lifted from my shoulders. I could not help but smile an even bigger smile. The birthdate Wolfgang provided was different than the birthdate of the Marcel who died in Ravensbrück. Wolfgang had just provided evidence confirming *my* Marcel was *a different* Marcel. *My* Marcel was real. That meant *all* of this was real: his love-filled letters, his affection for Vérane, Suzanne, Denise, and Lily, his cherry, pear, and plum trees. *It was real.*

But a second later, it felt as if every brick landed back on my shoulders with a heavy *whump.* It was real: the Russians, the hunger, the desperate longing.

As Hoover and I continued our swing around the block, I calculated Marcel's age. Marcel had started working for Daimler two weeks before his thirty-first birthday. *He had been even younger than I guessed.*

Forty-five minutes later, when I returned to my office showered and dressed for the day, I jotted a quick email to Wolfgang expressing my gratitude for his response. I confirmed my interest in the chapter he offered, and noted I would consider his request for the letters.

I yearned to look at the good news again, so I opened Wolfgang's email and reread his message. A third of the way through, every cell in my body seemed to freeze. I stared at the monitor. I had initially misread something.

Wolfgang's information could not be correct.

It just wasn't . . . possible.

Chapter Nine

White Bear Lake, Minnesota

Late February 2012

Wolfgang's record had to be wrong. *It had to.*

Marcel could not have left Marienfelde on November 11, 1943, because the second letter Tom translated had been sent from Marienfelde four months later: March 12, 1944. For a few long minutes, I sat motionless, processing the information in Wolfgang's email, attempting to cobble together any answer that made sense.

Hours later, another email from Wolfgang arrived. He attached a black-and-white image of two expressionless men standing at long machines with belt-operated spindles. Neither man was Marcel, Wolfgang clarified, but he wanted me to see the type of work Marcel would have done as a *dreher*. Dreher, turner, lathe operator: these men ground, shaped, and polished metal pieces. The work required precision and specialty training.

As I imagined the scream of grinding metal and pictured those two men laboring at those machines day after day, week after week, I wondered: *Did it seem as if hope was the thing they were grinding away?*

Wolfgang also attached the chapter on Daimler-Marienfelde, as promised. It was in German, which meant I had to hire yet another translator. I corrected myself: I did not *have* to. But no doubt existed I was *going* to.

As I scrolled through the chapter's pages, black-and-white before-and-after photos of the Marienfelde factory entrance caught my attention. The before photo showed a stout brick wall with a large arched entryway. A road ran below the center of the arch with pedestrian entrances on each side. Forty or more people flooded through the archways; I guessed they were workers leaving at the end of a shift. Three men walked bicycles. Two women walked arm-in-arm.

Above the center arch was a large sign showing a swastika inside a gear. Three words arced above the symbol; smaller words flanked each side. The small words were hopelessly indecipherable. But I did not even need an official translation to make sense of the large words. One year of high school German was enough. *Wir marschieren mit.* We march with.

The after image showed the same entrance. The bones of the archway still stood, but the stout brick wall had been obliterated and its rubble had been piled high. The two pedestrian entrances were blocked by debris. Three men, holding shovels or hoes, stood as a handful of pedestrians walked down the single-lane path open through the center.

It would be another a year and a half before I learned about the International Tracing Service in Bad Arolsen, Germany. The International Tracing Service is the central repository for documents on World War II incarceration, forced labor, and the Holocaust. Their mission is to "keep the memory of the millions of victims of Nazi persecution alive."

Some documents in their archives came from the Red Cross; others had been confiscated by military units as camps were liberated. The International Tracing Service claimed to have materials indexed in a way that linked thirty million documents to more than seventeen million people.

For decades, their archives were only accessible to survivors and immediate family members, but in 2007 they were opened to researchers and other "interested parties." I puffed up when I realized I met the definition of an *interested party*, and I submitted an inquiry.

Days later, an email arrived from a researcher named Birgit. A preliminary examination of their archives revealed "multiple references" for Marcel Heuzé, she noted. She wondered if I could provide any additional information. I speculated if Birgit found *multiple* Marcel Heuzés, she had also found the Marcel who had been murdered at Ravensbrück. In my reply, I clarified the Ravensbrück Marcel was a different man, and outlined everything I knew about *my* Marcel.

Birgit ultimately found nine documents. There was no cost for her research time, but she included a small invoice, payable via bank transfer, to order scans of those nine documents.

I was simultaneously surprised—and not surprised—that Birgit found nine records within an archive of thirty million documents in a matter of days. I had repeatedly read the Germans had been meticulous record keepers.

A nondescript brown envelope arrived a week and a half after the bank transfer went through. I popped Birgit's CD into my computer and tried to make sense of the pages filled with columns of typed names and dates: *Geburtstag*. Birthday. *Geburtsort*. Birthplace. *Frankreich*. France. *Dauer des Aufenthaltes*. Length of stay.

One particular date caught my eye: 11.11.43.

The date sounded familiar, though it took a while to realize why. When I figured it out, my heart dropped like a stone: November 11, 1943, was the date Wolfgang claimed Marcel had left Marienfelde. Wolfgang's information never made sense, but according to the scan in front of me, it had been true. Marcel indeed left Marienfelde on November 11, 1943.

On that day, Marcel had been transferred to Spandau Prison.

For a moment, I could not breathe.

The single document typed in French, not German, listed offenses committed by the men transferred to Spandau. Five were imprisoned for theft, three for concealment. Others had been imprisoned for contraband, forged handwriting, disloyalty, or for providing a false name. Two men were imprisoned for "*faute c/règl. de consommation*."

That was Marcel's offense. He had "run afoul of food regulations."

"Punishable acts"—infractions considered disobedient but not criminal—were exempt from judicial review. Accusations did not require proof. Workers like Marcel could be transferred to a prison or a "corrective" camp without trial.

To add to the humiliation, "Foreign workers . . . absent from their working place for reasons such as serving a prison term . . . were to be considered as having stayed away from their work by default, 'just as if they had been absent because they went "on a spree" or for some similar reason.'" Work contracts were extended by the length of the prison term.

A spree? A spree! Anger roiled through me.

I would read an account of one French prisoner in Sachsenhausen "battered to death for taking two carrots from a sheep pen," and another account of a Frenchman executed after a German's sandwich went missing. I tried to wrap my head around a world where starving men were killed for stealing food, others broke food rules and were spared, and time in prison was considered a spree.

"You're *really* trying to make sense of that?" Aaron's words felt less like a question and more like an accusation.

I asked Wolfgang if he would go through Daimler's records once again. Within days, he found a record showing Marcel's reentry into the Marienfelde camp on February 7, 1944. My heart ached when I realized Marcel had spent Christmas 1943, New Year's 1944, his Name Day, and his thirty-second birthday in a prison with such a horrific legacy for hate and abuse that when it was demolished, its bricks were ground to dust, then buried.

Frenchmen rallied around fellow citizens when—*if*—they returned to the labor camp, I read. They pooled money to buy food and help others "get on their feet." I hoped that happened for Marcel. I hoped the men he befriended embraced him upon his return, and enveloped him with as much kindness and assistance as they could muster. Once again, gratitude swelled for these men I knew only by first names.

To my surprise, Wolfgang sent scans of the ledger pages documenting Marcel's two entries into the Daimler-Marienfelde camp.

The records, which began on left-hand pages and continued all the way across the right-hand page, were inscribed in an efficient looping script with smooth black ink. Abbreviations in crimson ink identified each man's nationality: French, Belgian, Italian, Dutch. The twenty-five vertical lines that created columns filled with names, places, numbers, dates, and departments were like bars of a jail cell. Marienfelde, it seemed, was no different than Spandau Prison.

Top: Left-hand page of two-page ledger showing Marcel's entry into the camp on January 13, 1943, and his exit on November 11, 1943. Bottom: Left-hand page of two-page ledger showing Marcel's reentry on February 7, 1944.
Courtesy: Mercedes-Benz Classic Archives

My heart sank as I realized what one of those numbers reflected. Marcel had been assigned a number. He was worker 210737.

The second ledger page—the one that showed Marcel's reentry into the camp in February, 1944—did not include an exit date.

"That's not a surprise," Aaron said with a shrug. "Everything was chaos at the end. Keeping good records would have been the last of Daimler's priorities."

November 11, 1943—the day Marcel had been transferred to Spandau—sounded familiar for another reason, though for weeks I could not figure out why. The date rolled around inside my brain: November 11. *November 11.* N-o-v-e-m-b-e-r e-l-e-v-e-n-t-h.

Hoover and I were walking around the block when I realized what had been eluding me: November 11 was Vérane's Name Day. It was a day for celebrations, for gifts, for flowers. But Vérane's 1943 Name Day had to be a day of shattering heartbreak—that was, if she even knew what happened to her husband eight hundred miles away.

The letter Marcel had written eight days before he was transferred to Spandau did not hint at problems. In fact, it sounded as though he believed he might be heading home soon. I hoped one of the other men had been able to notify Vérane of what had happened. But maybe Marcel had been transferred to Spandau without a word. Maybe, for a desperate two and a half months, Marcel was missing. Absent. Unaccounted for. I could not fathom the worry that must have tormented Vérane as she waited for one of his letters. Letters, I had come to understand, that were not just proof of love. Marcel's letters were proof of life.

"Why do you think Wolfgang wants them?" Aaron and I sat in the living room, finishing dinner as the news played in the background.

"Do you think he wants to bury them?" Aaron asked.

"That's what I'm afraid of," I confessed.

Wolfgang contacted me twice more making a case for Daimler's acquisition of the letters. "For our archives only. We would handle them strictly confidential," he assured me. "We want to do all to keep the memories of this chapter of our company's history," he said in another email. "The contents of Marcel Heuzé's letters from Berlin-Marienfelde are very important."

It was unthinkable. Giving Marcel's letters to Daimler would be returning the one thing Marcel had control over—his private thoughts and feelings—to those who imprisoned him. *If Daimler had custody of the letters, could they hide what happened inside their camp? Could Daimler make the only tangible proof that seemed to prove Marcel even existed disappear entirely? What would giving Daimler the letters mean for the font? Could that mean I might not be able to release it? Could that mean I might never be able to mention Marcel's handwriting as the source?*

Aaron's eyes lit up with a familiar spark of mischief. "What?" I asked.

"See if you can trade 'em for a car!" I drew in a breath of fake indignation and hissed his name as we laughed. I knew he had been kidding. Or, I hoped he had been kidding.

I would never trade them. I stole a glance at Aaron.

I was not as sure what he would do.

His idea was not entirely far-fetched. I probably *could* trade them for a car. *What would a car—even one that cost $50,000—be to Daimler?* I envisioned a shiny black Mercedes pulling into our driveway, carrying a team of corporate lawyers wearing bespoke suits. "We'll give you this car right here right now if you give us the letters," I imagined them offering. Then I imagined them demanding.

The next day, I took Marcel's letters to our safe-deposit box.

"On one hand, I question whether Daimler should benefit in *any* way from such personal letters," I wrote to Wolfgang. "On the other hand, at the core, these letters are a testament that love can transcend any situation. Once I release the contents of the letters to you, the company can do whatever they choose with the contents, and I am trying to consider the ramifications of that. You said the content would only be used for archival purposes, and I believe your intent. But that isn't to say someone else couldn't make a different decision."

I marked my calendar for six months from that day, and promised Wolfgang I would check back with him then. It seemed impossible to believe it would take another six months to find out if Marcel lived.

But I had already been searching for six months and had barely found a trace.

The promise I made to Aaron to work on the font only after client work was done extended to the search for Marcel, too, I figured. But it was getting harder to keep that promise. I searched for him first thing each morning. I wedged fifteen minutes of time between client projects. I took Hoover for a quick walk, then searched as I wolfed down lunch. Often, by the end of each workday, a list of places to look would be scribbled on a scrap of paper. As often as I could, I would devote entire evenings to finding Marcel. When Aaron worked long shifts at the hospital, I searched until the wee morning hours.

At times, Marcel felt so present it was as if he were in the room, watching me search, patiently waiting to be found.

Aaron occasionally asked if I wanted to go out to dinner or a movie, but I usually suggested we have a quiet night in. He would watch sports on television; I would sit on the couch, my nose buried in my laptop. It was unfair to Aaron, but searching for Marcel was the only thing I wanted to do.

I began writing letters. Lots of letters. I drafted each letter in English, then used the online service to translate it into French. Each letter began: "*Avec le plus grand respect, je suis en espérant que vous pouvez me aider avec une recherche.*" With utmost respect, I hope you can help me with a search.

I outlined what I knew about Marcel and posed the core question: do you have information on his fate? Letters were mailed to museums, war organizations, and archives in France. A few letters went to Germany, with the all-too-familiar apology for errors translated into German. Inquiries were mailed to museums and archives in the United States, too.

Sometimes the search for Marcel felt like trying to find the end of a roll of cellophane tape. The end had to be somewhere, even if I could not see or feel it. Meanwhile, I scratched and picked and spun in circles, knowing once I finally found something to grab onto, I could unroll and unwind it until I reached the core.

I began repeating the mantra "people do not just disappear."

In France, births are recorded at *La Mairie*. Local town halls had been the keeper of civil records since the 1700s. If I was lucky, I heard, additional information such as a person's marriage or death might be scribbled in the margin. Some registers, apparently, had wide margins filled with annotations about a person's life.

My problem was that in France, personal records are private for one hundred years after a person's birth. Marcel had been born January 26, 1912. In theory, Marcel's information should have been made available a month earlier. But there was no telling how many years it might be before 1912 records would be digitized and posted online. And I could not wait years for an answer.

"It's a meat Ho Ho," I said as I tapped my chin. Aaron pretended not to hear me. "It's the perfect way to describe it," I added with a whine. When he still refused to acknowledge the accuracy of my description, I gave him a playful swat.

We were having four friends over for dinner: Laura and Adam, and Karrin and Jim. Laura was the first friend I made when I moved to Minnesota as a teenager, and most of my high school memories include either Laura or Karrin. The first time we got drunk, cruel boys, bad haircuts, band concerts: those were the memories we shared. We went to colleges in different cities, but we remained friends in the way a river can split into braided channels, then flow back together in one swift and seamless rush.

A couple of years after college, Laura and I rented an apartment together. It was a horrid beige, two-bedroom, one-bathroom apartment near a freeway. Furniture had been picked up at garage sales or borrowed from family. We occasionally had to hot glue the kitchen floor tiles back into place, but we relished our first taste of independent adulthood. Aaron and I met a few weeks before Laura and I signed the lease, and as the months progressed, the three of us spent countless hours together. Aaron once remarked Laura was the closest thing he had to a sister.

Laura, Adam, Karrin, and Jim were foodies, and Aaron wanted to impress. He prepared a roasted squash soup with homemade croutons; a beet, apple, and chèvre salad topped with hand-candied walnuts; and the meat Ho Ho, which was a pork-belly roast rolled so that it looked like the chocolate and vanilla-creme snack cakes we had as kids.

For an hour after everyone arrived, we visited in the kitchen. The conversation meandered from politics to headline news. Karrin told us about her new job. Laura and Adam announced their plan to move in together. Eventually, we moved to the dining room. We had more wine and savored Aaron's exceptional dinner.

When Karrin asked how work was going for me, I told her about a multi-month corporate rebranding project I had been hired to spearhead.

"How's the font coming along?" Laura teased. She knew it was not done.

"Getting closer." A lilt at the end of my answer made it sound more like a question than a statement.

"That's what you said last year!" Laura added with a laugh as she grabbed my arm. It was as if she had caught me telling a lie.

Neither Jim, Karrin, nor Adam knew anything about the font, so I explained what it was based on. "This is going to sound like an excuse, but I haven't worked on the font lately because some interesting things have happened with the letters." I outlined what I had learned so far. As I recited some of Marcel's tender words, Laura and Karrin cooed in unison.

"It makes me want to cry," Laura said as she held her hand over her heart. Laura turned to Adam and asked if he would write her love letters like that. He gave her a quick kiss and told her yes, he would be happy to.

I looked at Aaron, then swiveled back to Laura and shook my head. "There's no point in asking."

I confessed I had become obsessed with finding out if Marcel made it home. "Obsession" is not a bad thing for graphic designers; it makes us good at what we do. I've obsessed over the color of camel-brown paper, the tone of silver ink, the width of pinstripes, the position of clear wafer seals. None of that is weird or unusual for a graphic designer. So, being obsessed with Marcel's fate did not seem unusual. *At first.* But the obsession had grown uncontrollably. It had expanded like foam to fill every crevice of spare time and energy.

"Daimler, as in the *car* company Daimler?" Jim asked.

"They made tanks during the war," Aaron said.

"Marcel's family was in Germany?" Jim asked as he cocked his head.

"No. They were in a village in the French countryside, though I don't think that was home. I'm guessing they might have been staying with family during the war," I said.

"And you don't know if he made it home," said Laura.

"Right! That's what I'm trying to find out."

"Was he Jewish?" Jim asked. My heart lurched as I thought about the hand-drawn swastika.

"I don't think so." I had wondered that, too. I had even searched for Marcel in Holocaust databases. But the more I learned about STO, the more it seemed Marcel had been summoned because the Germans needed his labor, not because he was, or wasn't, Jewish. I also did not sense Marcel worried his family would be deported.

"Where did you get these letters?" Jim asked.

When I said "Stillwater," Jim's eyebrows shot up. "Eight, nine years ago now," I added with a shrug.

"Why were they in Stillwater?" he asked.

"I have no idea!" I said through a laugh. I doubted any of them could guess the amount of time that question consumed. "Considering what's in them, I can't believe family would have gotten rid of them. But maybe somebody decluttered their house and the letters were inside of something. Maybe they got rid of them without realizing it. I don't know . . ."

"Or there was an estate sale, and everything was sold," Laura offered.

"Right. Or the family had to abandon the house near the end of the war. Maybe they never came back and the house was cleaned out." After a pause, I offered another scenario: "Maybe Marcel survived, but no one else did." My heart sank at the notion he might have returned to a burned-out, bombed-out shell of a house that would never again echo with the laughter of his young girls. But if that had been the case, Marcel might not have needed—or wanted—to keep his own letters.

I drew in a deep breath and offered yet another scenario. "Even though his letters are full of love, maybe the war ruined him. Maybe no one wanted the letters because they were a reminder of who he had been before the war, not who he was after." I paused, saddened by the thought anyone who could write such beautiful, loving messages could be irretrievably broken. "It's possible, right?" War could destroy people.

"Maybe someone in the family needed money, so they sold them," Adam offered.

"That's my theory," Aaron muttered.

"But I bought the letters for something like five bucks each. So the store had to buy them for a buck or two. If someone is going to sell a family heirloom, I'd hope they'd get more than that."

"If some college kid wanted to buy a bottle of wine, they might not think twice about selling anything they could," Aaron said. He had offered this scenario before. I refused to believe it.

Karrin had an idea, and when she shared it, I was too stunned to move. "What if the family moved to the US after the war? Maybe no one speaks French now. Maybe they got rid of the letters because no one could read what they said." The possibilities in this new scenario made my head spin. *Why hadn't I thought of that?*

"How many letters did you get?" Adam asked.

"Five."

"There were other letters, though," Aaron added.

Karrin's jaw fell open. "There were other letters?"

"Oh, trust me," I said, knowing the thought racing through her mind. "If I knew then what I know now I would have bought every single one. I picked the five letters that provided good raw material for the font. That's all I cared about."

"Which store was it?" Laura asked.

"Yeah, yeah!" Jim jumped in. "Ask the owner where they got the letters."

"They wouldn't remember something they sold so long ago," Karrin said.

Laura interjected. "—Wouldn't it be cool if they knew who bought the other letters?"

"The store has been out of business for years," I said. "I don't even remember which building it was in. They probably went out of business after 9/11." Stillwater had been hit hard by the recession. For a while, it seemed every third or fourth building sat vacant.

After a moment of silence, I looked at Karrin and nodded. "I'll see if I can find any family in the area. That's a good idea." Maybe whatever remained of the family emigrated to the US. Maybe they brought Marcel's letters along as a treasured relic of all that had been lost. But, sixty-some years and a couple generations later, maybe the letters no longer held sentimental value. Maybe no one alive today remembered how Marcel fit into their family tree. If the family was in the area, it wouldn't be hard to think of a dozen ways the letters could have ended up at the store.

The conversation shifted to other topics: Karrin's teaching job, Karrin and Jim's family vacation, each of our parents' health. But in the back of my mind, I was planning how to search for the Heuzé family in Minnesota.

Hours after everyone headed home, after Aaron and I washed dishes and cleaned up the kitchen, I went into my office and began searching. I did not find anyone in the Minneapolis/St. Paul metro area, so I expanded the search to greater Minnesota. Then Wisconsin.

"You're going to be up half the night, aren't you?" Aaron leaned on the frame of my office door. I swiveled to look at him and shrugged.

"What are you going to say if you find the family?" The sharp irritation in Aaron's voice surprised me. "'By the way, I bought these letters that meant so little to you that you got rid of 'em'?" Aaron stepped forward and kissed my forehead before turning and walking away.

He had a point. *What would I say?*

I could tell by Aaron's furrowed brow and the posture of his body he needed to say something. My mind raced to think of what I had done wrong. *Had I misassembled the food processor when we cleaned up after the dinner party a few nights earlier? Had I thrown a shirt in the dryer that should have been hung instead? Had I forgotten to put something on my calendar?*

"Just because I don't write you love letters doesn't mean I don't love you," he said.

My head snapped back.

"I tell you I love you all the time." His face hung with sadness. "When I bring you coffee in the afternoon, I'm telling you. When I fill your car with gas, I'm telling you. When I cook dinner, I'm telling you. When I scrape ice off the driveway so you don't fall, I'm telling you . . ."

We had been married sixteen years. I should not have needed him to point that out.

It hurt my heart to realize I did.

The summer Aaron and I began dating, he worked the night shift as a nurse's aide. As patients slept, he whiled away moonlit hours writing rambling, love-filled letters. They were five, ten, fifteen pages, written longhand on blue-lined notebook paper in ballpoint pen.

Sometimes he wrote about his patients: a cancer patient yearning to live, or a psychiatric patient navigating some unmapped reality. Other times he described coworkers, or family members I had not yet met. More than once he described the vivid oranges and fluorescent pinks of the sunrise over downtown St. Paul.

He made numbered lists of the reasons he loved me.

He laid bare his dreams for our future with a candor I was unused to.

He wrote about the times we made love.

He promised to be true.

His letters stopped once his college classes resumed in September. The notes he now wrote were hastily printed and left on the kitchen counter: "we need dishwasher soap," "I picked up an extra shift Saturday," "Hoover is almost out of food." Occasionally instead of notes, he would send me a text message or an email.

One evening, more than a year after learning Marcel's fate—as I was still trying to make sense of everything I learned and felt—I retrieved Aaron's letters from a dusty box in our basement and read them for the first time in twenty years. The biggest surprise was not reading his introspective thoughts or his sweetly sentimental words. It was seeing Aaron's ornate, curled cursive handwriting. The unfamiliarity was jarring; I had not seen him write in cursive in years.

Chapter Ten

White Bear Lake, Minnesota

Mid-March 2012

I stared at the unopened email. Waiting until evening to read it would have been the responsible thing to do. But within minutes, curiosity gnawed through self-control. I set client work aside and began reading the translated text of the chapter Wolfgang provided.

At its highest count, more than 3,600 foreigners had been assigned to the Daimler-Marienfelde factory. Workers were from Belgium, Czechoslovakia, Denmark, France, Greece, Hungary, Italy, Netherlands, Poland, the Soviet Union, Switzerland, and Sweden. Most were involved in production of the Panther tank.

Some workers had been conscripted. Others had been abducted—swept up like dirt filling a Nazi dust pan.

An account by an Italian stated the factory where he worked was raided and two thousand workers had been stuffed into cattle cars. Once in Germany, they were divided up and distributed to various factories. Most of the Italians allocated to Daimler-Marienfelde had been assigned to Workshop 40, the part of the factory that made tanks and military vans. It was also the same part of the factory, I would eventually learn, where Marcel worked. My heart ached at the thought that those workers had not been able to say goodbye to their loved ones, or that their families might not have known for days or weeks or months—if they ever found out—what had happened to their husbands, sons, fathers.

Marienfelde was described as a collection of fourteen wood and stone barracks on Buckower Chaussee. The camp, called D4, was divided into three sections, each surrounded by barbed wire. D4 East housed Soviet "East Workers," including women and children. D4 South housed Belgian, Dutch, French, and Italian workers. D4 West primarily housed French and Italian workers.

D4 West. My heart skipped. D4 West had been the return address on Marcel's postcard! When I initially provided that address to Wolfgang, a shadow of doubt existed whether Marcel's letters were even real. But this meant not only had I provided a return address of a godforsaken but actual camp, I had provided a return address for a *section* of the camp that held French workers! Within seconds, though, the soaring, validating joy of discovering the corroborating information was replaced by shame. *How could learning about D4 West result in any kind of joy?*

"By the end of 1943," the chapter said, "most of D4 had been destroyed." Workers were moved to Mariendorf, a camp composed of twenty-three stone buildings. The larger Mariendorf camp held six to seven thousand workers. Some were assigned to Daimler. Others were assigned to the machine and tool factory Fritz-Werner-Werke, or to the electrical part manufacturer Siemens. The chapter mentioned other locations, too: camps on Albanstraße and Benzstraße, and additional camps for East Workers on Daimlerstraße and Säntisstraße.

Daimlerstraße! Wolfgang had listed Daimlerstraße as Marcel's "home." But that was for East Workers. My head began to pound.

I read the paragraphs several times, but making sense of the names and locations felt like trying to see detail while looking through gauze. It wasn't until I studied a map of Berlin that I finally understood: Marienfelde was not just the name of a camp or a factory. Marienfelde, and its neighbor, Mariendorf, were suburbs. They were *places.* Albanstraße, Benzstraße, Daimlerstraße, Säntisstraße, and Buckower Chaussee were roads—roads that were still there.

Months earlier, when I first learned 170 camps had been located in Berlin, the number seemed too preposterous to be true. But by the count in Wolfgang's chapter, it seemed Marienfelde and Mariendorf alone had been home to eight or more camps.

Perhaps the first description I found—the one that said Berlin-Marienfelde was a camp with "six or seven" barracks—referred to one section of D4. Perhaps it referred to a camp on Albanstraße or Benzstraße. The two descriptions did not match, yet in some inexplicable way things also began to make perfect sense. Workers, it appeared, had been shuffled around based on which companies needed their labor, and based on which barracks, which workers, remained after bombings. The workers were no longer individuals with names, families, histories; they were playing cards to be shuffled, dealt, then played again.

By February 1944, the standard workweek at Daimler's factory was seventy-two hours. Saturday shifts were mandatory. Prisoners worked two or three Sundays each month. When not toiling in the factory, the German army might force them to clear rubble or dig anti-tank trenches.

French workers initially received the same rations as German workers, but those larger rations were eventually suspended. After that, one French worker described his daily ration as "a portion of margarine, some sausage, one soup, and that was all." One Italian worker recalled a day he received a small piece of sausage with his soup. "It was really something special," he said, until he cut it open and noticed worms in the sausage. He ate it anyway. "We were that hungry," he said.

The same man explained, "On the way to work and back I was always looking down on the road, hoping to find a potato peel, a piece of carrot or some other root. We were also taking grass or herbs from the side of the road or from hedges. Whatever was possible to eat."

I had to stop to take a few deep breaths. *In the second letter Marcel mentioned cooking veal bones and potatoes. Marcel said he made crêpes!* Maybe it had been true; maybe Marcel had been able to steal or buy those items. But maybe he lied. Maybe he claimed to have veal bones and potatoes to protect his wife from the truth. "Hunger haunted the barracks," I read elsewhere. "[Inmates] fantasized about cooking the dogs of

SS men. Often, prisoners talked about lavish meals, seasoning and frying imaginary steaks."

Wedding rings, I would read elsewhere, were sometimes traded for bread.

"Civilian workers were entitled to leave at any time," the chapter stated, a claim that surprised and confused me. On weekends, Western European workers could go swimming or meet other foreigners at Alexanderplatz (a large public square in Berlin) or the Friedrichstraße station (a major railway station). I speculated trips outside the barbed-wire perimeter were to buy food and supplies. I guessed swimming was more for hygiene than recreation.

The chapter listed movies and soccer games as favorite diversions, and stated that factory management organized occasional outings for music or theater. That was surprising and confusing, too, since it seemed impossible that lice-infected, unshowered foreigners would be welcomed into any venue used by Berliners. "Participation was, as is obvious, under constant watch," the chapter stated.

The only clothes some workers in Marienfelde had were the garments they had on the day they arrived. "The few things we had with us wore out very fast," one man said. One worker traded his watch for a shirt, which wore out in weeks. After that, he cut a hole in a blanket, draped it over his shoulders, and tied a string around his waist.

When Marcel told Suzanne, Denise, and Lily he had "quite a bit of mending to do," I envisioned reinforcing a frayed cuff, replacing a button. I had not imagined fibers and seams dissolving like salt in water, and I berated my naïveté.

"We protected our feet with rugs because we had no socks. No work clothes were given out by Daimler-Benz," another worker claimed, though the chapter contradicted that by noting management provided clothes to some foreigners after everything had been lost in a bombing.

"Employers are only permitted to issue these clothes when absolutely necessary, that is . . . [if] the worker would not be able to continue his work," I would read elsewhere. And in 1942, the policy changed from *giving* clothes to workers to *renting* clothes. "In order to prevent foreign workers from taking working clothes with them . . . a certain sum shall be deducted from their wages as deposit. . . . For the use of the clothes, the worker must pay a fee, which is to be deducted from his wages," read an Order by the Reich Director for Clothing and Related Industries.

When it came to wages, Western European workers like Marcel were paid directly. And they were paid more than other workers based on the perception that Western European workers were more productive. For East Workers, companies like Daimler paid the SS "for the privilege of using the camp inmates."

Wages, I would read elsewhere, were a farce. Any mistake was a pretext for a fine. Deductions were made for lodging and food, and up to 30 percent of a worker's wage might be withheld for taxes, compulsory "donations" to various German funds, or mandatory membership fees to the German Labor Front, the Nazi organization that replaced individual trade unions.

Hygiene inside the Marienfelde and Mariendorf camps was catastrophic. Tuberculosis, typhus, and meningitis were rampant, yet people were forced to work even if they were seriously ill. Clothes were boiled to kill lice. Cotton was stuffed in ears to prevent parasites from crawling inside. Showers required a permit issued by the factory foreman, though showers were "generally avoided" since people had to undress outside and soap was unavailable. Trips to the toilet were "always urgent" because they often ate only soup.

As bad as it was for Western European workers, conditions were profoundly worse for East Workers. East Workers were beaten bloody for not understanding orders barked in German, or locked up for work infractions as minor as "leaning back for support." Their camp was infested with vermin. Hygiene was disastrous. Their food situation was dire, and they were unable to afford food on the black market. East Workers were also not allowed to join French and German workers inside air-raid shelters, which made aerial bombings even more treacherous.

A selfish relief washed through me that Marcel, as a Frenchman, was better off than others. Compassion should have poured out of me for the East Workers, but it did not, and its absence made me feel horrible and ugly. Yet my mind kept circling back to a brutal truth: better conditions increased the probability Marcel might have survived.

Was it Marcel's fault French workers had privileges others did not? Was it his responsibility to forfeit any advantage he had?

Charity, I read, could be "suicidal."

After reading the translation of Wolfgang's chapter, it was impossible to turn my attention back to client work. For the rest of the day I was in a stupor, my mind churning through the camp conditions and testimony provided by survivors. That night, as I attempted to fall asleep, one particular passage rattled around inside my head: "Civilian workers were entitled to leave at any time."

I had spent months being angry at Daimler, at Germany, at the Vichy regime, at STO, at the entire war. For the first time, my anger was directed at Marcel. The unkind thoughts were gone nearly as fast as they appeared, but I could not deny I had them. *If Western European workers were entitled to leave at any time, why the hell didn't Marcel pack his belongings and go home? Why didn't he escape when he ventured out to buy food? Couldn't he have walked back to France? Why didn't he do something—anything!—to avoid going to Germany in the first place?*

Within France, I would learn, "in areas where there was a heavy German presence"—areas that included both Paris and Berchères-la-Maingot—men stood little chance of evading STO. German officials "would enter French factories and choose workers by name, or demand lists of workers from the French employer." Selected workers would be summoned to appear before a German labor office representative. "If he failed to appear, the French labor inspector signed a contract in his stead."

French police ruthlessly enforced summons. "If the worker did not appear at the appointed place and time, he was brought forcibly to the station; if he could not be found, a relative was conscripted in his place or his family was deprived of its ration cards." Those who refused to appear for their summons faced five years in prison and a fine of up to thirty thousand francs. Radio broadcasts warned that the family members of those who evaded STO might face reprisal.

French workers were led to believe they could return home once their term of service expired. But "as time went on, it became more obvious that STO was a one-way ticket." In late 1943, the Germans authorities made that formal by announcing, "all French workers . . . had their 'contracts' extended . . . for the duration of the war."

Once someone was inside Germany, it seemed they were caught in an inescapable web. Any foreigner leaving or entering Reich territory needed a police-issued visa. Soldiers guarded roads and bridges. The tattered clothes covering Marcel's back might have been painted with a red acetone *X* identifying him as a prisoner. Bounties were paid for the arrest of fugitives.

Even if he had made it to Berchères-la-Maingot, he would have been unable to stay. Breaches of labor contracts could be punished by "hard labor, imprisonment or fine, and even, in serious cases, by the death sentence."

So as unbearable as life in camp seemed, perhaps the most clear and certain path for survival—perhaps Marcel's *only* chance for survival—was to do what he was told, try to stay healthy, and wait for the war to be over.

I let out a long sigh. There did not seem to be a single thing clear or certain about that path.

In the days that followed, I often caught myself staring at my computer monitor. Routine tasks were bewildering. Simple client revisions felt like Herculean puzzles. I made several humiliating errors: I sent a proof to a client with "Minneapolis" spelled wrong; I released a project to a print vendor, then had no recollection of doing so.

Guilt began to gnaw at me when I ate, when I put on clean clothes, when I indulged in the obscene luxury of a daily hot shower.

Night after night, I searched for Marcel until the wee morning hours. Other nights, I would awake with a start when images of the camp filled my dreams. On those nights, I would slip out of our bedroom, settle into the living room couch, and resume the search. If I was lucky, I would fall back asleep by 4:00 or 5:00. Mornings when Aaron got up early for work, he would wiggle my foot to wake me and send me back to bed so I would be near the alarm when it began to chirp. Other mornings, Hoover roused me when it was time for our walk.

After showering and dressing, no amount of under-eye concealer could mask my gray tiredness.

Hoover trotted to the kitchen to greet Aaron when he got home from work. I remained cocooned inside the zigzag afghan, my laptop balanced on my outstretched legs. I glanced at the clock; it was just before midnight.

Aaron walked into the living room, folded his arms onto the back of the stuffed chair, and kissed the top of my head.

"How'd your shift go?" I asked.

Aaron began to tell me about his last patient, but he stopped mid-sentence as the grid of information displayed on my laptop drew his attention.

"What are you looking at?" He did not even attempt to mask his irritation.

I knew he would not like the answer, and I hesitated before responding. "Bombing records of Berlin."

The chapter Wolfgang provided on Daimler-Marienfelde listed the results of several aerial bombing raids. In one August 1943 nighttime attack, forty-five or more East Workers had been killed. A thousand foreign workers lost housing. Parts of Workshop 40, the section of the factory where Marcel worked, burned. Another part of the factory, Workshop 90, was destroyed. Afterward, some of the Workshop 90 workers were transferred to a factory in Poland.

I became convinced the answer to Marcel's fate hid behind the questions: *When was the factory bombed?* and *How bad was it?* Maybe military records would reveal the entire Daimler-Marienfelde complex had been destroyed. Maybe I would find a list of casualties. Maybe I would learn Workshop 40 workers had been transferred, too. Maybe I would learn all French workers had been released. Or that French workers had been shipped to an extermination camp.

"Carolyn—" Aaron said as he abruptly stood. "Stop. Just stop!" I flinched at the anger in his voice. "He made it home. He didn't make it home. It doesn't—"

"Don't say it doesn't matter," I snapped. It mattered. Marcel mattered. For several long seconds, we glared at each other.

"I was going to say . . ." Aaron sharply enunciated each syllable to emphasize his irritation, "it doesn't change anything." He stormed out of the room, muttering, "You're never going to sleep tonight."

He was right.

I did not care.

During the first years of the war, strategic bombing raids of Germany and occupied Europe were conducted by the Royal Air Force. In November 1943—the same month Marcel had written the third letter—the RAF began an intense, four-month-long bombing campaign of Berlin. By February 1944, Berlin had seen sixteen major raids.

In late February 1944, the US Eighth and Fifteenth Air Forces joined the RAF in targeting aircraft factories and airfields across Germany. Immediately after, their combined sites shifted to Berlin. In the first week of March, the Eighth Air Force launched three major attacks on Berlin. In the third of those attacks, a 125-mile-long column of 730 heavy bombers targeted the city.

I scoured records for any mention of the Daimler-Marienfelde plant. Most records, though, listed frustratingly unspecific "war industry targets" or targets "to the south of Berlin." That description—"to the south of Berlin"—incited a wave of anxiety each time I saw it; Marienfelde was eight miles due south of Berlin's city center.

The anxiety was heightened by a fundamental conflict: the same bombings that were bringing Germany to its knees, and in turn an end to the war, were the same bombings killing workers like Marcel.

One of few documents I found specific to a bombing of Daimler's Marienfelde factory was a black-and-white montage of aerial reconnaissance photos in the US Library of Congress archive. Along the top edge, handwritten block letters identified the target: "Marienfelde—in Berlin—August 6, 1944. This plant specializes in Panther Tanks." On that hot summer day, more than one thousand B-17 and B-24 US Army Air Force bombers, escorted by seven hundred fighter planes, attacked oil refineries, aircraft factories, and other sites in Berlin, Poland, and France. From what I had been able to sort out, eighty-three of those B-17s targeted Daimler's Marienfelde factory. "The bombing is very effective and ten major [targets] are severely damaged during one of the best days the Eighth [Air Force] experiences," the mission record stated.

The first photo in the montage—the before photo—included a thick, hand-drawn border around the massive factory complex. Sections were labeled: Tank Factory, Communication Equipment, Machine Tools.

The photo taken during the attack reminded me of a satellite image of a forest, not unlike satellite images I had viewed of the countryside surrounding Berchères-la-Maingot. But instead of lush canopies of foliage, every plume was a cloud of smoke and debris. Overlapping plumes of white, gray, and black filled the perimeter. Fifty or more plumes billowed from residential-looking areas beyond the factory.

Aaron guessed the small photo in a lower corner—the after photo—was taken an hour or two later. Smoke still streamed from some buildings. Others appeared flat and lifeless, choked by a layer of ash. It reminded me of images of Manhattan's streets after the Twin Towers collapsed on 9/11.

The full fury of Allied air power was brought to Berlin in 1945. On February 3, more than one thousand B-17 bombers dropped more than two thousand tons of explosives. It was the single largest aerial attack on the city. The scope of destruction was almost beyond comprehension. Fires raged for days.

Images of Berlin seared into my brain like an iron brand scarring flesh. German soldiers sprinted past buildings engulfed in flames. A woman cradled a child as she skittered past bodies abandoned in the street. Legs with feet still laced into boots laid in a gutter, the torso nowhere to be seen. Men and women in tattered clothes cleared mountains of brick with shovels and bare hands. Cables and axles had been rolled together and tossed like balls of yarn. Buildings were fleshless skeletons, with trusses and beams jutting out like bare ribs.

On March 24, 1945, one hundred and fifty B-17s—nearly twice as many as the eighty-three that caused the destruction shown in the Library of Congress photo—targeted the Daimler-Marienfelde plant. They delivered a fatal blow. Damage made it "impossible for production to resume."

My stomach dropped. *What happened to Marcel after Daimler no longer needed him?*

My head knew the likely answer. My heart refused to believe it.

I quietly got out of bed and went to the living room. Once again, nightmares made sleep impossible. I was too exhausted to look for Marcel, so I grabbed the remote control and flipped to a television show on forensics that ran throughout the early morning hours. Each half-hour episode focused on a brutal crime and explained how the tiniest detail could crack open a case. Despite the show's topics—murder, rape, arson—I chose it because the narrator's silky-smooth voice sometimes lulled me back to sleep.

Exhaustion was not the only thing that had taken up residence inside of me. It was anger. I was angry at Aaron for not helping with the search; at Marcel's family for not cherishing his letters; at my clients for consuming time and energy; at every person who had not returned an email or letter. Most of all, I raged at myself for not finding him—and for allowing the search to devour time, money, energy, sleep.

As the third episode rolled into the fourth, I tried to dissect the hold Marcel's letters had on me. Thousands of men and women wrote letters during World War II. They were only words on paper. Every day I was surrounded by words on paper. I made a career of designing words on paper. *Why were these words different?*

I did not have a driving interest in genealogy.

Or French history.

Or World War II.

I was not searching because I was bored, or because I had vacuous blocks of time to fill. A hundred better uses of my time existed: I could finish the font, market my business, swim laps at the YMCA. Even more basic: Hoover needed a bath, I needed a haircut, the mound of laundry in the basement grew ever larger.

Marcel's words of love were undeniably intoxicating. But his letters were not written to me. His letters would never provide *me* with love. Sliding into this obsession might have made sense if there was a gaping emotional hole in my life. But I was married to a wickedly smart and funny man. We were good together. I liked my work as a graphic designer, and I was fortunate to have good clients. Yet I could barely wait for each workday to be done so I could search for Marcel.

Aaron had been correct when he said finding Marcel's fate would not change anything. There was no practical reason I *needed* to know. The answer would not cure cancer, prevent homelessness, stop wars.

Yet finding out if Marcel lived seemed to be the only thing that mattered.

It haunted me that his letters had been at an antique store halfway around the world, sold for a handful of dollars. Marcel loved his wife and daughters so openly, so deeply—his desire to return to them was so palpable—I could feel it in my bones. If Marcel loved his family that much, he *had* to be loved by them in return. *Didn't he?* So why hadn't they treasured these letters as much as I, a complete stranger, did?

The word to describe what I had been feeling hit me: beholden. Somewhere along the way, the search had changed from a curiosity to an irrevocable responsibility. It was as if not stopping until I found out his fate would prove someone cared what happened to him. It would prove the fragment of life captured in his letters mattered. Even if I did not know anything else about Marcel, I knew this: He existed. He mattered.

So despite the fact that every physical record of Marcel seemed to have disappeared—every record other than Wolfgang's ledger—I refused to let Marcel disappear, too. I refused to allow the love he had for his wife and daughters to be lost to history, even if that love was only ever remembered by a non-French-speaking, novice type designer in White Bear Lake.

"I will remember you," I whispered.

"Fromage, dinner will be ready soon," Aaron said as he poked his head into my office.

"Fromage?" I repeated minutes later when I stepped into the kitchen.

"It's your new nickname," he said with a smirk. *"Ma petite fromage."*

"My little . . . *cheese?*" I said with a laugh. "Why would you call me your little cheese?"

"It's perfect. You *are* from Wisconsin."

The nickname was a peace offering. The angry exchange over the bombing records had been forgiven.

I sensed Aaron wanted me to declare the search a good effort and let it go. But I was grateful he accepted that was not going to happen. After I cleaned up the dinner dishes, I settled into the couch, pulled my laptop onto my outstretched legs, and resumed the search.

Three short notes accompanied Tom's translations of the final letter and the postcard. First, Tom noted the date on Marcel's letter was confusing. "It had been written February 1, but he told his wife to go see 'them' on February 1. It's not clear how timing could work," Tom wrote.

Then, Tom noted the letter included a reference to *"fridoline cuisine,"* which even stumped older native French speakers he consulted with.

Finally, Tom noted he changed the three-letter acronym DCA, which stood for *défense contre avions*, to AAA to reflect its English-language equivalent: anti-aircraft artillery.

My heart sank before I read another word.

Marienfelde le 1er-2-43

si tu peux envoie moi une photo, car je n'en ai pas beaucoup. Souhaite le bonjour à tout le monde, ton grand qui t'embrasse avec ... et qui pense bien à toi Marcel

Ma petite femme chérie

Je ne sais pas si tu auras cette lettre là plus vite, mais il y a un copain qui doit partir pour Paris et je lui donnerai ta lettre. Ce soir j'ai eu des nouvelles du patron, il me dit que tu dois aller les voir le 1er février. Là je vais pouvoir te donner un peu de détails sur ma vie de prisonnier. Ce soir j'ai réussi à avoir un beau morceau de Colin, je l'ai fait au court bouillon et à l'huile et au vinaigre. Tu vas peut-être dire que je te boules, mais il y a peut être des lettres que tu n'as pas reçues

The text at the top of the page, above the salutation, is a continuation of text from the fourth page and is the end of the letter.

Marienfelde, Germany

February 1, 1943

My darling wife,

I don't know if you will receive this letter the quickest, but there's a friend who is leaving for Paris and I will give him your letter. This evening I received news from the boss. He told me that you need to go see them on February 1st. Now I can give you some details about my life as a prisoner. Tonight I succeeded in getting a beautiful piece of cod. I prepared it in a court bouillon and with oil and vinegar. You might say that I'm boring you, but there might be some letters that you didn't receive.

    In the morning at 6:10 we leave for the workshop, arrive at the canteen at 6:30 to drink the juice that costs 5 pfennigs, that means 20 centimes, without sugar. Then to work, when we arrive we chat until 7 o'clock. At 8 o'clock it's 20 minutes in the toilet for a cigarette when there is one. Quarter to 9 we go down to the canteen to have a snack and another coffee. At 9:30 we go back to work, another trip to the shitter waiting for quarter to noon, then we leave quickly for lunch. At ten past noon the meal is finished and we go back down to the canteen for the third juice. At 12:25 we go back to work with several trips to the toilet, waiting for 5:30, the time when we clean the machinery.

At 6:00 it's the evening meal, 6:10 everything is done. We run errands in town or go back to the barracks to get letters and to make food because as soon as we leave the table we are hungry again. What we eat doesn't stick to our ribs. When I come back I will make you some fridoline cuisine and you can tell me the news. The other day we ate chicken.

As for the tough times, let me tell you about a big event the other day. At 7:30 pm the sirens go off, we hurry down to the shelter, leaving all the just-served plates of food on the tables. At 8:30 the sirens have been blaring for an hour, then strangely even in the shelter we feel a blast, because nearby there is an AAA battery. At 20 minutes to nine somebody yells that the barracks are burning. Everyone hesitates to go out because the AAA bursts are still going off all around us. Then the battery takes a big hit and everything quiets down. I'm able to go out with a buddy. The moment he opens the shutters to go out through the window, the window panes blow up, the barracks was already an inferno inside. At 9:30 we see the results of the operation. All around us houses are burning and so is the battery with six krauts killed off. In our two French barracks, five Russians and one Russian dead. The worst is the prisoners' camp. 80 guys burned alive because the Germans locked them in their barracks. Talk about some real bastards.

The next night it happened again but it's Berlin that really suffered the most. The ambulances kept going all night and the next day. Yesterday I saw the damage and you know that matters for us. Now the morale is good and I'm waiting for business. Now for the packages, everything that you can think to send me go ahead, because the black market is king here. 160F for one kilo of bread, 160F for one pack of cigarettes, 80F for 20 grams of tobacco, 3000F for one kilo of butter, 1200F for one kilo of pork, and everything is in keeping. Today I sent you 50 marks. If I receive some packages think of how much money we'll make. Above all send me tobacco because I am too sad without it. The time is already very long without you and without my daughters. What are those three doing? I think I'll get a letter from you soon that will tell me some news. My boss tells me that you are strong. I was proud of my darling wife and I send her my biggest kisses. Please hug and kiss my dear daughters for me, as well as Grandma, and also my father who must be worried too. I'm waiting for news from Pierre. You saw that the krauts are taking a beating in Russia, but you know there are still lots of partners even though there are still many who are sulking. Your bum who loves you, kisses you so tenderly, before going to sleep.

If you think of it, send me a photo because I don't have a lot. Say hello to everyone for me. Your big guy who kisses you again and who thinks about you all the time.

Marcel

April 13, 1944

My darling,

Finally Tuesday evening I received a letter from Berchères, dated March 15th. Can you believe it, almost one month. I was so happy to have some news. Actually the garden is not very early this year. And it's the same everywhere. But can't you find someone to till it? There must be some late or lost letters, because I don't know the little Marc. I suppose it's Madame Vallet's grandson. For Henry I was not surprised. He must have many of them in his case. As for the Maillard girl she only gets what she deserves. There are too many women like that.

One girl who must be happy that I didn't come in person is Grisette, she can take advantage of life. I started working here 15 months ago today. I would love to take a little trip to see all of you. The longer this goes, the more I miss you. Maurice was extremely proud of himself when I told him that he was your favorite. As for the others, they are looking forward to meeting you, and they all say hello.

My little treasure, I leave you for today while always keeping the hope that I will see you again soon. Give a big kiss to my little hoodlums for me as well as my dear mother. I send you my biggest kisses and above all be careful with your health.

Your big guy who only dreams of you.

Marcel

Absender: Heuzé Marcel
Lager D 4 West chambre 21/3
① Berlin Marienfelde Deutsch...

Sprache Französiche

Postkart

le 13 avril 1944

Ma petite chérie

Enfin, mardi soir, j'ai reçue
une lettre de Berchères elle
est datée du 15 mars. Tu te
rends compte presque un mois.
Tu penses si j'étais heureuse
d'avoir des nouvelles. En effet
le jardin n'est pas très en
avance cette année. Et c'est

Madame Marcel Heuzé

Route de St Prest

Berchères-la-Maingot

par Chartres   Eure et Loir

France

---

partout pareil. Mais ne peut tu pas
trouver quelqu'un pour le retourner.
Je dois avoir quand même, des lettres en
retard, ou perdues, car je ne connais pas le
petit marc. Je suppose que c'est le petit fils
à madame Vallet. Pour Henry je n'ai pas été
surpris, il doit y en avoir beaucoup dans son
cas. Quant à la fille Maillault, elle n'a que ce
qu'elle mérite, des femmes comme cela il y en a trop.
Une qui doit être contente que je ne sois pas
venu en panne, c'est la grisette, elle peut
profiter de la vie. Il y a aujourd'hui 15 mois
que je commençai à travailler ici, moi aussi je
voudrais bien, aller faire un petit tour pour vous
voir toutes plus ça va, plus vous me manquez.
Maurice lichait comme un vieux poux, quand
je lui ai dit qu'il était ton préféré. Quant aux
autres, ils sont impatients de faire ta connaissance
en attendant ils te souhaitent le bonjour.
Mon petit trésor, je te quitte pour aujourd'hui
en gardant toujours l'espoir de te revoir bientôt.
Embrasse bien mes vagenese pour moi ainsi que
ma bonne maman. Je t'envoie mes meilleurs baisers.
Et surtout fais bien attention à ta santé.
Ton grand qui ne songe qu'à toi   Marcel

Chapter Eleven

White Bear Lake, Minnesota

Late March 2012

After reading the translation of the fourth letter, I sat in silence with a hand locked over my mouth as if I were trying to prevent a gasp from escaping. When I stood inside the store in Stillwater, I selected that letter because it included so many numbers, and I knew I needed numbers for the font. I never imagined the horror those numbers would reveal.

I walked out of my office and tried to think about something else. Anything else. But it was impossible. As Marcel's words swirled inside my brain, messages of love—"your big guy who only dreams of you"—seemed to rebound off news of men burned alive. Tender kisses ricocheted off hunger. Affection and brutality were like oil and water: coexisting but refusing to mix. The two seemed impossible to reconcile.

I went back into my office and sent Tom an email. "Eighty men burned alive. Fuck."

Tom responded with a confession: he wept while he translated the letter.

Eight months earlier, before I gave Tom approval to translate the first letter, I ran a quick search on him as part of due diligence I would complete before sending money to anyone. A profile photo showed a man in his late forties. He wore a black T-shirt and had a shaved head. His arms were folded tight over his chest. The tough-guy image seemed surprising for someone who spent free time translating French love letters. It was even more surprising he would admit weeping to me, since I was essentially a stranger. Marcel's letters, it seemed, had wormed their way into Tom's heart, too.

Marcel had written the postcard fifteen months after arriving in Berlin. *Fifteen fucking months.* Nearly two more months would pass before Allied troops would storm the beaches of Normandy. Four months would pass before Paris would be liberated. Another year would pass before the war in Europe would come to a bloody end.

I read the two translations again and again. It was as if I hoped the words might magically rearrange themselves into clues or answers. The name Marc Vallet was new, though the lead was not encouraging. First names alone—Henry, Maurice—were worthless.

Sadness washed through me as I realized this was the end.

These were the last words I would read from Marcel.

It seemed like a logical guess that Marcel had painted the blue and red stripes with watered-down writing ink, but in a quest to uncover any overlooked clue, I wanted to test that theory. I scavenged through office supplies for a bottle of red ink used to refill a stamp pad I used to mark client approvals. I grabbed some scrap paper, went into the kitchen, and swirled drops of ink into a tablespoon of tap water. The stripes on Marcel's letters were about the width of a fingertip, so I dipped my finger into the pool of crimson and swiped it across the paper, trying to replicate the stripe.

Color-wise, the diluted red ink was remarkably close. But my stripes ended at three inches or so, and were wide where my finger first touched the page, then quickly tapered to a point. Marcel's stripes were long, with a uniform width. *Did he have a paintbrush? What if it wasn't ink? Could the red be transmission fluid? Ground-up bricks? Blood? Wouldn't blood have oxidized and turned brown?* The unknowns were maddening.

In the days that followed, I exchanged emails with a sales representative at a chemical analysis laboratory. He outlined two options for identifying what the stripes had been painted with.

The first option required the destruction of part of a letter, a condition which made the solution untenable.

The second option would not have harmed the paper, and it was considerably less expensive—only $500 per color—but the result would have been limited to the identification of a *class* of chemical compounds. That information would be meaningless since I did not know the first thing about the differences between one class of compounds and another. And I could not throw away $1,000 to get information that would not tell me whether he survived.

Ten more months would elapse before I learned how the blue and red stripes had been made. It would prove to be one of the biggest surprises of the entire search.

I was in our living room, curled under the zigzag afghan as January winds whistled outside, mindlessly scrolling through typography specimens on eBay. If I was lucky, I might find something to add to my ever-growing collection of handwritten ephemera: a splendid old letter, an envelope bearing a wildly flourished address, a ledger page with columns of scratchy numbers. But the prize I unexpectedly stumbled across was even better: a letter bearing familiar watery blue and red stripes.

The letter had been written in 1943 by a Dutchman, then mailed to an address in *Zweden*. The letter came with its original envelope, which also had blue and red stripes. The envelope had been sliced open, resealed, then certified with a blood-red *Oberkommando* stamp. My mind raced to understand what I was seeing. *Why would a Dutchman mail a letter to Sweden emblazoned with the colors of the French flag? Why would the Oberkommando open the envelope?*

My head snapped back when I noticed that the eBay seller described the blue and red stripes as "chemical censor marks." An online search confirmed chemical censoring had indeed been used during World War II, and within minutes I found a detailed report online about chemical censoring. The report had been written by a man in California—a stamp collector with a special interest in censored mailpieces. It was only 8:45 p.m. in California; I impulsively picked up the phone and dialed his phone number.

The man, Franklin, answered after the first ring. I introduced myself and, in the cheeriest voice I could muster, I inquired whether we might chat about his report. I guessed not many forty-three-year-old women called to chat about World War II chemical censoring. I held my breath as I waited for his response.

Franklin asked a few clipped questions, his skepticism palpable. But once I described the stripes on Marcel's letters, and explained they had been mailed from a Daimler factory in Berlin, Franklin believed me.

We talked for an hour. More accurately, Franklin talked while I absorbed every transfixing word. Letters written by conscripted laborers—men like Marcel who had access to valuable intelligence about factory production, armaments, and supply chain issues—were *highly* censored, he said. The blue and red stripes were not a gesture of Marcel's French pride, as I had assumed for years: they were chemical developers used by German censors to reveal messages that might have been written in invisible ink.

Franklin's words sounded surreal, and my mouth fell agape. Invisible ink seemed to be the purview of spy movies, or adolescent boys in tree houses, not font designers in Minnesota with affection for old handwriting.

Multiple brushes would be wired together, Franklin explained, which created the parallel stripes. With one dip into separate wells of developers, then with a single rake across the page, inspectors could apply multiple chemicals that would develop different kinds of "ink."

Red cabbage water revealed messages written in ammonia. Iodine solutions revealed messages written in starch or lemon juice. Ammonium hydroxide revealed messages written in copper sulfate. Plant tannin or potassium ferricyanate revealed messages written in iron sulfate. Other chemicals developed messages written in potato juice, semen, or urine. In addition to liquid chemical censoring, heat and smoke were used to reveal hidden messages, too. Formulas for inks and developers were constantly changing, Franklin explained. Censor offices were essentially small chemical labs. "It was a constant game of cat and mouse."

I asked Franklin whether he thought messages might have been hidden on Marcel's letters. He said it was unlikely. If messages had been found, the letters would have been confiscated. Marcel probably would have been killed. He would have been made an example of.

Franklin knew about traditional censor marks, too, so I described other marks that scarred and stained Marcel's letters. The large red "Ae" stamped on the postcard indicated that mail piece was to be forwarded to the Frankfurt office for review. Other small numbers stamped or scribbled in pencil—785, 4087, 5265—were identification numbers of individual censor clerks. "Clerks were trained to look for very specific things," he said.

Marcel would have been prohibited from affixing postage onto his own letters "to eliminate the possibility prisoners might hide a message underneath a stamp," Franklin explained. That was why Marcel had to go to the post office, wait in line, buy postage, and have the clerk affix the stamp. I had a new appreciation for the time and energy required to mail each letter—time that could have been used to procure food, sleep, or mend clothes.

In the days that followed, I learned the US government monitored mail for hidden messages during the war, too. More than fourteen thousand censors reviewed a million pieces of mail each day. More than four thousand suspicious mailpieces received additional testing in government labs. Four hundred contained secret writing and codes.

For the entirety of France, five telephone numbers existed for men named Marcel Heuzé. I know because I looked. I wished each listing included the man's age, but the information was limited to a city and a phone number. I located each city—Carnoët, Granville, Husson, Mantes-la-Ville, Saint-Georges-de-Reintembault—on a map of France. If one had been near Berchères-la-Maingot, Boissy-le-Châtel, or the Montreuil Marcel mentioned, I would have rooted around for more information. But none of the cities were anywhere near a place connected to Marcel. And deep in my bones, I knew none of the five men were *my* Marcel.

Writing letters to museums or war organizations was one thing, but it just seemed crazy to write a letter to every man in France named Marcel Heuzé. More accurately, I realized, it might make *me* look crazy.

Over the years, I have stumbled across information on other women named Carolyn Porter. I do not know any of them. I have never met any of them. I do not believe any other Carolyns exist in my family tree. So if someone wrote a letter asking if I knew or was related to a *specific* Carolyn Porter, I would be amused, but I probably would not respond in case the inquiry was some scam to acquire personal information.

I filed away the idea of writing to the five Marcels as the one last desperate, potentially humiliating thing I could do before folding my cards and walking away from the table.

Some days, that point did not feel far away.

Chapter Twelve

White Bear Lake, Minnesota
April 2012

I eventually transitioned from searching for Marcel to searching for Suzanne, Denise, and Lily. I was not particularly hopeful I would find answers because I figured any search for daughters would be complicated by the fact that if they married, they might no longer have the Heuzé surname.

As I searched for Lily, an eerie and inexorable thought entered my mind: *Lily does not exist.* The haunting thought seemed to materialize from nowhere, and it caught me off guard. As I tried to make sense of those four words, the only answer that made sense was that Lily had not survived the war. I did not abandon the search for Lily, but after those words echoed through my brain, I did not search as voraciously for her as I did for Suzanne, Denise, and Jacqueline.

I was almost positive Jacqueline was part of the Gommier family, not one of Marcel's daughters, but after so many false starts and dead ends, I was not going to eliminate any possibility. So I looked for any Jacqueline with either the Heuzé or Gommier last name.

Within days, I found a Jacqueline Gommier living in a town not far from Berchères-la-Maingot. As I drafted a short letter to her, I felt buoyed with optimism. I translated the letter into French, outlined an array of ways she could contact me, and included the standard apology for errors: "*Je m'excuse pour les erreurs dans la traduction; Je ne parle pas Français.*"

"Sounds like you're grasping at straws," Aaron said when I showed him the letter.

"Yep," I said defiantly. "Worst case is she's not the right Jacqueline and she thinks I'm a crazy American." Aaron's eyebrows arched in agreement. I stared back with a squint and a mock scowl.

A week later, I located a woman named Denise in northwest France whose maiden name had been Heuzé. I did not know whether Denise was twenty-eight or eighty-eight years old, but I wrote her a letter, too. Similar to the letter to Jacqueline, it did not reveal any secrets. But if she was the right Denise, I felt certain my letter would pique her interest.

Visiting the leading genealogy website would have been the first thing most people would have done. Perhaps it had not occurred to me to visit it earlier because I had scoured so many other World War II records. Or perhaps it was because my mom had already looked for Marcel.

For years, my mom has researched her branch of our family tree. She has special software to organize her records. She attends genealogy conferences and has taught genealogy classes. She has even tracked down distant cousins living in the Netherlands. Several weeks earlier, when I called to ask if she would help me look for Marcel, I waited through a long, bewildered silence. She heard me mention the font before; she knew it was based on old handwriting. But she had never heard Marcel's name, and she did not know I had had letters translated. My interest in his fate seemed confounding since he was not family, but she agreed to help. She agreed to try, anyway.

Two weeks later, she emailed the results of her search: "I could not find him in French military records. I could not find marriage or birth certificates for the girls. The Heuzé name isn't common, so I looked under alternate spellings. I mentioned Marcel to a couple of my friends, and they looked for him, too." Her email then transitioned to more excit-

ing news: she got tickets to a Marie Osmond concert! Then she went on
to tell me about my dad's most recent softball game before providing an
update on the weather.

I thanked her for her time and effort—though I was not sure she had
expended much of either—and I tried to mask the sting of how easily
Marcel had been dismissed.

The leading genealogy website offered a free fourteen-day trial, so I
set up an account. In a selfish way, I was relieved nothing came up after I
entered Marcel's name. It would have been embarrassing if, after all this
time, an answer appeared immediately. That first evening I searched for
hours.

After exhausting ways to search for Marcel, I shifted my focus to
Vérane, Suzanne, Denise, and Lily. It was not long before I found a
record for a Suzanne Bernadette Heuzé Cléro, born September 22, 1933
in Montreuil. My heart soared. *Marcel's letters mentioned Montreuil!* And
a 1933 birthdate would have made her about the right age.

A moment later my heart plummeted: the record showed Suzanne
had been dead for more than twenty years.

A digital family tree had been created by Suzanne's daughter, though
all information, including the daughter's name, was concealed for privacy.
The identities of Suzanne's parents were concealed, too, so I could not
confirm whether Marcel was her father. And, despite the connection to
Montreuil and the date, there was no way to be certain this was the correct Suzanne.

I should have been elated about finding the record, but it did not
feel like a victory. I did not know what I could do with her birthdate
other than scour obituary notices with the hope of learning her daughter's
name. I did not know how to search obituary notices in France, and the
language barrier made the task feel overwhelming.

During the days that followed, I spent every free moment searching
the website's archives, but each promising lead turned into a dead end.
It felt as if I were grabbing sand: every time I thought I had something,
I clenched my fist around it only to feel the tiny grains slide between my
fingers and drain away.

On the thirteenth day, I attempted to cancel my trial membership. The website froze part-way through the process, so I called customer service to have them close the account for me.

"I can help you," an operator with a thick southern drawl said. "But can I ask why you want to do that?" She sounded bewildered by my decision.

"I was looking for a specific person, and couldn't find anything."

"Well, hon, would you mind if I tried?" she gently asked. "Maybe I can find who you're looking for. If not, I'll close your account, but I'd sure love to try to help before we do that." Perhaps it was the way she effortlessly called me "hon," or the sincerity in her voice when she said she'd *suuuure loooove* to help, but I told her if she was willing to try, I was willing to give her the opportunity.

"Okay!" she hooted. "Let me log in to your account," she said more rapidly than anything she had said so far. "It looks like you searched international records for Marcel Heuzé, Vérane Heuzé, Suzanne Heuzé, Denise Heuzé, and Lily Heuzé. Is that right?"

"Marcel Heuzé is the person I'm searching for. Vérane is his wife. Suzanne, Denise, and Lily are his daughters."

"Do you have a birthdate?"

"January 26, 1912. I believe he was born in Boissy-la-Châtel. It's near Paris."

"Okay, hon, gimme a few minutes. Our tools are good, but if you don't know the ins and outs, sometimes they aren't easy to use. Know what I mean?" I envisioned her fingers hovering over her keyboard like a cat ready to pounce.

As synthesized music looped, I opened the font file. It had been nearly three months since I looked at the curves and lines of these letters; these beautiful, heartbreaking curves and lines. It felt selfish to want two things: for Marcel to live, and to someday finish the font. But if only one could be true, I decided, I wanted him to live.

"You still with me, hon?" Ten or more minutes had passed. The woman seemed surprised I was still on the line. "I'm gonna need more time. You okay with that?"

I told her to take all the time she needed.

"Well, I'll be," she said when she came back on the line after another fifteen minutes. "Usually I find something right away. Is it possible his name is spelled another way? I'm askin' because I found a record of a M. Heuse, spelled H-e-u-s-e, who sailed to the US from France in 1952. But that person was born in 1914."

"I found that record, too," I said. I found it after a couple of hours that first night.

"Let me look a few more places for you, okay?"

After another ten or so more minutes, she got on the line: "Are you there, Ms. Porter?" The tone of her voice was flat and apologetic. I already knew what she was going to tell me. "It's unusual not to find *anything*, especially when you have a birthdate."

"Marcel has been a bit of a mystery man," I said.

"I really am sorry. I can't think of the last time this happened." What had been a lilting, bubbling voice was as flat as a sheet of paper.

I felt sorry for her. She sounded so easily defeated.

My daily walks with Hoover were good for both of us. The morning walk helped me wake up. The noon walk provided a quick break from client work. The evening walk provided the opportunity to make a mental list of the day's loose ends. No matter how busy I was, we always went on those walks. Sometimes Aaron came along. Most often, though, it was just Hoover and me.

Those walks also provided the opportunity to make mental lists of new places to search for Marcel: new websites to scour, new organizations or archives to contact. But as the weeks and months progressed, I began returning from our walks without any fresh ideas.

One day, before I realized what happened, I spoke directly to Marcel.

"If you want me to find you, help me find you," I commanded.

I shook my head and let out a chuckle. *Why did I think that would work?*

The ridiculousness of it did not seem to be that I had spoken to Marcel—it was that I had spoken to him in English.

Chapter Thirteen

White Bear Lake, Minnesota

April 2012

In 2001, when I first began to freelance, a fellow graphic designer offered this grim warning: "Keep good records and expect a tax audit." Because of the fear that warning instilled, I made a point of keeping meticulous records. I earnestly tried to follow every tax rule.

So in January 2011, when I received a form letter from the Minnesota Department of Revenue announcing my business had been randomly selected for a sales tax audit, I was not entirely surprised. "I won the *you're fucked* lottery," I said to Aaron as I handed him the just-opened notice, the stark white piece of paper still bent in thirds.

Despite good record keeping, the prospect of the audit rattled me. Sales tax regulations for graphic designers were notoriously ambiguous, and people in my professional network warned that the outcome could vary wildly depending on how my auditor interpreted the rules. On top of that, I had recently heard about a small St. Paul firm whose audit resulted in more than $100,000 in penalties and fines.

The audit took place in our home. For three days, two auditors examined ledger pages, inspected credit card receipts, and scrutinized tax deposits. They flagged invoices with sticky notes, then crossed-referenced expense records filed inside job jackets. The two women were pleasant and professional, though I was acutely aware they were not on my side.

On the third day, as the lead auditor backed her car out of our driveway, I did the Happy Dance behind the closed front door. The amount I owed—$384.25—was the tiniest fraction of the worst-case scenarios that had plagued my sleep since the day the notice arrived.

In April 2012—more than a year after the audit had been completed—while I worked on client paperwork, I thought about the audit. Once the day's immediate deadlines had been met, I pulled several three-ring binders off the office shelves, sat on the floor, and began leafing through old business receipts. I had looked for the receipt for Marcel's letters before, but I had only looked in the font's job jacket. I had not looked in the general business ledger.

I had started tracking time on the font in May 2004, but I knew I had worked on the font before that. I began examining receipts and ledger pages from May 2004, then worked backward. In the years that had elapsed, dye in thermal-paper receipts had almost entirely disappeared, so each strip of paper required careful inspection. At one point, Aaron poked his head into the office. He did not even ask what I was doing, as if sitting cross-legged on the floor, surrounded by piles of feather-like receipts and a flock of black three-ring binders, wings spread wide, was a perfectly normal thing to see.

An hour later, I jumped into the living room, waving a piece of yellow paper in the air. The paper was about the size of a playing card. A smile stretched from ear to ear. "Belle Époque. January 6, 2002!" I repeated the year, emphasizing the last two: "Two thousand, *two!*"

"What's that?" Aaron asked.

"The receipt for the letters!" I smiled even bigger and stretched tall, inflated by the find.

The yellow paper was the bottom layer of a carbon copy receipt, the handwriting no more than a doughy shadow from the sheet above. I read the details aloud: five French letters, on sale for $6.40 each, for a grand total of $34.08. The receipt included a note, in my handwriting, confirming the total included $2.08 in Minnesota sales tax.

If it had not been for the fear of being audited, I *never* would have kept this receipt. I wanted to throw my arms around the two auditors in gratitude.

"Gimme your laptop," I said as I plopped into the armchair, motioning for Aaron to slide his laptop across the coffee table.

A listing for Belle Époque appeared immediately. My head snapped back in astonishment. "It's still in business. It moved!"

I recalled visiting the store at this new location once with Laura, seven or eight years earlier. At the time, though, I had not realized it was the same business as the store in Stillwater. I recalled stately pieces of furniture, antiques, and artfully displayed French décor: pillows, frames, vases. The store might have offered custom upholstery services, too. I thought I recalled books filled with fabric swatches tucked into a case along one wall.

"Unbelievable," I muttered as I grabbed the phone and dialed. *Would the owner recall where they acquired the letters? What if they still had some?* My heart soared at the possibility.

"No answer yet," I said as I tapped my finger against the phone.

I hung up, jumped from the chair, and raced to the kitchen to grab my purse and keys. "I'll be back in an hour and a half," I said with a grin. "Two if the owner is there."

As I backed out of the driveway, I recalled I had promised a client I would be available all afternoon for a phone call. But I did not stop. She would have to wait.

50th and France is an upscale neighborhood west of downtown Minneapolis with a collection of one hundred or so street-level shops selling designer clothes, jewelry, paper goods, and gourmet kitchenware. It only took thirty minutes to get there in light midday traffic. Plus I sped.

I *thought* I remembered Belle Époque's location, but the building now held a clothing store, so I scurried down the sidewalk, scrutinizing each window sign and scalloped awning for the store's name. At the end of the block, I turned and retraced my path, certain I must have breezed past it. Back at the corner of 50th and France, I pulled out my cell phone and dialed the store's number.

After eight rings, I hung up. Every bit of hope that had surged during the previous hour drained away. *I knew.*

I took a deep breath and stepped into the store on the southeast corner of 50th and France. A sea of designer yoga pants, dresses, and cotton T-shirts silk-screened with geometric kolam patterns—clothes people wear when they seek bliss and balance—were perfectly displayed on racks and shelves.

"Can I help you find something?" The saleswoman's perky singsong lilt hurt my ears.

I pointed my thumb over my shoulder to gesture to the front door. "Is this 5-0-0-1?"

She stared back blankly.

"Building 5001," I clarified, certain my false cheeriness sounded unconvincing.

With a pasted-on smile she responded, "I don't know. Let me ask." She walked to the store's far corner and consulted with a second, older saleswoman. They both walked back to me. My question, it seemed, made the older woman deeply suspicious.

"Yes," the perky one said, "this is 5001."

"How long has this store been here?" I snapped.

"About five months," she said with pride. The older saleswoman stood a few feet back, monitoring our interaction.

"Do you know what it was before?"

"An Ann Taylor store, I think."

My shoulders fell. "How long was *that* store here?"

The women looked at each other. "Five years?" The younger saleswoman shrugged. "Can I show you some spring dresses? We just got them in and—"

"—No." I knew she was just doing her job, so I added a curt, "Thanks."

"Well, how about—"

"No!" I could not stand to hear what she wanted to sell me next, and I knew I was not going to remain polite for long. I turned and headed to the front door, fighting the impulse to reach out and throw every stitch of perfectly folded bliss and fucking balance merchandise onto the floor.

I slumped onto a frozen metal street bench, took my phone out of my purse, and dialed our home number. It had been reckless not to grab gloves as I raced out of the house, and the cold spring air felt like shards of glass cutting into my fingers. When I heard Aaron's voice, I choked back tears.

"What a fucking waste of time." I was humiliated I had allowed myself to be inflated with so much optimism. It was unlike me to run out so impulsively. I'm methodical! I have a level head! But Marcel's letters had a hold on me I could neither control nor explain. "Online it still looks like it's open. It even listed a fucking phone number."

Aaron could not fix the situation. He said the only thing he could: "I'm sorry."

"I don't know who else to write to. I don't know where else to look. Wolfgang doesn't know anything else."

"I know," Aaron said gently.

"I just . . ." I took a deep breath. "I just want to know if he made it home."

"I know," he said again. "Where are you now?"

"Sitting on a bench outside the store." The words caught and stuttered.

"Come home," he implored.

A cheery voice message from my client waited. But I did not call her back. I could not bear to hear her always-sunny disposition.

Aaron prepared a hearty dinner and served it with a big glass of white wine. Afterward, I did not go into my office to wrap up the day's loose ends. I did not search for Marcel. I did not even want to say his name. I lay on the couch and watched some stupid shit-com; the show's laugh track felt as ineffective as someone trying to fill the Grand Canyon with sound by whispering over the rim.

I had believed with absolute certainty I would eventually find some meandering trail that would lead me to Marcel. But after the trip to 50th and France, I faced the prospect I might never find him.

The thought made it painful to breathe.

The next morning I received a phone call from a freelance copywriter named Jon. We had never worked together, though we ran in overlapping professional circles. He was beginning a high-profile brochure for a medical device manufacturer. His go-to graphic designer had a family emergency, and he hoped I would be available to pinch-hit. The project was a good fit for my skillset, and the budget was generous, but the schedule was brutal. Layout concepts were due in less than a week despite the fact that copy had not yet been written. And in two days I would have to art direct a photoshoot for a product I had not yet seen—and knew nothing about. The project seemed destined to fail.

I agreed to help.

The only way to remove Marcel from my mind, it seemed, was to displace one all-consuming project with another.

The next day, I spent seven hours researching the client's product, downloading reference files, coordinating the photoshoot, and sketching cover designs. During the next three weekdays and over the weekend, I logged more than fifty hours on that project alone, which was time over and above other client work.

By the time I presented concepts to the client's marketing team, I was so exhausted I could barely string words into coherent sentences. I nearly fell asleep on the drive home.

But my plan had succeeded.

I had not thought about Marcel for days.

Chapter Fourteen

White Bear Lake, Minnesota

Late April 2012

Eventually, enough time passed that my impulsive trek to 50th and France felt more like a bruise than a cut.

Information had to be somewhere, I realized. A paper trail had to exist that would identify who had owned Belle Époque, who paid rent, or who remitted sales tax.

And with that, the search was back on.

Pages of results appeared after I typed "Belle Époque" into a search engine. The store showed up immediately, of course, like salt on a wound. The long list of other results included bed and breakfasts, books, hair salons, and wine bars named after France's "beautiful era."

Several pages into the results, I found a breadcrumb: a link to an eight-year-old magazine article profiling the style-maker behind Minneapolis's newest hip-and-trendy place to shop. A photo showed a petite woman with long blond hair standing inside the store at 50th and France. The first two words of the article were her first and last name.

"Gotcha," I whispered with a smile.

I typed her full name into a search engine. After the store closed the woman—Kim—moved to California to focus on building a furniture and interior design company. Images of sun-drenched couches in perfectly styled living rooms and chairs upholstered in bold stripes or lush silks filled her website. Accent pillows inspired by her world travels combined prints and patterns in vibrant blues, corals, and yellows.

I sent Kim a short email. More than ten years had passed since I purchased the letters; I did not know if she would remember them. But I had to ask. No particular reason existed to be optimistic, but I felt certain Kim would write back right away.

When Hoover was a twelve-week-old roly-poly ball of black fuzz, a friend came to our house to meet him. After fondling his oversize paws and nuzzling his velvet ears, she grabbed his tail and whisped his nose with it. He chomped on the tip and whirled in a circle until he fell over. She grabbed his tail and tickled his nose again. We laughed as he lunged, then whirled and whirled. Each time, it was as if Hoover had discovered his tail for the very first time.

As I continued to search for answers, I lunged at any resource that looked encouraging. But I was wasting time on databases I had already scoured, and documents I had already reviewed. Hoover outgrew his tail-chasing folly in days. I was still running in circles with no sign of stopping. Other than an occasional lunch with Kathy, business meeting, Type Tuesday gathering, or quick trip to the grocery store, I barely left the house. I had not talked with friends or family for months.

Aaron tolerated my emotional absence, but I could not help but feel I was being unfaithful. I thought about Marcel each night as I drifted to sleep. I thought about Marcel each morning before I opened my eyes. His presence was so real, so constant, so strong, it often felt as though he were in the same room, breathing the same air.

Yet he remained nowhere to be found.

France seemed to whisper to me. Accordion music played between stories on National Public Radio while I drank my morning coffee. People in the grocery store wore bedazzled T-shirts showing the Arc de Triomphe. On the rare occasion I watched a few minutes of television, stories about France seemed to be front and center.

I could not decide if I was being beckoned. Or mocked.

One Saturday afternoon I ran to the local superstore to pick up shampoo, garbage bags, toilet paper; it was a resupply run that could not be put off any longer. After picking out the items on the list, I wheeled my cart to the cosmetics aisles to buy lip gloss or fingernail polish—something pretty to lift my hollowed spirits. A bottle of purplish-gray fingernail polish caught my eye, and I tossed it in my cart.

Back home, after packing everything away, I thought I would delay my break a bit longer, so I sat down at the kitchen table with the bottle of fingernail polish. After brushing the color onto my nails, I lifted the bottle close to read the tiny label imprinted with the color's name.

It read: EIFFEL FOR YOU.

"How'd it go?" Aaron stood in the kitchen, chopping vegetables.

I kicked off my dress shoes and slung my blazer over a kitchen chair. Hoover leaned into my leg as I rubbed his ears.

"They like it, but they want to show it around," I said with a shrug. The meeting was about the ongoing rebranding project—the project with the always-sunny client I ignored on the day I drove to 50th and France. The presentation went well, though I suspected the final design solution would be a diluted mish-mash of layouts once everyone had their say. Any other month, any other year, I would have ferociously defended the designs. But I did not have any fight left. A margin's width, the paper's texture, the photo's composition: after spending twenty years obsessing over these details, they suddenly seemed shockingly unimportant. At one point during the meeting, I felt an escalating irritation with the clients' back-and-forth discussion of how they might change this or that. I wanted to swipe the presentation boards away from them and announce, "This doesn't fucking matter!"

What I wanted to do was spend every minute looking for Marcel. Finding out if he lived was the only thing that seemed to *fucking matter.* But I could not do that; it would have destroyed the business I spent a decade building. I had to let my client believe her project was the singular thing that mattered. For the first time in my career, I felt like a fraud.

Aaron used the knife to point to a stack of envelopes on the kitchen counter. "There's a letter for you."

The words *Liberté, Egalité, Fraternité, République Française* were printed below blue and red stripes. "It's from the French National Archives!" I announced, realizing Aaron already knew that. Without any shred of delicacy, I ripped the envelope open. The letter was, of course, in French.

I recognized a handful of words: *Seconde Guerre Mondiale.* Second World War. *Date du décès.* Date of death.

After skimming the page, I cobbled together a best-guess translation for Aaron: "Regarding your letter, it's not possible to retrieve information about Marcel Heuzé . . . French man affected by Second World War *a la* Daimler-Marienfelde. I suggest you contact the civil service at Boissy-le-Châtel."

The next paragraph only made partial sense. But some words were devastating in their clarity: *Bombardements.* Bombings. *Décès de la personne concernée.* Death of the person concerned.

I silently read the closing paragraph, looked at Aaron, and shrugged. "Then, I think he's wishing me good luck with my search."

"Or he's telling you to *le fuck off.*"

I forced a slight smile. "No, I don't think so."

"It was nice to get something back," Aaron added after a few moments of silence.

During the previous months, I had begun looking forward to Sundays. Not for the extra hour or two of sleep it sometimes allowed; it was the only day mail was not delivered. It was the only day I was guaranteed a respite from disappointment.

I had received two other responses from various letters, one- or two-sentence emails noting they could not help, then wishing me luck. The vast majority of inquiries, though, including the letters to Jacqueline and Denise, and the email to Kim, remained unanswered. Apathy, it seemed, was my biggest adversary. This was the first piece-of-paper, stamp-on-envelope response, and despite the lack of answers, I was grateful. The signature at the bottom of the page made me feel someone cared enough to pick up a pen and sign their name.

"Are you going to send a letter to, where is it? Bossy-*le*-something?" Aaron asked.

"Already have. Boissy-le-Châtel. Berchères-la-Maingot."

I had not heard from either one.

"How are you doing?" I stood up and gave Kathy a tight hug.

"Better this week," she said with an exaggerated nod, as if she were trying to make the answer true. As she slouched down across from me, it looked like her petite frame was going to be swallowed whole by the restaurant's large booth.

"Getting laid off sucks," she said with a long sigh.

Again, I thought. *Getting laid off again sucks.* The economy was no longer in recession, though our industry was recovering in fits and starts. Kathy had only been at this job for one year. Dark circles pooled under her eyes, but she had a smile on her face. Kathy always had a smile on her face.

"Any leads?"

"I'm not ready to look." She waved her hand to change the topic, though it looked like she was shooing an invisible fly. "What's going on with you?"

After ordering lunch, I told her the medical device brochure was nearing final review, and that the corporate rebranding project was keeping me busy, but was on schedule. "Searching for Marcel is like a frustrating second job," I said. The words caught in my throat and I immediately regretted my word choice. "Job" made it sound like it was something I was being *forced* to do when it was, in fact, the only thing I *wanted* to do.

"I think I've run into a dead end. I've written all these letters to France, right? I haven't been able to find anything else online. Personal information is protected for one hundred years. Did I tell you I tracked down the antique store owner?"

"No!" Kathy said as her head bounced in surprise.

"It doesn't matter. She's not emailing me back. It feels like I am out of options. And I'm running out of ideas."

The server arrived with our food; we picked at our lunches without saying a word.

"Have you given thought to the possibility he's still alive? It would be possible, right?" Kathy offered a gentle smile. "How old would he be?"

Marcel had been born in 1912. "One hundred. He would be one hundred," I said.

"So, it's possible! Wouldn't that be amazing! What if—" Kathy said as she slapped the tabletop. Her voice fell half an octave. "What if you find out he's alive? What if he's in a nursing home somewhere? What would you do? Would you go meet him?"

"Hell, yes! I'd be on the very next plane!" In my bones I knew it was not possible, but I was happy to play along.

It was silent for a few moments. "What do you think he looked like?"

Kathy's question surprised me. As graphic designers, Kathy and I constantly thought about what things *looked* like. But I had to confess I never thought about it. I had spent a thousand hours looking at the tiniest details in his handwriting. I had tried picturing the barracks, the place where his girls lived, the trees and pond in Berchères-la-Maingot. It felt as though I had a crystal-clear picture of what was in Marcel's heart, but I had never wondered what *he* looked like. *What does a Frenchman look like?* The visual that came to mind was a Hollywood stereotype: a lanky man wearing an off-white turtleneck, dark slicked-back hair, a cigarette hanging from his mouth.

An uncharacteristic seriousness filled Kathy's face. "Do you think he made it home?"

Her question took my breath away. This *was* the question I had thought about a hundred times. A thousand times. Ten thousand times.

But no one had directly asked me before. Not even Aaron.

I did not want to answer. I did not want to commit to words the only possible outcome where I was not being naïve and foolishly optimistic. Seconds passed. It was as if waiting could allow the answer to be untrue for a while longer.

"No," I said. Time stood still as that word—cruelly definitive in its verdict—hung in the air. I offered a silent apology to Marcel. It felt as though the answer meant I was abandoning hope. Abandoning him.

Kathy did not say anything, so I explained: "It didn't seem there was any intent to release him. We bombed the factory until it was obliterated. He was always hungry. Sanitation was non-existent. People were worked to death . . ." I could have continued, but the list was already insufferably long.

"Why are you spending so much energy trying to find the answer, then?" The question was gentle, but blunt. The kind of question only a close friend could ask.

"Because I hope I'm wrong."

The complete absence of World War II stories that ended happily was too unbearable to comprehend. If there was one story somewhere, somehow, that resulted in a prisoner returning to the people he loved, I wanted it to be Marcel. *Why couldn't it be Marcel?*

"I just have to know before I can let it go," I said in a tone more defensive than it needed to be.

"So, what's next?"

I shrugged. I could write letters to the five Marcel Heuzés in the phone book, though I did not expect it would lead to anything new. I had not made progress on the font since Aaron and I were in the accident, so I explained I would turn my attention back to the font. I still was unsure if I could sell it if it was based on the words of a man killed in a labor camp, but it was the only *what's next* that came to mind.

"Have you talked with a genealogist?" Kathy asked.

"Yes and no. My mom looked a while back, but she didn't find anything. I looked on a genealogy website," I said with a shrug. "They have a personal research service, but it starts at eighteen hundred bucks."

Kathy's face lit up and she cocked her head to the side. "You know, a couple years back when I needed help tracking down my mom's Canadian birth certificate, I worked with someone." Kathy had looked on and off for years, and had run into one dead end after another before asking a friend to help. "Dixie found it in a week!"

"A week?" My eyebrows soared.

"She knows how to do it! Dixie would love this story. I'm going to see her next weekend. Can I ask if she'll help?"

"Sure," I said, then added under my breath: "Let's see who else can take my money."

Kathy offered a disclaimer: "Dixie doesn't take all the jobs people approach her with. Because I think a lot of people ask."

I nodded and shrugged. "Ask. What can it hurt?"

A couple nights later, I saw Marcel. It was not the first time I dreamed about the search. But it was the first time I saw *him* in a dream. He walked ahead of me on a narrow, gravel-covered country road. The back of his thin frame was in sharp focus; the fields and trees in the periphery were mottled like a painting. He wore old trousers, worn brown shoes. Rolled-up, threadbare shirtsleeves pooled around bony elbows. Marcel's arms hung at his sides, swinging slightly as he walked. His hands were empty.

I watched and waited for Marcel to glance left or right, hoping to see his profile. But he never wavered from his straight-ahead, singular focus. I listened for birds or cars, cows or wind, but the only sound that echoed in my ears was the rhythmic crunch of his footsteps.

Marcel never broke from his steady pace. Sometimes I lagged behind and had to take running steps to regain my place. Other times I tried walking faster. But no matter what I did, I could not close the distance between us.

I tried determining the color of his hair, the conversation with Kathy undoubtedly still on my mind. *Was it black? Brown? Blond?* I could not tell. Colors seemed to shift in the light. *Was he tall or short?* He was too far ahead to know for sure.

I longed for Marcel to turn and extend an invitation for me to join him. I wanted to walk beside him, to hear the timbre of his voice. There were so many questions I wanted to ask, so many things I wanted to know. Somehow, in my dream, we would understand each other. I was certain we would somehow speak a common language.

But Marcel never noticed I followed behind. Or perhaps he did notice. Either way, deep down, I knew why he did not turn around.

Deep in my bones, I understood.

I awoke from the dream wrapped in a blanket of sadness as thick and heavy as the comforter covering me. I lay motionless as I attempted to cement into memory each and every detail: Marcel's gait, his swinging arms, his rolled-up shirtsleeves, his worn brown shoes.

I did not have to work hard to interpret what my subconscious understood with absolute certainty: I was never going to catch up with him.

I was never going to find Marcel.

Lunch with Kathy made me want to try again to connect with Kim in California. Instead of sending another email, I called and left a message with her office manager. I made a point of saying I did not have a complaint about an item I purchased from her; rather, I simply had a question. The woman promised to send Kim the message right away.

Sure enough, an email from Kim arrived a short while later. She asked me to outline which piece I was inquiring about. I wrote back immediately. "My question has to do with letters I purchased from you in 2002 when you owned Belle Époque in Stillwater. I am hoping you can recall where you acquired them. An extraordinary story is emerging."

"Of course I remember the letters!" Kim emailed back. "It killed me to sell them off as they were such a personal thing."

She remembered them! My heart skipped and soared. *Why was I not surprised Marcel's letters touched her in the same way they touched me?*

"I would love to know the story," she wrote. "I purchased them in France, but I can't remember what city I was in. It was undoubtedly at one of the many flea markets I went to."

My head snapped back. *They were at a flea market? Why were Marcel's letters at a flea market? Did this make the situation better? Or worse?* The theory that no one in the family survived the war roared back to the top of the list. *Maybe there really hadn't been anyone left to cherish these letters.*

"I will put more thought into it and reach out to my friend and former partner who was with me on the trip." Kim noted she was busy and at a trade show, but promised to call me once she returned home.

Two weeks later, when I still had not heard from Kim, I sent a follow-up email.

That email went unanswered.

Two weeks after that I sent another email.

That email went unanswered, too.

Chapter Fifteen

White Bear Lake, Minnesota

May 2012

"Dixie's going to do it!" Kathy squealed as soon as I picked up the phone. "For free! She wants to know whether Marcel lived, too!" Kathy's enthusiasm made me grin from ear to ear.

Kathy suggested I begin by assembling a list of everything I knew for Dixie. I started immediately. I outlined names, dates, and places I had looked, what Wolfgang's records showed, and what I had found on Suzanne's death, though I admitted I had no proof she was the correct Suzanne. I listed what I knew about Berchères-la-Maingot, though I noted it did not feel like it was home. Finally, I noted Marcel had mentioned Montreuil and Paris, though it was still unclear how, or if, those two puzzle pieces fit into the bigger picture.

"Sounds like a great mystery!" Dixie wrote in an email later that night. "I have zero experience with research in France. I have some in Germany, but not a lot. I'm experienced at working the genealogical data system and finding help where I need it." Dixie suggested we find a time to get together, and noted she would have me pre-approve document fees, but reiterated the offer to help for no charge. "My reward is in the adventure," she wrote. As Dixie's offer sank in, I was unsurprised Kathy and Dixie were friends. They exuded the same kind of abundant generosity and infectious positivity.

I agreed it would be a delight to meet, but I told her I wanted to send her everything I had without delay.

Within days, Dixie posted Marcel's information on French genealogy boards. Help began to trickle in.

A man named Guy reviewed civil records from Boissy-le-Châtel and reported he did not find any mention of the Heuzé family between 1896 and 1911. More-recent records were not yet available. He offered to look elsewhere, but questioned whether the Heuzé surname might be incorrect.

A woman named Nathalie reviewed birth and death records from Berchères-la-Maingot between 1882 and 1902. She did not find anything, either. The closest surname had been Herve, and she, too, wondered if my information was bad.

Guy and Nathalie's actions left me flabbergasted. *Who were these people?* Dixie seemed to be a member of some secret, amazing network. Hope surged in a way it had not in months, yet Guy and Nathalie's comments also made me question what I thought I knew with certainty. *Was it possible I didn't even have Marcel's name right?*

Dixie seemed cautious and offered a warning, "Don't be surprised if some facts turn out to be incorrect." I attempted to decipher whether she meant *their* information or *mine*.

Dixie noted she would have time the forthcoming Saturday to dig in and do some serious research. I tried to be patient. Time slowed to an excruciating crawl.

In the hours and days after the airplanes careened into the Twin Towers, Aaron and I could barely tear ourselves from the televised images of New York's dust-covered streets, the twisted metal, the trails of smoke. We watched police and firemen standing atop Ground Zero's smoldering rubble, digging for life. Digging not only because *their* loved ones were missing—digging because *someone's* loved ones were missing.

Images showed sidewalks filled with candles and walls and bus stops plastered with flyers of the missing. Every letter of every word—ragged handwriting on some, blocky computer type on others—held a desperate plea: *Have you seen my husband/brother/wife/mother/friend? Please call. Please email. Please, please, please.*

Their hope seemed desperate. Impractical. The candles, flyers, and vigils seemed pointless.

How could they not know their loved ones were gone?

Yet who would dare tell them to abandon hope? Who would dare point out that if they were lucky, a wedding ring, a watch, a trace of DNA might someday be found? If they needed to cling to the belief that *their* loved one might be in a hospital, *their* loved one somehow survived, *their* loved one beat the odds, who would dare tell them it could not be true?

As the knee-buckling reality of the terrorist attack sank in, I began to feel irritated by the images of glowing candles. It did not seem right a candle's flame should represent hope. Its shape and size were too easily measured, too easily seen. Hope was more like the silent, black space around the flame: infinite, invisible, unfillable, inconsolable.

"Hope is the thing that destroys you," I heard one mother say in a radio interview weeks later. She begged for relief from the agonizing hope her daughter would walk through the front door one more time. She prayed hope would release its suffocating grip so she could grieve.

Yet there I was, my arms thrown around the same desperate, all-consuming, impractical, insidious hope. Maybe Marcel survived. Maybe Marcel beat the odds. Maybe *my* Marcel had been lucky! The better part of a year had been consumed digging through the rubble of records, sending out flyers and emails: *Do you know what happened to Marcel? Please write. Please email. Please, please, please.*

My head knew what Dixie would find in the same way people in New York had to have known. But as long the answer remained uncertain, my heart could pretend anything was possible: Marcel *could* have made it home, he *could* have lived. For a split second, I considered telling Dixie to stop looking. Maybe it would be better to always believe it was possible than to know for sure. Hope left room to dream. Hope left room to be foolishly optimistic.

But hope had already taken a toll. *I had to know.*

I made a silent vow to travel to Germany someday—wherever Dixie discovered Marcel had been buried—and lay flowers on his tombstone to show him he had not been forgotten. To show him the love he had for his wife and daughters had not been lost to history. But a shiver ran down my spine as I realized his body could have been incinerated, tossed into an unmarked ditch, buried under a blanket of quicklime. A tombstone probably did not exist.

As I waited to hear from Dixie, my head's practical certainty waged a fierce battle with my heart's foolish optimism, each side gaining or giving up ground as hope and despair alternately swelled. I abandoned any attempt to concentrate on anything meaningful and just tried to keep occupied. Kitchen counters were scrubbed, floors swept, loads of laundry cycled. Inevitably, though, I wandered back into my office, slouched into my chair, and stared at the computer monitor, waiting for answers.

"Anything yet?" Aaron asked on one of the trips wandering between my office and the living room. Aaron was on the couch. Hoover was splayed on the floor.

I shook my head, and looked down at Hoover. "Want to go for a walk?" He did not move, so I asked again, forcing more enthusiasm into the question. He continued to lie on the floor, looking up with apathy. We had already been on twice the usual number of walks. I twisted to look at Aaron. His shoulders jiggled as he tried to prevent laughter from breaking free from his lungs.

"It's not funny," I whined.

"Oh, yes it is," he assured me.

Hoover agreed to go on a walk only after I bribed him with treats. Aaron came along, too, though I suspected it was solely to mock my impatience.

When we returned, I checked email again.

I emptied the dishwasher, folded laundry, fluffed the couch pillows and positioned them so they looked *just so*. I tried a few yoga poses, reaching my arms high to heaven.

"Let's go," Aaron said.

I took a deep breath in and let my arms fall to my sides. I could not will an email from Dixie to appear. Maybe she would not find anything for days. Maybe it would be weeks or months. Maybe she would not find him either.

When we returned from dinner—burgers with a mountain of greasy fries—we sat on the deck and listened to birds sing while Hoover patrolled the back yard. Flowerpots, which by this time of year should have filled the deck, were still stacked inside the garage. The plants in the yard that budded and bloomed had done so by luck or their own sheer will.

"I'm turning in," Aaron said through a yawn. I nodded to indicate I would stay outside until Hoover was ready to come in. I gazed heavenward, forcing myself to take slow, deep breaths. My mind was blank. I was out of prayers and wishes.

By the time I stepped into the bedroom to wish Aaron goodnight, he was fast sleep. I went into the office, slumped into the chair, jiggled the mouse, and watched as the monitors dissolved to white.

An email from Dixie awaited.

I read the four-word subject line and gasped as my vision became a mottled field of white stars. I burst into tears—abundant, shameless tears—as I processed her words: "Got 'im. He survived."

Through tear-filled eyes, I opened Dixie's email and looked at the record she found. Birth: January 26, 1912. Death: January 4, 1992.

Thoughts seemed to dissolve into fractions. My brain seemed incapable of processing the information. *Was I seeing right? 1992?* I looked at each number: 1-9-9-2. *He lived. Marcel lived!* I did the math over and over, as if my calculation had to be wrong. Marcel had lived to be seventy-nine years old. *Was that true? Could that really be true?*

A second attachment listed his marriage: December 31, 1932 to Renée Duthé in Montreuil-sous-Bois. *His wife was Renée, not Vérane?* As

I processed this new information I pictured how the two names might be linked: Vérane > Rane > Rene > Renée. The record showed Renée lived until 2005. She had lived to be ninety-five. All the air seemed to leave my lungs as I realized Marcel's letters had been in my possession while Renée was alive. *How could that be? How could I have had Renée's letters while she was alive?*

Dixie's email continued with a record showing Suzanne had been born in Montreuil, and had died March 22, 1990. *It was true, Suzanne had been dead more than twenty years.* The record showed Suzanne had married in 1955 and had four children, though their names and ages, even genders, were concealed. Suzanne had been an *aide comptable*, a bookkeeper.

The record Dixie found included a small black-and-white photo. I stared in wonder at this first glimpse of Marcel's family. Suzanne offered a proud, full smile. Grommets in the corners made it seem the photo had been attached to some kind of official document. I guessed Suzanne had been in her early twenties. A side barrette held back wavy, shoulder-length hair. The photo had a warm sepia tone, but if the photo had been in color, I would have seen emerald eyes and auburn hair.

A calculation worked its way through my brain: Suzanne had only been nine and a half years old when Marcel inquired whether she fetched milk and bread while Renée had been in Paris. That was years younger than what I had guessed. *What silly thing had I been doing at nine and a half? Sleeping in a bed piled with stuffed animals? Standing along the fence at the edge of our yard, singing songs to the neighbor's cows after I got home from school?*

I scrolled back to the top of the email to read the text of Dixie's message—a message I initially skipped over. "Some good news here, though still sketchy. There's only one daughter listed, Suzanne, the same Suzanne you found. Notice Montreuil—the place of Marcel and Renée's marriage and the birthplace of Suzanne. We're on the right track!"

Tears streamed down my face. I leaned forward and cradled my head in the palms of my hands as one fat tear after another dropped onto the hardwood floor. *Marcel survived.* Plink. *He lived!* Plink. *He lived to be an old man!* Plink. It seemed impossible to express to Dixie the gratitude that filled my heart. It was as if she had been the one to save him. It was as if she alone had brought Marcel home.

I walked to our bedroom, crawled on top of the covers, and lay next to Aaron. He heard my sobs and wrapped his arm around me to offer consolation. I shook my head and tried to tell him they were happy tears, but the words were locked inside of me. I should have been dancing, jumping, doing cartwheels. Brass horns should have been playing fanfares. Fireworks should have been exploding. Instead, I was curled in a ball and I could not stop crying. Many minutes elapsed before I could tell him the news. His response revealed disbelief. And relief.

I eventually returned to the office to send Dixie an email: "Kathy was right, you *are* amazing." I did not know how or where Dixie found the answers. In that moment, I did not care.

"Got another clue!" a new email from Dixie read. "This is Denise." Fresh tears blossomed as I read her email. *Denise was alive.* Suddenly, Denise was no longer a name scrawled across a piece of paper, a young girl who had been told to pick violets. She was a woman of seventy-seven. Twenty-five thousand days had passed since Marcel told her he wished she would help mend his clothes. School, work, love, marriage, children, loss, laughter: I knew nothing about her life. But Denise was *alive.*

"I'll bet this is little 'Lily,'" the next email said. My head snapped back as I read Dixie's email. The strange feeling I had weeks earlier had been true: Lily did not exist. "Lily" had been a nickname. Lily wasn't *Lily!* Dixie did not have any information other than that Lily—Eliane, I corrected myself—was alive, too. Eliane was seventy-three years old.

"Because Denise and Lily are alive, their records are private. But their maiden names are Heuzé so it's probable they are the two you are looking for," Dixie wrote. She then added something that made me gasp: "I found a record which showed Marcel and Renée had four children (a fourth child must have been born after the war)." I stared at my computer monitor, dumbstruck.

By the time Dixie signed off, it was well past midnight. I went to the living room, collapsed into the couch, and read the translations of the four letters and the postcard. For the first time, I could read his glorious words through a filter of life, not death. Hoover crawled next to me and licked the tears from my face. As I rubbed his silken ears I assured him they were happy tears. *The happiest ever tears.* For the entire night, he remained vigilantly by my side.

My mind wheeled with all the new information. They had another child. Lily wasn't Lily. Marcel's wife's name was Renée. Denise and Eliane were alive. Dizzying swells of joy were tempered by waves of guilt and confusion that Marcel's letters had been in my possession while Renée was alive. And fresh tears flooded my cheeks every time I thought about the most astonishing news: he lived. *Marcel lived.*

Hours later, bright morning sunlight flickered between the closed living room blinds. Aaron, I realized, must have shut them while I slept. As I slowly sat up, I kicked to free myself from the zigzag afghan, which had twisted around my legs. A pounding echoed inside my head. It felt as if I had a raging hangover. My eyelids were raw, and I could see my swollen cheeks in the periphery of my vision. The hair on the right side of my head was matted to my face; the hair on the left side was a spaghetti-like tangle.

"How are you doing?" Aaron reached forward with a cup of hot coffee.

Tears began to well. Through a series of choked-back sobs I squeaked, "I'm so happy."

"Mmmhmm, I can see that."

Other than having another child, I did not know anything else about Marcel's life, yet my heart overflowed with joy. *How could it be possible to feel this much happiness for someone I would never meet?*

On Sunday afternoon, Dixie sent a couple more emails, one that included Denise's mailing address in Paris. As I stared at the letters and numbers that defined her physical existence, two things were immediately clear: this was a different Denise than the woman I had written to months earlier, and I had to write *this* Denise.

Questions swirled: *Was it even my place to contact Denise? The all-consuming question had been answered; I didn't have to know anything else. Would my letter be welcome? Or, if the letters were at a flea market because of something horrible that happened, could my letter usher home an unwelcome relic and break her heart wide open?*

Despite unknown consequences, the fire of curiosity still roared. *Not* writing to Denise was an impossibility.

I realized it would be prudent to include proof I was not running some cruel scam, so I decided to include a copy of the sweet letter Marcel had written to Denise and her sisters. That letter mentioned cherry blossoms, fetching milk, picking violets—not bombings, men burned alive, boiled veal bones. The letter did not include the swastika.

Dear Denise—

I am searching for relatives of Marcel Heuzé. I have been working with a researcher who believes you may be related, and I hope that is true. To be sure, though, the Marcel Heuzé I am seeking information on was born January 26, 1912 in Boissy-le-Châtel and worked as a turner. Is this the same Marcel Heuzé as your father?

Let me tell you more. My part of the story starts in 2002, when I purchased several letters in a local antique shop. By local, I mean in Stillwater, Minnesota. I do not speak French, but I purchased the letters because they were beautiful, and it was clear that they had been written with love. The letters begin, "*Mes chères petites.*"

I am a graphic designer and I have been designing a font inspired by the letterforms in the letters. I wish I could tell you that the font was done.

Even though I don't speak French, I could pick out words here and there: Paris, Berlin, 1,300 kilometers, and names such as Denise, Lily, and Suzanne. Last year, I began to wonder who wrote them. I paid someone to translate the letters. The letters were written by Marcel while he was conscripted into labor at the Daimler factory in Marienfelde. The letters describe many things: how hungry he was, what his daily work life was like, that his clothes needed mending, and how desperately he wanted to come home. In every letter, he expressed deep love for his wife and daughters.

After spending so much time with the letters, I began to consider Marcel an old friend, yet I knew nothing about him other than what was written in the letters.

This led me to wonder about the fate of Marcel and how his letters ended up in a small antique store halfway around the world. I could not find anything about Marcel searching online, though I looked for many months.

I even contacted Daimler seeking information. An archivist confirmed Marcel worked as a turner at the Berlin-Marienfelde factory. Their records indicate he was released November of 1943, which could not be true since I have a letter from April 1944 expressing how much how much he hoped to be able to go home.

Later, I was connected to a genealogy researcher, who was the one who found you.

When she discovered Marcel returned home, I am not ashamed to tell you that I cried I was so happy. Based on his letters and everything I've read, it seemed unlikely that he would have survived. I understand he lived to be seventy-nine. I would love to learn more about him, if there is anything you would be willing to share. I have so many questions:

Did he share stories about his time at Marienfelde?

The letters were filled with love for his wife; were they together the rest of their lives?

Where did he work before and after the war? Was he always a "turner"?

What was he like? Was he kind or hot tempered? Funny or serious? Quiet or loud?

Do you have any photos of him from that time? Do you have any photos of Marcel and your mother together?

The genealogy researcher said that they had another daughter after he returned home. Is that true?

During the war, the family lived in Berchères-la-Maingot, but it didn't seem like "home." Were you staying with extended family during the war?

Do you have any idea how his letters wound up in an antique store halfway around the world?

I have enclosed a copy of one of the letters. This letter is the sweetest of all of the letters, and has a section written to you. This is the only letter signed "Papa," the other letters were signed "Marcel."

If you are so inclined, I would love to learn more about the life of Marcel. If you are not interested, I send great apologies for the intrusion.

After considering what to—or what not to—reveal, I decided not to tell Denise that Marcel's letters had been purchased at a flea market, instead asking the gentler question of whether she knew how the letters might have ended up in Stillwater. It seemed like a small kindness. *What if being at a flea market meant someone in the family had sold them?*

I folded my letter—translated into French with the standard apology for errors—over the copy of Marcel's letter, and slid both inside an envelope. When she opened the envelope's contents, she would see Marcel's letter first.

Using the most delicate handwriting I was capable of, I inked Denise's address onto the envelope. When I set the pen down, my eyebrows arched in surprise. The left side of the *M* in "Mrs." swooped just like Marcel's *M*. Without realizing it even happened, my handwriting had started to look like his.

Chapter Sixteen

White Bear Lake, Minnesota

May 21, 2012

Early Monday morning, Dixie sent an email noting she had received a brief message through a genealogy website from a member of the Cléro family in France. Cléro was Suzanne's husband's surname. I assured Dixie it was fine to pass along my contact information, and figured if the person was a distant relative of Suzanne's husband, they might be reaching out as a curiosity. They might not know much about Marcel.

As I showered I planned my day: final revisions were due on the medical device brochure, the rebranding project needed attention, some administrative tasks needed to be done. The day sounded delightfully mundane compared to the weekend's emotional roller coaster.

As soon as the post office opened, I took Denise's letter to the counter so a clerk could confirm I had enough postage. I was bursting to tell the woman behind the counter what was inside the envelope, but I refrained. The story seemed impossible to summarize.

On the drive home, I swung by a coffee shop and ordered a fancy drink with a towering ruffle of whipped cream. It was a splurge reserved for special occasions. As I waited for my drink, I reminded myself this was really happening. Contact with Marcel's family was five or six days away.

But it wasn't *just* five or six days. It felt as if sixty-eight years were about to fold down and disappear like an accordion's bellows.

Hours later, an email arrived with the subject line "Marcel Heuzé." The sender's name was unfamiliar; it did not include "Cléro."

The email was in passable English, and after reading four sentences, it felt as if I was back in Aaron's pickup, sliding sideways. I rolled the chair away from the computer monitor, distancing myself from the words on the screen.

"What the fuck do you mean by that?" I whispered as my fingers covered my mouth.

I reread the first four sentences as a sourness flooded my mouth. The room felt like it was tilting. As I stood up, my office chair skittered across the room.

"What the fuck do you mean by that?" I said again. This time, the words were loud.

I scurried into the bathroom and leaned over the toilet, anticipating a wave of convulsions. *Fuck! What have I done? WhathaveIdonewhathaveIdone?* I wanted to race back to the post office and retrieve the letter to Denise. By now, though, the envelope had certainly been processed and shuffled into a mountain of a million other pieces of mail.

The email I received had not been from some shirttail relative. It was from Suzanne's granddaughter, Natacha. "My mother who doesn't speak and write English read Dixie's mail, which I translate for her," Natacha wrote. "We were so surprised to know that Marcel's letters travelled so far. It's just unbelievable and so exciting. My mother is quite sad to think that Suzanne, her sisters, and Marcel's wife Renée never received those letters."

I read the last sentence ten times. Twenty times. My head began pounding and it hurt to focus my eyes. *They never received the letters? How could that be? That was not a scenario I considered!*

"If you want to receive a picture of Marcel as army suit, we could send to you. My mother, Nadine, and her sister, Agnès will meet tonight, because they have so many questions they would like to ask you. Will you accept to reply?"

"I would love to see a photo of Marcel," I wrote to Natacha. I decided to proffer answers to questions about who I was, why and how long I had Marcel's letters. I explained Marcel's letters had been purchased at a flea market in France before being sold here in Minnesota—a tidbit that seemed essential to disclose after learning the family never received the letters. I attached a scan of the first letter, promised I would answer any question her mother and aunt had, and noted I had many questions, too.

It was impossible to concentrate on anything else, so I sat on the couch trying to puzzle together any scenario that could explain how letters spanning fifteen months could have remained together, yet not have been received by the family. I felt like a toddler clumsily trying to pound a square peg into a round hole: nothing fit. As hour after hour passed, emotions ranged from disbelief to amazement to near-suffocating anxiety.

"What's going on?" Aaron stepped into the dark living room after finishing a sixteen-hour shift.

"In a couple of days I'm going to go to prison."

He sat down in the stuffed chair. "Elaborate . . ."

"I got an email from Suzanne's granddaughter. She said they never *got* the letters." Aaron's eyebrows shot up; his surprise reflected the astonishment I had felt all afternoon and evening. "So, in what? Five more days, Denise is going to open a letter that includes a photocopy of a letter her father mailed from a fucking Nazi labor camp. A letter she's never seen before. She's going to have a heart attack and fall over dead, then I'm going to go to prison for killing her."

Aaron started to laugh. "It's not funny," I whined. "This could kill her." I reached behind me, grabbed a pillow, and threw it at Aaron.

"You're not going to kill her," he said, tossing the pillow back to me.

At midnight—early Tuesday in France—Natacha sent another email. She wanted to share her family history. "Marcel came into the world January 26, 1912 at Boissy-la-Châtel, a little country town near Coulommiers and died in 1992. They had three girls: Suzanne in 1933 (who is my grandmother, she died in 1990), Denise in 1934, Eliane (nicknamed Lily) in 1939. After the war they had Marcel."

A son. They had a son! Dixie had not specified whether they had a girl or a boy. In my letter to Denise I mentioned a fourth daughter, an incorrect assumption I blamed on not thinking clearly in the hours after learning Marcel lived.

"His whole life Marcel lived in Montreuil-sous-Bois, a town adjacent to Paris," Natacha continued. "In 1939, Renée and her three girls moved to their country house at Berchères-la-Maingot, close to Chartres, a town famous for its cathedral. During World War II, Marcel was imprisoned at the STO, then a prisoner of war interned in Germany. It was a forbidden subject."

"Forbidden" rattled in my brain. The word sounded sharp. Inflexible. Many people did not talk about the war afterward, yet this seemed different. "Forbidden" represented something infinitely more damaged, and my heart ached.

The words "prisoner of war" surprised me, though they should not have. It made sense, unfortunately. After the Daimler factory was destroyed, I speculated the Germans might have held on to him to prevent him from returning home and fighting with the Allies.

"Marcel was tall and slim, to my mum, he was often sad, and not talkative at all. Serious and quiet but not hot tempered." Quiet, sad, not talkative: Natacha's description unmoored me. *Marcel had been so expressive in his letters. He had been filled with hope and optimism!*

"Renée received so many letters of him. If I can find it I will let you know. We think the letters were taken by a German soldier, and after the war, to get money, they were sold to a flea market shop."

The suggestion a German soldier had taken the letters seemed impossible since the letters spanned so many months. *But what did I know?* Perhaps the mail had been confiscated before it left Germany. Perhaps mail had been held by the French postal service.

"At the end of the war they went back to Montreuil-sous-Bois. He was still a 'turner'—do you know what that is? They lived there until Marcel died in 1992. Renée died in 2005. And they were still in love."

Natacha's announcement "they were still in love" made thick drops pool in my eyes. Guilt stabbed at me for having entertained the notion Marcel had been unloved, or that he had been forgotten. *Nothing could be further from the truth, it seemed.*

Natacha attached a file with photos. As I looked at the first image, the tears that had pooled in my eyes began dripping down my cheeks. Marcel stood tall in a military uniform with a proud, stoic expression. Straight, dark hair swept over the crown of his head. His nose was thin and straight, his complexion flawless. His right arm bent at his elbow and his hand grasped the buckle of a thick garrison belt. Numbers were pinned to his collar; chevron patches sat above his cuffs.

The next photo took my breath away: it was Marcel and Renée's wedding portrait. Marcel seemed to have a slight smile, and he wore a tuxedo, complete with a bowtie and white pocket square. But it was not so much that he wore the tuxedo. Marcel held his body with so much confidence it was as if he wore a tuxedo every day.

Renée sat next to Marcel. Deep, dark, perfect finger curls framed Renée's temple. Her expression was regal. Her floor-length black dress had a simple scoop neck. The skirt's waves of silk reminded me of water shimmering in moonlight. I wondered whether simple black wedding dresses had been the fashion in 1932, but I later learned she wore black as a sign of respect for Marcel's mother, who had recently passed away. Renée cradled a bouquet of roses and hyacinths. A wicker basket filled with additional flowers sat on a table next to Marcel.

Together, they were a vision of confidence. It was as if neither of them doubted their marriage would last forever.

The file Natacha sent included other, unlabeled family photos: baby photos, a young girl embracing a terrier, decades-old class portraits, a scratched photo of a stern old woman wearing a black bonnet tied with a big bow. Later, I would learn one of the wallet-size photos was Renée, though I could not yet see the thread that tied the stunning twenty-two-year-old in the wedding portrait to the small portrait taken fifty or more years later.

I extracted Marcel and Renée's wedding portrait from Natacha's file and placed the image in emails to Kathy, Tom, and Dixie.

I was so honored to make this introduction.

With tears in my eyes, I typed the words: "Meet Marcel."

Chapter Seventeen

White Bear Lake, Minnesota

Late May 2012

I did not hear back from Natacha, and fretted her mom or aunt had reined in additional communication. *Did they want to contact an embassy? A lawyer?*

"Maybe," Aaron said, "they're busy."

Busy? I wanted to scream. *What could be more important?*

At times, the thoughts that raced through my mind were paralyzing: astonishment at Natacha's claim the family never received the letters, confusion about Natacha's silence, curiosity about when Denise would receive my letter, anxiety about what her reaction would be. Other times, swells of emotion made me want to throw my arms around anyone and everyone, cup my hands and shout, "Never-before-seen words of love are on their way to Paris!"

By Tuesday evening, I was glad to have a reason to get out of the house. Aaron was happy to see me leave, too, since my constant speculation had become irritating chatter. Instead of a typical Type Tuesday lecture or presentation, the plan was to gather at a local letterpress print shop to celebrate the completion of a serif font by the group's founder, Craig.

As I stepped inside the shop, jazz music echoed off the high tin ceiling. Sturdy oak cabinets with drawer after drawer of movable metal type sat along one wall. A center worktable was covered with snacks and beverages. Grandpa and Cutie-Pie, two of the shop's century-old treadle-powered presses, sat in a corner near The Beast, a press that incorporated an axle assembly from a Ford Model T. Hand-cut woodblock illustrations filled one tall shelf, tins of ink filled another. The letterpress shop was like Santa's workshop, though instead of toys, the owner, Kent, created wonders of words and paper.

Craig offered a welcome, followed by a round of introductions and a social hour.

It would have been reckless to make any kind of announcement about Marcel's letters before learning Denise's reaction to seeing her father's words. During the social hour I adopted the taciturn composure perfected in childhood. But the self-control didn't feel admirable; it felt more like wearing a too-small coat, zipped tight. I could barely move. I could barely breathe.

I hoped telling just one person might release enough pressure so I could remain composed for a few more days, so when no one else was nearby, I told Craig about the letter in transit to Denise. Craig's jaw dropped and his head bobbed like a jack-in-the-box. I smiled, imagining I had worn that same silly expression for days.

Wednesday and Thursday were devoured by final revisions to the medical device brochure. The work required every ounce of concentration I could muster, and I was grateful to have something to consume my time and energy.

My heart would skip whenever the letter crossed my mind. *Was it already in France? When would Denise receive it?* Each hour that passed meant I was one hour closer to hearing from Denise. I was certain of it. Or maybe confidence became absolute because silence would have been devastating. Aaron tried to prepare me for disappointment by reminding me of the other times I believed responses had been imminent: from Kim, from Berchères-la-Maingot, from Boissy-la-Châtel, from Jacqueline.

I assured him this time it was different.

I was going to hear from Denise.

I had to hear from Denise.

I had to.

Chapter Eighteen

White Bear Lake, Minnesota

May 25, 2012

"My name is Tiffanie," the email said. "I am the granddaughter of Denise Heuzé, so I am also the great-granddaughter of Marcel. Today we received your letter and it was such a pleasure to read a letter of Marcel. We are amazed by the situation. We are interested by the letters you have and will be happy to answer any question that you have about Marcel. He was an amazing man and even if I didn't know him very well (he died when I was four years old), I remember his passion for life and his love for his family. My grandmother doesn't speak English, so I will translate your questions and her answers. Thank you very much for this lovely surprise."

And with Tiffanie's short email, I could breathe again.

"I am amazed by this entire situation, too," I typed back immediately. "I received a couple of emails from Natacha. She made it sound like the family never received the letters. Could that be true?" I told Tiffanie I did not have Lily's address, and asked if she could please share the letter with her.

"I don't know Natacha," Tiffanie noted. In fact, I later learned Tiffanie had had to ask who Natacha was. "As you may know, Suzanne died twenty years ago so we didn't build a relationship with her family. As for 'Lily' her real name is Eliane and she will come next week to my grandmother's house to see your letter. My grandmother also informed their brother, Marcel, who was born after the war. We have so many questions, like how did you get the letters and how many do you have? My grandmother thinks they were taken by a German soldier so that is why she doesn't remember the one that you sent to us."

"I purchased the letters at an antique store here in Minnesota," I wrote back. "The store owner bought them at a flea market in France." The letter to Denise had not included that information. However, after being told the family never received the letters, it seemed important to disclose everything I knew about the letters' journey.

"I am sad to report there were other letters I did not purchase. That was ten years ago. I have three other letters plus one postcard. I will email them to you." A short note accompanied each scanned image: "I hope Denise and Eliane laugh when they read he called them 'hoodlums.'" "It brought tears to my eyes he ended this letter, 'Your big guy who only dreams of you.'" "This letter included a reference to '*fridoline cuisine*,' though we don't know what that means."

I presumed the swastika would be a surprising—potentially painful—symbol to see, so when I emailed the scan of the March 1944 letter to Tiffanie, I gently proffered a reason it might have been there. "I assumed he needed to include that to get the letter past the censors."

"Do you know when he came home?" I asked.

I did not hear back from Tiffanie, and I began to fret my comments had been unwelcome. Perhaps I had stepped over some invisible boundary. *Were long-forgotten memories rushing to the fore? Were they overwhelmed by the swastika?*

"You can't change what you don't have control over," Aaron said as he attempted to calm my frayed nerves.

It was days before I heard from Tiffanie again. "I showed them the letters today. They were really happy, and they cried. I asked the questions you wrote, and I took some pictures. Marcel was released in 1944. *'Fridoline cuisine'* is German cuisine." I chuckled as I realized Marcel had been making a joke: he had been promising to cook Renée German food when he got home.

Tiffanie attached several photos to her email. The first was Marcel and Renée's wedding portrait. My heart swelled to see their quiet elegance again: Marcel's slight smile, his cocksure stance, the perfect finger curls that framed Renée's face, the skirt that looked like water in moonlight.

The next photo, taken a few years later, was of Marcel and Renée standing together. Marcel wore a dark blazer and a necktie with wide stripes. His face was mostly hidden in the shadow of his fedora. Renée was to his side, her face fully illuminated by the sun. The front of her hat flipped skyward; a silk flower and a wide-ribbon bow adorned the underside of the brim. Renée's close-mouthed smile curled into full, round cheeks. Their fingers were knit together in front of them. *Did they know?* I wondered. *Did they know in just a handful of years they would be swept up and separated by a world consumed by fire?*

The next photo had been taken the summer of 1991, six or so months before Marcel died. Brown trousers billowed around Marcel's ankles. A white sleeveless T-shirt hung from rounded shoulders. It seemed as though an old man with a shrunken frame had replaced the vibrant man in the wedding portrait. Marcel's arm wrapped around Renée, drawing her body into his. Her outside leg was extended, as if she had just been pulled off balance. Her hair was a pillow of white, wind-blown and cottony, and the camera caught her mid-laugh. Behind them, gardens exploded with color, and hotel balconies hinted at a far-off view. I imagined they were near the ocean and that the air was thick with salt.

The wedding portrait and the photo from 1991 were like bookends of a life. But, other than the months in Marienfelde, and the fact they had another child, I knew nothing about his life.

"They told me that after his return he didn't talk about what he saw," Tiffanie wrote. "They didn't remember ever seeing those letters. Of course Eliane was really young so she didn't remember any of it. Apparently, my grandmother took some letters when they moved from Berchères but I didn't find them, we wanted to compare the date. I will maybe find them another time."

Chapter Nineteen

White Bear Lake, Minnesota

June 2012

Tiffanie and Natacha had answered some of my questions, but so many other questions remained. I tried to release them. I tried convincing myself the details of Marcel's life were not my business. But curiosity's chokehold was unrelenting. *Which passages made Denise and Eliane laugh? Which ones made them cry? Were particular words or turns of phrases quintessentially Marcel?* I often woke in the middle of the night, my brain churning. *Did Tiffanie find the other letters she mentioned? When exactly did Marcel get home? What was their reaction when they saw the swastika?*

Both Natacha and Tiffanie suggested Germans had taken the letters. Collaborating to concoct a story seemed impossible since they did not even seem to know who the other one was. *But if Germans took the letters, how would they have ended up at a flea market in France?*

In the weeks that followed, I made an effort to devote attention to Aaron to make up for the months he came second to Marcel. We went out to a movie. I baked his favorite rhubarb crisp. We ate long dinners on our deck and took Hoover for extended visits to a dog park.

For the first time in a year, I ventured out to graphic design industry events. I attended the opening of a friend's art show. I finally took Laura out to dinner for her birthday. I had missed her birthday by more than five months, but it was a twenty-year tradition I was not going to break. Over dinner she told me she and Adam had started to plan their wedding.

Word began to leak out about Marcel's letters. Aaron shared the story with a few co-workers. I told one client and a handful of design friends. I told a neighbor one evening when we took a break from mowing our yards. Sometimes the words that came out of my mouth sounded too preposterous to be true and a couple of times I stopped mid-sentence, as if I had caught myself inventing some fantastical story: A man in the labor camp wore a tuxedo! Someone sang a Maurice Chevalier song! Marcel told his daughters to pick violets!

I delighted at people's dreamy expressions when they heard Marcel's words of affection. And I learned to anticipate their questions after learning about STO. "The government could do that?" they would ask with wide eyes. "They could make anyone work for the Nazis?"

More than one person wept when they learned Marcel survived.

Evenings when Aaron was at work, or when he spent evenings watching television or puttering in the garage, I worked on the font. I felt an even deeper responsibility to make it as beautiful as possible to honor Marcel, though the software's technicalities still confounded me.

I took a stab at kerning and spent hours writing lines of code to define incremental spaces between letters. It was time consuming and impossibly tedious, and it would be months before I learned I had approached it in the most inefficient way possible.

At some point, I accidentally double-compiled the code, which meant every kerning adjustment was amplified: if the code added space, twice as much space appeared; if the code subtracted space, letters were twice as close as they should have been. I scoured FontLab's user guide for answers. I pored through online problem-solving forums. But the solution remained elusive, and the only remedy seemed to be to start again from the beginning. Anyone who had the misfortune to ask about the font's progress would hear me hiss about kerning.

Designers at one of the Type Tuesday gatherings mentioned an upcoming typography conference. When I learned a pre-conference workshop was being offered on a different piece of type design software, I sent in my registration and reserved a spot. I had reluctantly concluded I had no hope of conquering kerning on my own. The two options, it seemed, were either to abandon FontLab or abandon the font.

One Saturday morning I walked the mile and a half from our home to White Bear Lake. It was the first time all year I had the time and opportunity to walk to the lake. Once I arrived at the water's edge, I sat on a granite boulder that hugged the shore. Hoover did not come with me; this walk was too far for our old boy. Aaron did not come along either. He was not much of a sit-along-the-shore kind of guy. These walks, these quiet minutes alone, were time to be by myself.

Bullfrogs croaked. Far-off outboard motors purred. Reeds rustled in the wind as mallards drifted between lily pads. I took long, deep breaths and reflected on the previous weeks. It was impossible to measure the happiness that came from learning Marcel's fate, connecting with his family, and knowing they were happy to read his letters. Yet I felt something more complicated—something that made no logical sense. I overflowed with joy, but what spilled over the edges was a sad emptiness.

As I tried to parse the contradictory emotions, I slowly came to understand why I felt sadness: He was not *my* Marcel. He had never been *my* Marcel. He was *their* Marcel.

I had held Marcel close in my heart when I believed no one else remembered him. Now that his family had been found I had to let him go. Knowing he had been loved—that he had never been forgotten—should have provided closure. But Marcel's tender words still inhabited a place inside me. Letting him go felt akin to purging him from my heart, and I was not ready to do that.

I could not do that.

I tried to find peace with the fact I might never hear from Tiffanie or Natacha again. Maybe everything I knew about Marcel was everything I would ever know. But I was no longer even sure what I knew; the impression I had had been muddled by their descriptions. Tiffanie said Marcel had a passion for life and love for his family. Natacha described him as sad, serious, and not talkative.

Knowing Marcel lived was no longer a complete-enough answer. I needed to know that the war had not destroyed the loving man who poured his heart onto paper. I knew it was not my business, but I had to know if Marcel had had a *good* life.

Reeds to my left swayed and rustled. A majestic heron with an impossibly long *s*-shaped neck stepped into view. I held my breath and sat still as a statue as I watched it swivel its tufted head. "Don't fly away," I begged.

Let him go, I told myself. *Let Marcel go.*

Life had returned to a familiar routine. Days were spent developing layouts, making text revisions, retouching photos. But that work suddenly felt too small, too disconnected from the world. *How could Marcel's letters have changed nothing—and everything—at the same time?* I took several long, deep breaths and asked the Universe for some kind of sign. I wanted to know what was next. I wanted to know whether releasing Marcel from my heart was the final step, or if something else needed to be done first.

I eventually inched up and whispered goodbye to the heron. I began to walk home, though at the last moment, I decided to take a slightly different route. Pinstripes of fresh-cut grass covered yards, and newly planted annuals sat in garden beds and pots on porches. Tree blossoms sweetened the air, and my ears vibrated with the hum of distant lawn-mowers. As I tried to fill my head and heart with the sounds and smells of early summer, my body came to a stop so abrupt it felt as if I had walked into an invisible wall.

For a moment, it felt as if my lungs did not work.

I stood at the end of a driveway and looked at the house in front of me. I tried to pick out some clue about who lived there. The shades were drawn tight as if the house had sworn to keep its secrets.

I blinked again and again. My eyelids felt heavy and slow. Each time I opened my eyes I half expected the view to be different. I twisted from side to side, hoping someone might be jogging down the sidewalk or walking their dog. If so, I would have grabbed their arm, pointed, and asked them to tell me what they saw. I was certain I could not trust my eyes.

The Universe, it seemed, wanted to provide a sign impossible to ignore.

In multi-colored chalk, one word—one *name*—had been boldly and joyfully written across the driveway: Marcel.

This wasn't *my* Marcel. But as I stood at the end of this stranger's driveway looking at that name, I knew what was next.

I was going to Paris.

Chapter Twenty

White Bear Lake, Minnesota

June 2012

After stepping behind the podium, a flush of heat encircled my neck. Standing in front of *any* audience made me uncomfortable. Standing in front of an audience that included a type historian and renowned type designers meant I hurtled past being just *uncomfortable* to the point of breaking out in red, hot, splotchy hives.

My presentation was the result of an email Craig had sent months earlier to everyone in our Type Tuesday group; he asked for volunteers to talk about work in process. As the date of my talk got closer, Craig generously promoted it as a "not to miss" event. I began by sharing my affection for old handwriting, and the epiphany I had the day I saw the font Texas Hero. I projected an image of the letter Marcel had written to his three girls, then showed corresponding favorite glyphs from my font: the swash *M*, the *p* with a high lead-in stroke, the double *ss* where the second *s* swept under the first.

"That's yours?" someone asked. The lilt in their voice revealed more than a hint of surprise. I nodded. *One thousand parts Marcel's and one thousand parts mine.*

What I looked forward sharing the most—hives or not—was Marcel's story. I wanted everyone to hear about the man behind the letters. I read Marcel's first letter in its entirety, followed by passages in other letters describing life in the camp. I shared what I learned about STO, and highlighted twists and turns of the search. When I revealed Marcel lived to be an old man, and that he loved Renée until the end of his life, one woman in the audience wiped tears from her eyes. Exactly one month had passed since the day I learned Marcel lived. On several occasions— random moments that felt like gusts of wind that came out of nowhere— every emotion I felt when Dixie told me he lived rushed to the surface and I had to wipe away tears, too.

Hands shot in the air once my presentation finished. "Where are the letters now?" *Still in my safety deposit box.* "Does the family still live in Berchères-la-Maingot?" *No.* "What does his family think of the font?" *They haven't said a word about it.*

Time after time, questions circled back to the letters' long journey: "How did they end up at the flea market?" *I don't know.* "Where was the flea market?" *I don't know.* "What happened to the other letters at the store in Stillwater?" *I don't know.* When I mentioned I had repeatedly tried to reconnect with the woman who owned the store, the audience seemed nearly as frustrated as I was with her lack of communication.

When someone asked if I hoped to meet Marcel's family someday, I smiled and nodded. I did not tell them about the "Marcel" that had been written in chalk, or that as I stood at the end of the driveway I knew I would be meeting Marcel's family with the same certainty I knew his handwriting would become a font. I had not discussed the trip with Aaron yet, or with anyone in France. But I knew I was going.

Afterward, as I packed up my laptop and notes, one of the few unfamiliar faces in the audience quietly came near to thank me. I got the impression he lost family in the war. Or in *a* war. Hearing how I refused to stop searching for Marcel touched him deeply, he said.

He went on to insist on something I would hear again many times: he did not believe I found the letters. He believed Marcel's letters had found me.

Two days after the Type Tuesday presentation, with curiosity freshly stoked by the questions asked by audience members, I sent Kim another email. I tried to keep my frustration hidden, and cheerily noted some extraordinary things had happened since we had last been in touch.

Kim called the next day. For a few long seconds after answering the phone I was too stunned to talk. Her voice had the distant echo of a speakerphone, and she explained a business associate was with her. I sensed Kim was guarded, so I reassured her that more than anything I wanted to share what I learned. I told her about the font, then recited from memory some of Marcel's tender words to Renée. When I told Kim I had established contact with the family, two of Marcel's daughters were still alive, and the family claimed they had never seen the letters before, Kim and her associate screamed.

She bought the letters because she loved the handwriting, she explained. And despite her inability to read French, she also innately knew they were love letters. She intended to reproduce the letters as wallpaper, or to incorporate the writing somehow into a product for her interior and furniture design business. The right project never materialized, she said.

I inquired whether she had been able to recall anything else about where she bought them. She explained she and her business partner rented a truck and drove from flea market to flea market. "We went to so many places."

I asked whether she had any recollection of how many letters they bought.

"Thirty or forty," Kim said, though her answer sounded more like a question than a statement. I let out a long sigh, astonished at the high number.

"If I had known!" Kim said.

"Oh, trust me," I said with a slight laugh. "I would have bought every single one." After a pause, I asked if she had any idea what happened to the rest.

"Some sold in the store. I had more until a year ago. People kept telling me I needed to get rid of stuff. I think I sold them off in one big lot."

"In California?"

"Yes," she confirmed. *She had more until a year ago?* I silently berated myself for waiting so long to begin the search. It seemed far-fetched, but I asked that if she ever ran across any of them, to please let me know.

"I will," she promised.

As the call drew to a close, I thanked her again for calling. "You're part of this story. I'm glad you were able to hear it." Kim thanked me for my perseverance. She traveled a lot, and acknowledged she could be hard to get a hold of.

After hanging up, I turned back to the project I had been working on when she called. I typed a few words, then stopped. Nothing on the screen made sense. I put my elbows on my desk and knitted my fingers together. *Imagine reading thirty more. Why, why, why did I wait so long to have that first letter translated?*

Twenty minutes later my phone rang. "I have more," the voice blurted. I did not have caller ID on my office phone, so I scrambled to identify the voice. *It was Kim.* In my mind, I replayed the words to try to make sense of—to *verify*—what I thought I heard.

"You have more . . . letters?" The words sounded preposterous as they fell out of my mouth.

"I didn't want to say anything because I wasn't sure I still had any." Once our call ended, she explained, she had looked in storage. "They were in an envelope marked 'French Love Letters.'" The hair on my arms stood on end and I smiled. *Of course they were.*

"Some are signed Marcel, some are signed with a different name." Kim was on speakerphone again. "This handwriting is different," Kim or her assistant said.

"They could be signed 'Papa' instead of Marcel," I offered.

I heard additional mumbles, and shuffling of paper.

"Most of Marcel's letters begin '*Mes chères petites.*' Do you see that?"

After a few seconds, Kim confirmed, "Yes."

"Were they written 1943, 1944?"

She recited some dates: May 1944. January 1943.

"That was the month he started his conscription," I whispered in astonishment.

Silence enveloped the line, as if both of us were trying to determine the next step. "Can I buy them from you?" I asked. The words sounded as fragile as an eggshell.

After a slight hesitation, Kim slowly said "no."

My heart plummeted as I tried to make sense of her refusal. Her voice sounded laced with irritation, as if she could not believe I asked. *Why would she call to tell me she had them, then?* Hearing Kim claim she had more letters—then hearing I could not buy them—was confounding. It seemed cruel.

After an unbearably long silence—it felt like minutes, though it was probably only seconds—Kim followed the word "no" with the kind promise: "I will give them to you." As my brain processed those six words, my heart nearly exploded with joy.

"Really?" I asked, as if I needed confirmation I had not misunderstood.

"I'm happy to," she said.

I could not think of words that adequately expressed the depth of my gratitude—and my wonder. After our call ended, I sat motionless. Then I jumped up and did the Happy Dance. I sent emails to Kathy, Tom, and Dixie. They were not going to believe this amazing news either.

In the weeks that followed, in separate emails, Tiffanie and Natacha each asked whether I ever traveled to France—or if I might one day. I did not tell them about Kim's letters; it felt premature to do so. But we began comparing schedules and discussing dates for a visit.

Every time a FedEx truck rumbled down our street, my head swiveled to look out my office window to see if it was going to stop. Day after day, week after week, those boxy white trucks drove right by. I feared Kim had changed her mind.

On the day a FedEx truck finally rolled to a stop in front of our house, I barreled out the front door and met the driver halfway across the yard. Kim's return address was written in a loopy upright cursive on the delivery slip adhered to the cardboard envelope.

"Want to see something amazing?"

The driver cocked his head to one side.

"Really," I said while I opened the envelope. "This might be the most incredible thing you deliver your entire career." He did not walk away, willing, apparently, to give me the opportunity to prove my claim.

I slid a thin stack of bone-colored sheets out of the envelope. My heart swelled to see line after line of the handwriting I knew so well. "*Mes chères petites*" was scrawled at the top of some pages. Blue and red stripes swept across others. A faint blue background grid pattern filled one page. Water damage left writing indecipherable on another. One had been written in pencil. One had a burn hole. One was held together with cellophane tape.

I pivoted so the driver could get a better look. As he leaned in, I explained where Marcel had been, and said his family in France claimed they had never received these letters.

The driver's eyebrows shot up. "That *is* amazing," he said.

I continued to slowly leaf through the letters, but when I realized the carelessness of exposing the fragile pages to searing sunlight, I abruptly slid the letters back into the envelope.

"Thank you for this," I said. The driver smiled and nodded, then jogged back to his truck.

Back inside our home, I carefully laid each letter on the dining table, unruffling edges and unfolding dog-eared corners. The inks were familiar murky shades of blue and brown and black. The paper had the familiar soft-yet-brittle feel. The pages seemed to hold on to old folds and creases in the same way skin holds on to scars. One page had droplets of blood along an edge. Another included a half-page section that appeared to be written to the girls.

Once all the pages were laid in a row, I slumped into one of the dining room chairs. I counted, then recounted before letting out an astonished sigh.

There were twelve more letters.

Chapter Twenty-One

White Bear Lake, Minnesota

Late July 2012

The corporate rebranding project had launched. The medical device brochure had been printed and delivered. It had been slightly more than a year since I established contact with Tom, and for the first time in those twelve months, I had room to breathe. So when Tom asked if I would be willing to come to his office to hand over copies of the new letters, I happily obliged.

Tom strolled into the lobby and extended his right hand. A handshake seemed too formal after sharing Marcel's intimate words; I raised my hands in the air, reached forward, and gave Tom a hug.

We walked a maze of halls, which opened to an enormous cafeteria. After purchasing lunch, we claimed a table near floor-to-ceiling windows that overlooked perfectly manicured grounds.

"How did you learn to speak French, anyway?" I asked while we ate. Tom had studied French in high school and college, then spent a year studying, then two years working in Aix-en-Provence. With a smile, he confessed his secret to learning the language: beautiful French women. His desire to communicate with them provided incentive for "disciplined study."

He returned to the States for graduate school, then moved back to France. He was certain he had never driven through Berchères-la-Maingot, though he imagined it was filled with quaint stone buildings and vine-covered walls like so many other villages he explored. When Tom returned to the States for good, he took a job in Minneapolis and began offering translation services on the side. "One or two jobs per month," he said.

After we finished eating, I retrieved a manila folder from my bag and slid it across the table as if it were some top-secret file.

"I still can't believe you tracked these down," he said. I related to the wonder in his voice. Several times during the previous days, I had slipped the letters out of the envelope to confirm they were real. That they were *really* in my possession.

Tom silently read a few paragraphs. I did not rush or interrupt. "I can't imagine," Tom said as he shook his head. "How helpless he must have felt. When I think about how much he loved those girls, and how he . . . I just . . . I just can't imagine . . ." Tom's eyes bloomed with tears. He lifted his glasses off the bridge of his nose and wiped his eyes. I did not imagine men cried in the cafeteria often, so I was careful not to say anything more. I changed the subject by asking Tom when he had last been to Paris.

"Too long," he said with a wistful smile.

The day before, Aaron and I had purchased our airline tickets. If it had been up to me, I would have left for Paris immediately, but late October was the first time that worked for everyone in France. Twelve weeks existed until our departure. Translating one letter per week was an aggressive goal, but Tom assured me he would complete them in time. Besides, he was curious to know what Marcel said in his letters, too.

Kathy, Dixie, and I had one requirement for our celebration dinner: the restaurant had to serve French food. I made a reservation at a place in downtown St. Paul known for classic brasserie cuisine. I arrived first, and as the maître d' escorted me to our table, I smiled at the lively accordion music echoing off the tall ceiling.

Moments later, a petite woman with long gray hair and wire-rim glasses stood near the door. I stood as Dixie began walking my way. "Nice to finally meet you!" we said in unison as we wrapped our arms around each other. By the time Kathy arrived, Dixie and I were chatting away like old friends. Kathy gave each of us a hug, then looked at me, and wagged her head.

"What?" I was unable to decipher her expression.

"I can't believe it," she said. I was unsure if she was referring to the fact Dixie found the family, the twelve new letters, the trip to Paris, or the cumulative whole.

Kathy handed me a small white bag. Tissue paper billowed out the top like a volcano exploding with lime green and royal blue. Dinner was my treat, so I did not understand why she brought a gift. She offered a broad, close-mouthed smile, and lifted her shoulders to her ears. I peeled away the tissue. A small linen pillow was embellished with delicate black stitching that spelled PARIS. The *A* had been replaced with an intricately embroidered Eiffel Tower.

"I just had to get it," Kathy blurted. Days earlier, when I told her we purchased tickets to Paris, she had squealed with delight. "This just keeps getting better!"

As our waiter filled three glasses with Champagne, he asked if we were celebrating anything special. It seemed impossible to summarize an answer, so I told him we were celebrating a *very* long story. I thanked Dixie for her amazing detective work and Kathy for putting us in touch. "To Marcel," we said as we lifted our glasses and toasted our favorite Frenchman.

After ordering dinner, I retrieved pages showing the font. Dixie had asked to see it, and I thought Kathy might like to see the most current iteration. I had made hundreds of additional revisions since Kathy had last seen a test print.

"This is beautiful," Dixie said with the note of surprise I was learning to expect. I described the beautiful first letter Marcel had written to his girls and explained how it was the standard for the angle and width. "There are so many variations," Dixie commented.

I brought copies of the twelve new letters to show Kathy; she said she wanted to see them. "*Mes chères petites,*" she said wistfully as she looked at one of the letters. Her index finger traced lines of writing as she cobbled together a translation with vocabulary from decades-old French lessons. "I received your letter. Imagine . . . good . . . I was counting hours and . . . and I can't stop reading it. Kiss . . . for me . . . Say hi to everybody in Berchères and Montreuil . . . As for you . . . treasure, your guy who loves you . . . you beautiful kisses."

Kathy remarked it was more difficult to read Marcel's handwriting than she expected. But even the ragged translations were enough to make us melt at his words of love.

"I just can't get over how expressive he was," Kathy said.

Dixie asked if I knew anything about his education. I had posed the same question to Tom months earlier. Based on grammar and word choice, Tom speculated that Marcel had a solid high school education, which would have been typical for the time.

We set the photocopies and test prints aside when dinner arrived. Kathy had stuffed rabbit, Dixie had corn fritters so delicious she raved about them for months, and I had seared tuna served with *haricots verts* and capers sprinkled like confetti.

"Have you heard from the family recently?" Kathy inquired.

I nodded. I had received an email two days earlier from Natacha's mother, Nadine. I was touched Nadine had translated it into English.

"We are Agnès and Nadine, grandchildren of Marcel," her letter began. "We are happy to have details of the life of our grandfather in Germany, because we've never heard of it. His memories must have been too painful. So everything we know, we've heard it from you, like where he worked. Since our grandparents died we haven't had any contact with our family. We are very happy to know they are in touch with you. It's a miracle to learn a little bit of our history because of you. We hope you understand those letters are a real treasure."

"What you did for them was extraordinary, you know," Dixie said. She meant it as a compliment, but her words skewered me. I began the search to satiate my own curiosity. I only searched for Marcel *for me*. The possibility that these letters held missing pieces of Marcel's life puzzle had never been a consideration.

"I hoped we'd have one big meeting with everyone in the family, but I get the sense that's not going to happen." I explained. Nadine's side of the family had not had any contact with aunts or cousins in the seven years since Renée's funeral: no calls on birthdays, no Christmas cards, no congratulations on graduations or on the birth of babies.

"Don't give up," Dixie said with a gentle smile. "Maybe you'll bring them together." I hoped that could be the case, though it would not be *me* bringing them together. It would be Marcel; it would be *his* letters.

"I don't know even how you found him," I said, changing the subject. Nine weeks earlier, asking *how* Dixie found him had not crossed my mind.

Dixie confessed the first days of "the hunt" had been unusually frustrating. She posted requests for help on various genealogy message boards only after exhausting all standard search routes. "I had all oars in the water on this one," she said.

What ultimately broke the case was the listing I provided of Suzanne's death, she said. Dixie searched permutations of the name I found—Suzanne Bernadette Heuzé Cléro—until she found a close-but-not-exact variation: Suzanne *Marcelline Jeanne* Cléro. That name led to information on a different website, which in turn confirmed Suzanne's death and revealed Marcel and Renée's fates. Dixie sent a message to the person who posted the information about Marcel and Renée. She could not tell who the message went to, but that had been the message Natacha referred to when she had written, "My mother . . . read Dixie's mail, which I translate for her."

The website did not include Denise or Lily's first names, but it included what Dixie guessed were married surnames. Dixie mixed first names with surnames until she found answers on yet another website. The information listed on the last site revealed Lily was actually Eliane. The labyrinth left my head spinning.

"You are amazing," I repeated, though Dixie dismissed the compliment. She assured me if that path had not led to answers, something else would have turned up.

For you, I thought. *Something else would have turned up for you.*

For the next hour or so, conversation meandered. Kathy listed some of her favorite markets and museums in Paris. Dixie told us about her genealogy projects; Norwegian research was her specialty. Kathy and I listened with mouths agape as Dixie explained it was possible to identify which valley in Norway a person's ancestors lived in based on autosomal DNA.

Months later, when I told a friend about the search for Marcel, she interrupted me when I mentioned Dixie's name. "You're working with Dixie Hansen?" she exclaimed. "Do you have *any idea* who you're working with?"

I wanted to shrug and explain that Dixie was Kathy's friend, but I sensed she meant something larger. "She is *royalty* in the genealogy world, you know," my friend stated emphatically. "Having Dixie help with your research is"—my friend waved her arms as she searched for a comparison—"is like getting songwriting help from Paul McCartney! If *anyone* could have found him, it was Dixie."

I smiled and thought of the day I told Marcel, "If you want me to find you, help me find you." Maybe he heard me after all. Maybe somehow— some *way*—Marcel made sure Dixie got involved with my search.

"Oftentimes," Dixie wrote in an email after our dinner, "it's the older generation that holds a family together. When the parents or grandparents die off, it's not unusual for a family to grow apart or split apart. So, it's magical when—with some assistance and maybe a little well-placed connivance—the earlier generation comes back from the grave and gathers the sheep back into the fold. Maybe not so close. Probably not forever. But, for a time at least, into an elbows and knees cluster that in some way resembles the jostling essence of a family."

"Do you wanna see 'em?" Kent eagerly nodded at my offer.

I lifted my shoulder bag onto the large worktable in Kent's letterpress print shop—the same table that two months earlier had been covered with bottles and bowls of snacks on the Tuesday we celebrated the completion of Craig's font. I pulled taped-together pieces of a cardboard mock-up out of my bag, along with a spool of blue-, white-, and red-striped ribbon. Lastly, I brought out a large envelope that held Marcel's original letters.

I wanted Kent to create a presentation case to hold Marcel's letters. A plain envelope or a plastic sleeve simply would not do when I returned the letters to Marcel's family. I wanted the letters to be inside something that would protect them. But more than that, I wanted the letters to be inside something that would unequivocally demonstrate to the family I had cared for them.

I grabbed the wide grosgrain ribbon and tied a bow around the cardboard to show my idea for closing the case. I made a mental note to bring a small scissor to Paris so I could cut the ribbon ends into precise angles that looked *just so*.

Kent rifled through a back room stacked high with rolls of linen until he found a roll of buff-color linen that coordinated perfectly with the aged pieces of paper. Kent carefully measured the largest letter, made a few other notes, and provided an estimate for his work.

As I drove the letters back to the safety deposit box, I realized only Aaron—and now Kent—had seen Marcel's original letters. Kathy, Tom, and Dixie had only ever seen copies. Once the letters were returned to the family, the letters might not see the light of day again. That evening, I talked with Aaron about having an open house. He was amenable to the idea because he had witnessed friends barraging me with questions once they learned where Marcel had been writing from. He had seen friends wipe tears from their eyes when they learned Marcel lived. Aaron and I compared schedules. Only one option existed: Saturday, October 6. It was two weeks before we left for Paris, so it gave Tom as much time as possible to work through the translations.

"You've heard about these love letters," the invitations read. "Here's your only opportunity to see them before they are delivered to Marcel's family in Paris. We'll have the letters—seventeen in total, along with the translations—available for you to view. We'll provide Champagne and other treats from France to celebrate the letters' extraordinary journey home."

Responses flooded back from friends, family, neighbors: people were *thrilled* to have the opportunity to see Marcel's letters in person. But it made my heart heavy to learn three of the people I most wanted to be there—Kathy, Tom, and Dixie—all had scheduling conflicts. When Tom sent his regrets, he sent an update: he had not yet worked on the translations, though he assured me they would be done in time for our party.

In the weeks that followed, Aaron and I finalized details for our trip. Kathy suggested we rent a little apartment rather than stay in a hotel. It was a common thing to do, she explained. We did some research and reserved a charming little seventh-floor apartment two blocks from the Eiffel Tower.

Emails from the family became more frequent, and more comfortable. They even teased me that my translated emails read like Tarzan trying to speak French. We were establishing a baseline of trust and comfort, and as each day passed, I grew more eager to meet them.

I reluctantly concluded the font would not be finished by October. But I still wanted it to be as beautiful as possible, so I spent night after night refining lines, curves, and loops. I printed test pages, marked up revisions, made more adjustments, then tested it again.

And, every night, before I fell asleep, I tried to commit one French word or phrase to memory: *S'il vous plaît*. Please. *Droite*. Right. *Gauche*. Left. *Merci beaucoup*. Thank you very much.

Chapter Twenty-Two

White Bear Lake, Minnesota

August 2012

One weekday afternoon, eighteen or so years earlier—back when I worked for Tim at his design firm in downtown Minneapolis—my attention was abruptly diverted from whatever project I had been working on as music suddenly filled the office. Tim rushed from workstation to workstation, commanding his team of designers to come listen to his radio. I stepped into Tim's office, confused by the interruption, while also bewitched by the extraordinary sound echoing through the cavernous space.

As Tim silently gestured for us to absorb the music, I realized what was happening. *This was some sort of design lesson.* I leaned back against a wall, hands flat behind me. Edith Piaf's soaring expressions—both raging in defiance and crumbling with vulnerability—reverberated through the wallboard into my fingertips. I started at the sensation. It felt as if she were singing directly into my flesh and bone, and I found myself hungrily pressing my hands tighter against the wall. I did not understand a word, but as Piaf sang "Non, je ne regrette rien," I unequivocally understood her. Tim's lesson became apparent. He wanted his designers to experience how emotion could transcend words. How emotion could transcend language.

As hot summer evenings disappeared refining my font, I decided to set aside my go-to lists of animals, foods, famous people, cities, and states to test words in French. I wanted words nearer—truer—to Marcel. A Piaf anthem came to mind, and though I did not know the title, I knew I would recognize the chorus. I skipped through online audio files of Piaf's seminal recordings until I heard it. I turned the volume up so high my office ceiling fan began to vibrate. Piaf did not sing—she roared—and I experienced the same sensation I had when I stood in Tim's office: I felt Piaf's astonishing voice inside my bones.

"What the hell are you listening to?" Aaron's interruption ripped through the moment's magic like a needle scratching across a vinyl record.

"La Marsey . . . La Maraise . . ." Correct pronunciation eluded me. "It's the French national anthem."

"Well, can you turn *zee volume* down?" Aaron asked with irritation.

I obliged, but did not stop listening. The drumming anthem provided an infusion of energy.

Aux armes, citoyens! To arms, citizens!

Formez vos bataillons! Form your battalions!

Marchons! Marchons! March! March!

Qu'un sang impur Let impure blood

Abreuve nos sillons! Water our furrows!

I created a new two-column text document and filled each column with lyrics: French on the left, English on the right. I changed the *M* in the title—"La Marseillaise"—to Marcel's beautiful swash *M*, then changed the *ll* to alternate glyphs where the two *l*'s curled together like spoons.

The lines of French included fascinating letter combinations I had never seen in English: *u'u, êt, S'I, n'y*. I printed the pages, and with a red pen, I marked dozens of glyphs that needed revision. Yet it was also one of the first times I liked the appearance of complete words: *longtemps, sanglant, mercenaires, expirants.* One letter swept into the next with fluid grace. That had rarely happened before, and my heart soared.

It took days to work through the revisions. When I reprinted the page, an entirely new round of issues caught my eye. Over the following days and weeks, I printed pages with the lyrics again and again, each time marking spacing or individual glyphs that needed additional attention.

Chapter Twenty-Three

Milwaukee, Wisconsin

August 2012

TypeCon is an annual conference for type designers, type historians, educators, and serious type aficionados. Several Type Tuesday members regularly attended; some had even been featured speakers. I had never before attended because the prospect of traveling to a faraway city and mingling with strangers who possessed an encyclopedic knowledge of type made every introverted cell in my body want to shrink and hide. But this year was different. I had already signed up, largely to take the pre-conference workshop on the alternate piece of font design software.

TypeCon 2012 was in Milwaukee, which was an easy five-hour drive. As I drove past vast seas of soybeans and corn growing under the hot August sun, I hummed along to Edith Piaf and Maurice Chevalier. I tried to imagine what it would be like to meet Marcel's family, and what secrets Tom might unfurl in the twelve new translations. As Milwaukee grew near, I tried to keep the whispers of uncertainty at bay about how and when—and if—I might complete the font.

Three other designers attended the pre-conference workshop. Combined, they had created more than seventy fonts. Their fonts were on

books and cards. One of their fonts was even printed on the paper grocery bags at the store where Aaron and I regularly shopped.

It did not take long to realize everything I hoped would be quick and
easy in the alternate software—kerning, specifically—was still complicated. The problem was not the software: it was me. A thick black cloud
of self-doubt gathered over me, and by afternoon's end, I berated myself
for ever thinking I had the skill to finish. I resigned myself to the possibility I might only ever use the font on personal projects where I could
manually fix kerning and other problems.

The conference officially kicked off Thursday evening, and over the
following days, presentations were given on topics as diverse as optimiz-
ing type readability in airplane cockpits, designing fonts for Cherokee
and Arabic languages, marketing, legal issues, distribution, and licensing.
Pages were filled with careful lecture notes combined with sketches of
glyphs to add to my font. One particular sketch was of a lowercase *y* with
a loop that reminded me of a cat's tail; Marcel had not written his *y*'s like
that, but I hoped he would approve of the embellishment. Despite the
cloud that loomed large during the workshop, the presentations inspired
me to forge ahead. I resolved to figure out kerning no matter what it took.

I skipped the late Saturday afternoon presentations to attend an
exhibit at the Milwaukee Art Museum. The museum was hosting the
traveling exhibit, "Posters of Paris: Toulouse-Lautrec and His Contem-
poraries." I justified playing hooky by reminding myself Toulouse-Lautrec often incorporated organic lettering into his work. More than one
hundred posters from the late 1800s were on display. Fluid, expressive
illustrations promoted products like Champagne, chocolate, bicycles, and
bawdy Parisian nightclubs. Iconic prints showed women in can-can skirts
with legs thrown high in the air; multi-layer petticoats swirled around
their bodies like whorls of foam.

At the end of the exhibit, visitors were shunted through a gift shop
filled with prints, greeting cards, travel guidebooks, and Paris-themed
home décor. I was nearly out of the shop when a small plastic box caught
my eye. I carried it to a check-out counter. The box was filled with magnetic tiles printed with French vocabulary words. I hoped having the

words stuck on our refrigerator might help me reach my goal of learning one French word per day.

TypeCon wrapped up on Sunday afternoon, but not before the not-to-miss conference event: Type Crit. At Type Crit, first-time type designers presented a font-in-progress to three industry experts for a review and critique.

Often it felt as if I was making decisions about the font in a vacuum, so I wanted feedback that would help me make it as good as it could be. As soon as the Type Crit sign-up opened, I claimed the fifth of the ten available slots. I figured fifth was a good, anonymous middle option.

But I would soon come to understand there was not a single thing *anonymous* about Type Crit.

The critique was held in a room separate from main conference ballroom. When I arrived, a handful of people loitered around the perimeter. A single, round, cloth-covered table with four chairs sat in the center of the room. No one dared to get close, it seemed.

I leaned against a wall, pretending to read the conference program.

"If I was on the list today, I'd be in the bathroom throwing up right now," a man in a nearby cluster of three whispered.

"Oh, *gawd*. I can't imagine," a man next to him said.

"I'd be crying," a young woman added.

My heart started pounding. A knot started twisting in my core.

"Do you remember Craig Eliason?" My ears perked at Craig's name. Craig was the leader of our Type Tuesday group. "His hands were shaking so much he could barely hand over his sheet," one of the men snickered. I had seen Craig lecture on type history to packed auditoriums. Craig embodied cool, composed confidence. The notion he could be unnerved enough that his hand shook made my swell of anxiety feel like a tidal wave of panic.

What the fuck have I signed up for?

During Type Crit, a designer received invaluable feedback to revise and improve their font, but it was not necessarily a gentle review—it was more like a three-on-one typographic bullfight. If the designer was lucky, they would limp away with bruises and scrapes to their ego. If they were unlucky, their work would be eviscerated. The room was filled with spectators—including many veteran type designers—and there was no doubt that they were there for the entertainment. They wanted to watch novice type designers be gored.

Two of the judges stood near the windows. Their conversation echoed through the quiet room. While I focused on breathing, their words began to sound warbled and muffled. The room's temperature began to feel infernal.

By the time the third judge arrived, the room was filled with spectators. The judges walked to the table. "Welcome to the—*what is it?*—eleventh annual Type Crit," a judge announced. "Here's what will happen: I'll call the names on the list. When we call your name, take the seat and show us one style, one weight." He gestured to the concentric circles of spectators: "You're welcome to look and listen, but please hold your comments until the end of each session. I'll be the official time keeper." He gestured for the two other judges to take their seats. "Let's get started."

I do not recall whether the judges introduced themselves, but everyone in the room knew who they were. They did not need introductions.

For four decades, Roger Black designed magazines such as *Rolling Stone* and *Newsweek*, and newspapers including the *New York Times*. His design teams had redesigned *Reader's Digest*, *Esquire*, the *Los Angeles Times*, and the *Washington Post*. The second judge, John Downer, had been designing type since the early 1980s. He wrote about type design for magazines including *Emigre* and *House*. He was also an accomplished sign painter who specialized in gold-leaf lettering. The third judge, Akira Kobayashi, had a background in calligraphy, and early in his career had designed Latin typefaces to accompany Japanese fonts. During his twenty-year career, Akira had amassed numerous awards and had designed some of the world's best-known fonts.

Roger Black called the first name on the list. The designer sat in the empty seat. I took a deep breath, sure hives were about to bloom.

Fuck. How can I get out of this?

As the judges began scrutinizing the designer's specimen, the circle of spectators tightened around the small table like a noose.

"What we have here is a modern slab serif," John Downer said. "How long have you been working on it?"

"Six months," the designer said.

"And how do you see this being used?" John asked.

"Body text for a magazine."

"Proportions are unresolved," Roger stated as he pointed to something on the page. I was in the very back, so I only saw an occasional flash of paper.

"There is an issue with letterspacing. The *o* isn't balanced on the left and right," John observed.

"The vertical strokes on the *F* and *L* look too thick," Akira added.

The judges offered additional opinions about proportion, shape, balance. As the designer's ten minutes drew to a close, Roger handed the prints back to the designer. "It's a start," he said. With that remark, he dismissed both the design and the designer.

The judges pointed out problems with weight, balance, and scale on the second designer's font. Spectators chimed in with observations and opinions. The judges did not seem to know what to make of the third design; the experimental, geometric letterforms left them unimpressed.

As the fourth designer handed the judges her specimen sheet, she explained her uppercase serif font had been inspired by ninety-six-year-old letterforms inscribed on a building in Seattle.

"The spine of the *S* is too heavy," John said immediately and unequivocally after initial small talk concluded. In addition to thinning the spine, he suggested she shift the spine upward. "And the tail on the *Q* obviously needs more work," he added. "The proportions don't all conform. The *M* and *N* appear too wide . . ."

Roger pointed out problems with the *G* and *H* before asking whether she had researched other high-waistline typefaces from the era.

Akira made observations about the top-heaviness of the *A* and *K*. The judges pointed out problematic serifs, issues with the lobes on the *B* and the crossbar on the *E*, problems with the shape of the *U* and *Z*. They discussed the style of the *W* before asking the designer final questions about her process.

As each minute ticked by, my heart rate increased, my mouth got drier. When Roger called my name, I quietly said, "that's me," and began working my way through the crowd.

"My name is Carolyn and I have an affection for script fonts." The rasp of my voice was unsurprising since my tongue felt too dry to move. "This is my first TypeCon and my first font." I reached forward and handed the judges pages set with the lyrics of "La Marseillaise." The anthem's title was large at the top. Columns of lyrics sat below the title: French on the left, English on the right.

"The font is based on a letter written in French." That was the extent of what I intended to say about Marcel; this was not the time or place to talk about his letters. For these ten minutes, I wanted to absorb their expert feedback. I handed over additional pages with the Glyph Map, which was a multi-page grid showing the five hundred individual glyphs that made up the font. I hoped I was giving them an appropriate sample; I had only learned about Type Crit a week earlier and had to guess at what they might want to see.

abcdefghijklmn
opqrstuvwxyz

The crowd jostled to look over the judges' shoulders. As I waited for the critique to begin, it felt impossible to breathe. Yet, I also sensed something inexplicably comforting.

"This is lovely," Akira said as a hint of a smile crossed his face.

"Thank you," I said quietly.

"Have you studied calligraphy?"

"Not since I was a teenager." I should have disclosed I had a Letter-form class in college, but in my nervousness, I had tried to answer his question literally. "I tried to pay close attention to the thicks and thins of the original handwriting."

"This was an ambitious undertaking," Roger said as he leafed through the pages.

"I didn't know what I was getting into," I confessed. Now that preliminary niceties were over, I braced myself for their excoriating truth.

"I'm seeing a nice array of alternate swashes," John said. "And you've done a good job of capturing the feathering you'd see when ink bleeds into paper." John talked about techniques other designers used to capture an ink-on-paper look with a digital font.

"How long have you been working on this?" Akira asked.

"A long time," I sheepishly replied. I did not want to disclose it had been ten years. The judges waited for an answer, so I complied. "Years. Evenings and weekends."

"And your intent is to license this?" John asked.

I nodded. John passed his copy to the spectator behind him, and gestured for it to be passed around the room. He had not done that with any of the previous specimen sheets.

"It's beautiful," Roger said.

I was sure the bloodletting was now going to begin in earnest.

"You might want to look at the dieresis on the *ä*, it's a bit too close to the top of the letter," Akira commented. He asked about the placement of other accents. I explained I tried to follow placement on the original letters; that was true for the acute and the circumflex, anyway. For other diacritics, I researched and made a best guess.

John noted the crossbar on the *T* seemed too mechanical. He suggested I study how it might slope up or down a bit more. And Akira suggested I refine the curve of the apostrophe. "You might make it less hook-like," he suggested.

One judge asked if I worked much with steel-nibbed pens. *Not since the Schaeffer pens I received for my thirteenth birthday*, I almost confessed. As he talked about the aesthetic qualities of steel-pen writing, I scolded myself for not determining *specifically* what kind of pen Marcel had written with. It seemed like such an elementary thing to have overlooked.

I prepared for comments pointing out fundamental flaws in proportion or scale, weight or shape. I anticipated they might suggest a typography class, or propose a different avocation. But Roger concluded the session with the observation that their suggestions were minor tweaks. "This is close to being ready, congrats."

I blinked a couple of times, unsure I heard correctly. *Was I being dismissed?* I gathered my sample pages, slid them into my bag, and thanked the judges for the review. Without the benefit of having witnessed previous Type Crits, I did not understand "beautiful," "nice," and "congrats" were words rarely tossed around.

Later that afternoon, after everyone returned to the main conference ballroom, a woman stopped to speak to me. "You have got to be thrilled," she whispered. "I've been going to Type Crit for years and I can't recall a single time when all three judges liked a font as much as they liked yours." I could not help but smile. "You could feel the energy in the entire room change as soon as you handed them the pages," she said. "I've never seen anything like that happen before."

"Thank you," I stammered.

What I did not tell her was that I had felt the energy in the room change, too.

It felt as though Marcel had been right there with me.

On Monday evening, back at home, while Aaron cooked dinner, I cleared off the front of the refrigerator before opening the clear plastic box I had purchased at the museum.

"What's that?"

"French vocabulary words," I said as I snapped apart the small magnetic tiles. *Eau.* Water. *Temps.* Time. *Jardin.* Garden. *Grenouille.* Frog. In addition to a couple hundred nouns—*café, amour, derrière, lumière*—magnets existed for pronouns, prepositions, and conjunctions.

I froze as soon as I saw a magnet imprinted with the word "font." *What an odd word to be in the collection.* I flipped through the miniature dictionary that came with the set. I let out a long sigh, then walked out of the kitchen.

"Dinner will be ready in a couple minutes," Aaron called as I headed to my office.

I typed "font" into the translation website I had used for the myriad letters and emails I had sent to Marcel's family. I let out another long sigh, then tried a different translation service, hoping to see a different answer.

"*Font* is 'police' in French," I said after shuffling back to the kitchen.

I had assumed no one in the family expressed interest in the font because they did not know much about typography. "They might not have any idea what I'm talking about," I explained to Aaron. Considering Marcel's imprisonment, I could not imagine a worse word—especially since I talked about my *police project* with such enthusiasm.

"What's French for 'fuck'?" I muttered.

I sent emails to Natacha and Tiffanie apologizing for any confusion. I hoped we might laugh about it someday, though at the moment, I just felt like throwing up.

In the week that followed, legal issues raised at TypeCon gnawed at me, so I reached out to a lawyer I occasionally hired for client work and outlined my questions:

Did I need the family's permission to complete and sell the font?

Did I need their approval to name the font after Marcel?

Could I share the letters' contents?

The lawyer said he needed time to research French copyright and privacy law. Weeks later, when he called to report there were no issues with the font, I wanted to do cartwheels. He said I did not need anyone's permission to finish, license, or secure copyright on the files, and confirmed I could name the font whatever I wanted as long there was no other font using that name.

"The original letters? Those are a different story," he cautioned. And with that, my cartwheel seemed to collapse mid-whirl. Since the letters were, in whole or in part, written to Denise and Eliane, according to French privacy law, it was their right to keep the contents private during their lifetime. He warned I could not *publicly* show images of, or disclose the contents, without their explicit written permission.

It did not matter I bought the letters, he said. Physical custody did not count.

"Do I need permission from the *son* Marcel?"

"Since he wasn't alive when the letters were written, the letters weren't *to* him, so the same rights don't extend to him."

Chapter Twenty-Four

White Bear Lake, Minnesota

Late August 2012

Apologies filled Tom's email. His busy summer schedule meant he would be unable to translate the letters after all. Fury surged. *A precious month of time completely lost!*

After anger subsided, a bewildering loss remained. It seemed impossible to believe I would find someone else who would translate Marcel's words with the same thoughtful care. I sent emails to the translators I contacted the previous July, followed by frantic emails to Kathy, Dixie, and any friend or graphic design colleague who might have a connection to anyone who spoke French. I hoped to find someone trustworthy and affordable. I was willing to work with anyone available.

Within a day, a neighbor's mother—a retired high school French teacher—offered to help. Hope soared when she promised to look at one letter that evening. But the next day she apologized and confessed she had trouble deciphering Marcel's handwriting. She puzzled together words and phrases, but did not feel confident she could translate an entire letter. I thanked her for the attempt, and tried to mask my disappointment.

Before long, Dixie sent an email noting a friend's mother spoke French. The elderly woman wanted to help, so I emailed a scan of one letter and crossed my fingers. But the next day, when I was told she, too, had trouble reading Marcel's writing, hope plummeted. After recusing herself from the project, the elderly woman suggested I call a friend of hers who had been born and raised in Paris, and for decades had taught high school French in St. Paul. Without disclosing that one high school French teacher had already passed, I thanked her for the referral and promised to call her friend, Louise.

"Letters like that don't exist. Do you understand?" The wonder in Louise's voice made my heart swell. She absorbed the situation with exhilarating speed, and barraged me with questions: "Where did you get the letters?" "Why did you buy them?" "Do you speak *any* French?"

Two aspects of the story confounded Louise: the font—which did not surprise me—and STO. Louise confessed she had never before heard that ordinary French civilians had been forced to work in Germany.

"What happened to your head?" Louise blurted as she processed the various pieces and parts. She burst into laughter, assuring me her question had not come out as intended. I chuckled along. I understood where her question came from. At times during the previous year, I had wondered the same thing.

After a moment of silence—the only silence during our spirited hour-long conversation—Louise's voice fell flat. "So many men, so many French men, disappeared, you know. One day they were gone and they were never heard from again." She repeated her amazement that these letters existed, and asked me again: "Do you understand?"

Louise wanted to begin immediately. We discussed a fee, and I promised to email her a scan as soon as our call ended. Timing was my biggest concern. It had taken Tom weeks to translate each letter, so it seemed doubtful an eighty-six-year-old woman would be able to translate twelve letters in the six weeks before the open house.

The letter I emailed to Louise had the earliest date of them all: January 17, 1943. It had been written less than a week after Marcel arrived in Berlin.

Some words appeared as thick puddles of navy ink; others were hair-thin scratches. It was as if Marcel's pen intermittently clogged, and I imagined him violently shaking it to make it work. Lines and funny, fish-shaped pencil loops ran along the bottom of the first page and continued on the top of the second. On the last page, Marcel abandoned the pen and finished in pencil, the dust of the sixty-nine-year-old graphite no more than a whisper across the page. I presumed the last page included a section to his girls, since Marcel's handwriting suddenly became large and tidy, just like the very first letter. The thought of it made me smile.

I did not expect to hear from Louise for days, but I quickly learned not to underestimate the amazing woman who had just entered my life. Within hours, Louise emailed the translated text, along with a note begging me to email the next letter as soon as I possibly could.

Marienfelde, Germany

January 17, 1943

My little wolf,

As I wrote to you, I spent a weird kind of Feast Day. Just think, Saturday, around 8 o'clock, I saw the friends of Auntie. And it happened in a strange way, we had barely found each other when two barracks were completely roasted, including my own; so that's why now I don't have a darn thing, I mean absolutely nothing, not even a handkerchief to blow my nose with. So the first package you can send me is the suitcase with my things. Can you imagine, all my food gobbled up all at once. I'm going to make you a little list of what I need. Some stationery, some ink, envelopes, some soap, some shaving soap, a razor, a shaving brush, also two bath towels, two dish towels, two washcloths, one undershorts, socks, six handkerchiefs, two undershirts, some basic medicine, sewing kit, a kit for clothes and shoes, and a little bit of food. Outside of that, don't worry, my health is good.

Saturday afternoon, I went to Berlin for grocery shopping; the city isn't bad, but it's a big change from Paris. There's music in the streets, and food, and everything in the shops, lemons, oranges, candy, chocolate; the only thing is you have to have coupons to have all that. Fortunately I have good buddies;

while I'm waiting for new clothes, we're managing together. Well, that's past. Let's think of you all. Are you thinking of killing the pig soon, and how is it going in Berchères? I really would like to hear from you. I'm beginning to worry.

Yesterday, we got a down payment of 21 marks. We have to get used to the money. Especially don't forget to send me some tobacco, because I got my tobacco yesterday but it went with the rest. Put also a place setting and a plate. When you get a letter, don't worry if it doesn't have an ending, because sometimes it's the Post Office that decides, since it closes at 7. Until tomorrow for the news. In the meantime, I send you lots of kisses. Your big guy, Marcel

Today, January 18, we are at the dining hall. Don't worry, I'm going to send you one or two cards because some letters might not get through. Last night, at the same time, it started again; it promises to be jolly. I hope to go to the Post Office in a little while. I'll send you a card for your Feast Day, and also one for Lily. For me, I'll remember St. Marcel Day of 1943; let's hope my birthday will be better. I'm ending my letter by sending you all kinds of kisses. Your big guy who thinks of you. Marcel

Mes chères petites,

Daddy is in good health. I had put some chocolate aside for you, but the fire ate everything. I hope to get more. And is my little Lily a good girl? I think that Suzanne and Denise are good girls too and that they think of their Daddy who thinks so much about his dear little girls. Be good girls with Mommy and grandma and kiss them for me. Your Daddy who kisses the three of you.

Chapter Twenty-Five

White Bear Lake, Minnesota

Late August 2012

I picked up the phone and heard the sound of Louise's laughter. "Only one pair of underwear?" I laughed along, allowing chuckles to mask the intoxication of reading more of Marcel's words. It felt as if a friend I never expected to hear from again was telling me about his day. The image in my mind was so clear I did not need to close my eyes to picture Marcel strolling through Berlin, gazing into shop windows. In *my* image, though, Marcel walked on the sidewalk with his head held high. In reality, Marcel might have been forced to walk in the street's gutter. If he had to follow the same rules as French prisoners of war, he would not have been allowed to "sully the sidewalk."

The letters' lines and fish-shaped loops made sense once I had Louise's translation. The lines underscored the items he requested, though it was a mystery whether he, a censor, or someone else had made the pencil marks. French workers had been ordered to bring specific items with them: a complete set of work clothes, an overcoat, underwear, good footwear, sheets. They had been forewarned that opportunities to acquire clothes or shoes in Germany would be limited, so perhaps Marcel figured it would be easier to request replacements from home than to find the items in Berlin.

I asked Louise whether she had trouble reading Marcel's writing. "None," she assured me. She had been raised reading that style of handwriting.

"Paper was rationed during the war, you know. That's one reason these letters are so . . ." Louise's words dissolved to silence before she exclaimed: "I still can't believe these letters exist!"

Was it too much to believe the Universe conspired to make things so? I felt awe that Kim kept Marcel's letters all those years; that Kathy knew Dixie, the finder of people; that Dixie's friend knew Louise; that Louise could read Marcel's writing.

Louise confirmed the "Feast Day" Marcel mentioned was the same thing as a Name Day. After our call ended, I looked up St. Marcel's Day. It had been January 16, the day before he had written the letter.

Within an hour, I emailed the next scan to Louise. Within two days, she would translate three more letters.

The first of the three had been written January 18, 1943—the same day as the last paragraphs of the previous letter. It was the only postcard among Kim's batch, and the return address included *Werk 40*, Workshop 40, which identified where within the massive Daimler complex Marcel worked. Two adhesive-backed stamps, which had once been affixed next to the preprinted mossy green stamp with Hitler's profile, had been ripped away, leaving scars of glue and paper fiber. Marcel's writing was careful and vertical. Lines of bruise-blue ink extended to the edge of the paper. A large red "Ae" had been stamped over the Berchères-la-Maingot address. Marcel's signature was partly obscured by a cancellation stamp from Eure-et-Loir, which meant the postcard had at least made it from the Frankfurt censor office *into* France.

The next letter had been written ten days later, January 28, which was two days after Marcel's thirty-first birthday. He would spend his thirty-second birthday in Berlin, too. He would turn thirty-three before the war ground to an end. Grid lines covered the thin paper, and a perforated edge made it appear it had been ripped from a notepad. Marcel's writing aligned to every other grid line, neat and orderly. He must have had problems with his pen again since a string of thick letters followed barely visible words. That frustrating pattern—inky thick, barely visible—repeated across the letter. Yet Marcel should have considered himself lucky to have a pen at all. Pens were sometimes confiscated. In some camps, ink was forbidden.

The third letter was undated, but it had been written on the same grid-covered, perforated paper, so I guessed it might have been written around the same time. It did not include a greeting, so it was not even an entire letter. I guessed it was the last page of a multi-sheet letter. Unlike the January 28 letter, Marcel had written on every grid line. Handwriting filled the sheet.

Marienfelde, Germany

January 18, 1943

My darling,

I'm sending you this card to wish you a happy birthday, and also to give you some news. I'm fine except that I don't have any more of my stuff. I hope that you will receive my letter that I sent you by express mail. I've given you all the instructions that you need to send me my things. I just have the clothes that I had on when I took off from the Gare de l'Est. Don't let that worry you. It still hurts though to see all the good things I had disappear like that in five minutes.

My little wolf, I leave you for today. Your big guy who kisses you very tenderly, and also his daughters and Grandma.

Marcel

January 28, 1943

My little darling,

Today the morale went back up; I just received your first letter. You cannot imagine how good it feels. I was counting the hours, and finally it's here and I can't stop reading it. It is not surprising that you did not receive my first letter because it was mailed from the camp. Don't worry, until now I've written you on the run, but now I'll write you twice a week, Mondays and Thursdays, by air mail, they say that it goes faster. When it comes to the bombing, you can be reassured. I didn't get anything, it was just my things that were destroyed.

Until now, I have just touched up an old suit for work. There's one guy who was given an old tuxedo. As far as the tobacco goes, send me as much as possible. Ask Mignard for some. Today I got a letter from Emile. He was flabbergasted to learn that I am here, and to learn what happened to me afterwards. I haven't smoked for four days. Until now that's the hardest. Now that I have some news, I feel better. Tomorrow I'll write another letter. In the mean time kiss my little rascals for me; for you lots of big kisses from your big guy who thinks of you and who loves you.

Marcel

(No Date)

I treat myself to some joe at the canteen, and it's the start of the day. Then at a quarter to nine, another hop at the canteen to drink another coffee. Then back there at noon for soup time; we're done eating in five minutes because we have no bread and nothing to drink. The main utensil that we must not forget is the spoon. No need for a fork to eat at the canteen because everything is boiled. At 12:30, back to work until 6:00. I don't have to tell you that at 6 o'clock, we have to eat fast and hurry to buy things because the stores close at 7:00 and we can't let the tickets go to waste. The worst is that we are in a weird location, and I've only seen it twice in the daytime, because in the morning we leave when it's still dark, and when we go back in the evening it's night time, a night, a dark night like I've never seen. Then return to the camp in the mud, and since the fire we've been 22 in a room without lockers, without anything. Starting tonight we are in a new barracks part of a plant next to Daimler; it's at Fritz Werner. So that's bad because we're 50 meters from the plant. Fortunately there's a good shelter. My little darling, when I ask you for tobacco, don't find that too odd; just think, last night I bought a little Italian cigar for 15 francs; can you picture that? Well, anyway, anything you can send, even if you have to buy it in the black market. You understand why I want to make the most of it. If you have to be an idiot here, and go back as poor as before, what's the use? It isn't by working that I'll get rich. Next Monday I'll send you 50 marks. The only thing is, it's going to take at least a month before you get it. Well, you know, it's a weird life that we live here. And more and more people keep coming; they don't know where to put them. And with the lack of space and the fact that our barracks burned, it's even worse. Well, I hope that it will not last much longer, according to the news. For distraction, a beer once in a while, and that's all because I've never seen such a miserable country; it's nothing compared to Berchères. I'm going to end my letter. I assume that my little girls are good, and is Lily still afraid of the pig? Pretty soon, she will not be afraid anymore because if he isn't dead yet, he will probably be soon. It's 10, I just had my coffee, and I'm going to go to bed in our new room. Like the others, the beds don't have any box springs, they have boards. Tomorrow our ribs will be vertical. My little darling, I always picture you having to manage by yourself. I can't wait for it to end. In the meantime, I send you my best kisses, also to my little girls who will write to me soon, I hope. While waiting for my tobacco, I kiss you all with all my heart. Your big guy who misses you so much, my little loved one. Lots of kisses.

Marcel

Chapter Twenty-Six

White Bear Lake, Minnesota

Late August 2012

Aaron's eyes softened as I read the translations to him. "You know where the tuxedo came from, don't you?" he asked.

I slowly nodded. The garment, I guessed, had been packed inside a suitcase processed at some extermination camp. "Who would bring a tuxedo to a camp?"

"A maître d' or a sommelier," Aaron offered. "He probably hoped to provide his high-end service wherever it was he had been told he was being 'resettled.'"

I threw out additional options: a musician, a conductor, a butler.

Then Aaron slowly added another: a groom.

After emailing each translation, Louise called me on the phone. I was grateful for the opportunity to ask questions.

"What is *Gare de l'Est*?" I asked. Seeing those words made me recall Marcel had mentioned Gare de l'Est in one of the original five letters, too.

"That's the station in Paris for trains arriving or departing to the east," she explained. My heart swelled for the small mercy: leaving from a train station meant Marcel might have been able to say a proper good-bye—unlike the Italians in Wolfgang's article who showed up for work and by the end of the day were on their way to Germany.

Three times per week, "special trains" transported workers from Paris. Train station platforms would be crowded with friends and family seeing their fathers, sons, and brothers off. As the trains departed, the men often sang "La Marseillaise." *Which sound,* I wondered, *was the last one the people on the platform heard as the train carried their loved one away? Singing? Or the sound of steam pistons and grinding wheels?* The train trip to Germany could last for days, and "strict precautions were taken to prevent them from escaping during the journey."

"I was unsure of a phrase: *Fritz Warma*," Louise said in an apologetic tone. I speculated Marcel had written "Fritz Werner," which was a street near the Daimler plant. His remark, "so that's bad," probably referred to the fact bombing targets would be dangerously close. I felt surprised Marcel could be as candid about food and accommodations as he was. Certain topics were forbidden to write about. Prisoners were not allowed to complain.

I thought about Marcel's request for "anything you can send." I suspected he was selling things on the black market. *And why not?* Everything in camp had value, even rotten vegetables and kitchen waste.

I had only been in contact with Louise for days, but an easy, warm rapport made it seem I had known her my entire life. When I told her I would love to meet her in person, she eagerly agreed, and we arranged to have lunch the following Monday, Labor Day. By that time, she would translate three more letters.

The first of the three had been written August 8. I presumed it had been written in 1943. Familiar brushstrokes of blue and red covered the page. The dark brown writing ink was watered down in places in a way that made me think of how even the murkiest lake water can be translucent right before it hits a pebbled shore. A narrow rectangle of paper was missing from one edge, as though fingers had held the letter so long and often that a chunk of paper had finally given way.

The second of the three letters had been written a week later, August 15. The paper was similar in size and color, and the blue and red stripes were accompanied by a third gray chemical brushstroke. Thin, scratchy writing covered the first half of the letter; thick writing filled the second half. A censor had scribbled their mark in pencil along the top edge.

I understood why I had passed on these letters when I made my selection at the antique store a decade earlier. The handwriting was not remarkable. Stains covered the papers. The pages did not hint they contained words of love. These letters did not beckon: *buy me, take me home, transform me into something beautiful.*

The blue stripe on the third letter, written two weeks later, was wider and thicker than any other. Marcel's handwriting was not in the usual neat horizontal lines, which elicited an immediate swell of anxiety. I knew these loops and curves; the haphazard writing seemed to reflect some dangerous change.

Marienfelde, Germany

August 8 (1943)

Today no news. Surprising for a Sunday. Kisses
7:30, during a depressing weather

My dear little wife,

There we are, another Sunday has gone by. I just finished eating, and I'm smoking my last cigarette. As far as tobacco, I'm counting on the package that I will receive tomorrow, maybe. My letter might be short, but all I have to tell you about is what I did today. I'm in a dorm where all the guys are from Renault. And they just received a box with 100 books which are real neat. I thought a lot about you, talk about a great library; too bad to put that in such hands. Around 9:00 I got up and had a cup of coffee. Then sweeping of the room. Afterwards, bathing, etc. and I hurried to the dining hall for the noon meal. After returning I went to drink a beer with Bernard, and rain surprised us on the way. Since I received some potato meal, I got the urge to make some pancakes. Talk about a chore, with such lousy stuff. Well, they turned out good anyway. Then I started to read. [Name illegible] bugged me to play a game of Belotte. One game and it was over. With the rain that kept falling, we all had the blues. And also to see the buddies preparing their suitcases for Tuesday. So what did I do? I started packing my suitcases too. It kept me busy for a while and it gives an illusion. Then I prepared the food, tomato salad, green beans, all that eaten with vinegar, and to end with, each one got a big pancake. And the rain is still falling. So you see, I filled my day very well anyway. I still have my shirt sleeve to sew, then I'll go to bed with a book. The trains are still running full blast, and the evacuation is continuing. My little darling, all I have left to do tonight is to ask you to kiss my little ones very tenderly for me, and Mom also. Your big guy who loves you kisses you with all his strength and with all his heart. And now for all of you lots of kisses and good night from your absent Marcel.

August 15 (1943)

7:00 PM

My little darling,

There goes another August 15. This afternoon, I waited for Moutardier until 3 o'clock. We went for a little walk in the country. Now it's 7, I just came back. I ironed two handkerchiefs and a shirt. What can I tell you, it's the Sunday occupation, if you want to be a little clean. Only now I don't have any more soap, and my laundry is not very white; for what I have to do, it's good enough. You would have laughed. This afternoon, with Moutardier, I picked cigarette butts; I haven't smoked for four days. The worst is with the buddies in the room; otherwise I could do without. I assure you that I'm anxious to get my package. I believe that, except for my suitcase, I've never been so impatient to receive a package. Let me tell you the menu that I prepared tonight: tomato salad with potatoes cooked in their skin, and an oatmeal cake made with condensed milk without sugar. It will do as long as your belly is full. What I would like to eat is fruits, especially since we see them in all the gardens. But since we had green apples, I made applesauce because we never could have eaten them like that.

That took all the sugar and that's why I did not have any left for the cake. Tonight I'm going to go to bed early, because last night we went downstairs again from 2 to 3. Now that it's a full moon, it promises to be something. That's it for today. Kiss my little girls for me. Your big guy who adores you and who hopes to hold you in his arms soon. Lots of kisses from your Marcel.

August 30 (1943)

At the hotel of the drafty winds.

My little darling,

First of all, I have to tell you that today I am happy. I got your letter of August 10 and the package I was awaiting for so long. It is complete, although a little bit damaged, but nothing is lost. It so happens that today I bought 20 cigarettes for 200 fr. Now let's get to our new situation. A week ago we were all jolly and today we are down in the dumps once more. After many goings-on that I cannot tell you about here. This is how we spend our time. First off, we are about 60 in an old kitchen that is our lodging now. We bed down on straw. Do you picture it? Good thing that it isn't too cold. We don't have any light, that's why my letter is messy. I'm writing outside. I have my suitcase on my lap, and I'm hurrying because it will soon be dark. Today at the shop we were given some workclothes, and you'd laugh because they're workclothes for women. I have a little windbreaker with removable sleeves and American pants without a fly. All we need now is breasts because there are darts to push up the breasts.

Nothing new about leaves. They say it might be by the middle of September. Because of the events, it's total bedlam; orders contradict themselves at any time. Good thing I have my stuff; just a few things left in the shack. They're going to put up some tents for us until they rebuild the barracks. It will be beautiful! Well, my little treasure, don't worry about your old man. I cannot write anymore, and the buddies are shaking the bench. I'm going to end my letter because I still have to write to Pierrot and to Moutardier who are bawling me out because they haven't heard from me and they are worried. The Post Office wasn't working for a few days, and I was saving my writing paper for you. Kiss my dear little girls for me, and for you, from your big guy who adores you, lots of kisses.

Marcel

Chapter Twenty-Seven

White Bear Lake, Minnesota

September 2012

I wanted to be certain the three letters had been written in 1943, so I consulted a moon phase calendar to confirm the moon had been full on August 15. I chuckled at the things that had become downright normal: checking moon phases, sending letters and emails in a language I still could not speak, dipping my fingers into watered-down ink, scouring bombing records.

"He did love his cigarettes, didn't he?" Louise mused after emailing over the last translation. I smiled, adoring the shared affection for the *he* we talked so easily about. In another forty-eight years, Marcel's favorite bad habit would ravage his lungs and take his life. But for today—*just for today*—I was happy he found cigarettes to buy.

It was Monday morning, Labor Day. Louise fretted about how we would find each other at the restaurant, so she provided a description of herself: five feet tall with dark brown hair. "Dyeing my hair is the one luxury I allow myself," she said without apology.

Hours later, we greeted each other with cheek kisses and a long embrace. It looked as though Louise had taken great care to get ready, so I complimented her put-together appearance. "I don't have too much makeup on, do I?" she asked as we trailed the hostess through the nearly empty restaurant. "I would hate to look like a *Madame*, you know," she whispered with a little laugh.

I had gleaned fragments of Louise's life story during various conversations, but I was eager to hear how the pieces fit together into a whole. She began by telling me she was born in Paris in 1925 to Jewish-Polish immigrants. Her parents worked hard "to be French," Louise explained, then corrected herself: "To be *Parisian*."

Louise was thirteen years old when her mother died from tuberculosis. Though they were non-observant Jews, her mother had a traditional burial. Louise was unfamiliar with the tradition of tossing a spadeful of dirt onto a casket. She wailed and refused until her father cradled her shaking hand and went through the motion with her. That moment was the first of only two times she ever saw her father cry.

In September 1939, two and a half months after her mother's death, Germany invaded Poland. That winter, as soldiers from France and Germany faced off along their shared border, life went on as normal as far as Louise remembered. No one believed the Germans would invade France.

The Germans invaded Belgium and Holland in May 1940. When it became apparent France was next, millions of Parisians fled. They left by train, car, bicycle, horse. If no other option existed, they walked. Some people even pushed elderly relatives in baby carriages or wheelbarrows.

By June, the only Parisians who remained in the city were those like Louise and her father: people who did not have family outside the city, and who lacked the financial means to secure safe refuge. "What could we do?" She shrugged. "We prepared for life under German rule."

On the day the Germans occupied Paris, Louise and her father walked to Hôtel de Ville, the grand Renaissance-style hall that housed Paris's city administration. Louise was unsure how she and her father knew to go there; she speculated neighbors who owned a radio must have said something. Small clusters of people—"two here, three there"—gathered on the plaza. As they watched their beloved blue, white, and red flag silently lowered, Louise's father squeezed her hand so tight it hurt. "We were numb. We didn't believe what we were seeing." More than seventy years had passed, but she could not hold back tears.

"You don't have to tell me if it's too painful," I said. Louise took deep breaths and told me she wanted me to hear.

As the Germans raised their flag above Hôtel de Ville, the waving lines of the swastika reminded Louise of snakes slithering on a field of blood. She turned and looked up at her father. Tears were falling from his bright blue eyes. When they walked away, shocked into a stupor, Louise realized a German soldier was pointing his machine gun at them. Louise could not believe he was there, then clarified, "I could not believe *he* felt *he* needed to be there."

As months crawled by, a surreal sense of normalcy returned to the city. German soldiers were polite, she said. "No one had trouble with them." With a sadness I would soon understand, she said it was not the Germans they needed to worry about. "The French did their dirty work."

One evening, as Louise stitched the Star of David onto her father's clothes, she asked why she had the misfortune to be born to Jewish parents. The guilt over the hurt her question inflicted, she confessed, was something she had carried for seven decades. Louise did not think of herself as a Jew. She considered herself a *Parisienne*, no different than anyone else. Others, however, defined her by differences, not similarities. "It was humiliation piled on top of humiliation," she said of the anti-Jewish laws. Radios and bicycles were confiscated. Jewish music was banned. Jews were prohibited from using cafés, markets, theaters, libraries, and public parks. When Louise had her identity-card photo taken, she explained, she was forced to turn to her side so her nose could be shown in profile. "Humiliation is a form of torture; people don't realize that."

Despite recurring stomach ulcers, Louise's father never missed work. He could not risk losing his job. Louise did not understand how ill he was until he could not get out of bed. At the same time, it was their day to check in and receive their monthly ration coupons, so Louise went to the 4th Arrondissement La Mairie on her own.

Louise did not notice that two plain-clothed French policemen watched her pick up both sets of coupons.

She also did not notice they followed her back to her apartment.

The policemen pushed their way into the apartment behind her. Louise pressed her rail-thin body against the wall, as if she could make herself disappear into the ugly, apple-patterned wallpaper. She watched as the police pulled her father out of his bed. "To this day, I have no idea why they didn't take me, too," she whispered.

My mind raced back to our first conversation when Louise said, "So many men, so many French men, disappeared, you know. One day they were gone and they were never heard from again." I finally understood why it brought Louise so much joy to learn about Marcel's letters—and why she needed me to understand how precious his words were.

After the war, a man who had been locked inside the cattle car with Louise's father came to pay his respects. Between his illness and the anguish of leaving Louise behind, her father "had not lasted long." The French government provided a death certificate listing his death at Auschwitz, but based on the man's testimony, she learned he died inside the cattle car. "It was a consolation to know what really happened," she said. After the war she also learned the two policemen did not have orders to arrest her father that day. They did it for bonus money.

After her father was taken, Louise was alone. She was sixteen years old. It would be a year and nine months before Paris would be liberated; two and a half years before the war would end. She gave full credit for her survival to her friends, her friends' parents, teachers, neighbors, and a priest, Father Devaux, who secretly gave Louise money so she could continue to pay her apartment's rent. Father Devaux would ultimately earn a place on the Avenue of the Righteous Among the Nations for risking his life to save Jews.

On June 6, 1944, when the Allies landed on the shores of Normandy, everyone believed Paris would be liberated in no time, Louise said. But the next two and a half months turned out to be the scariest time. The Germans were angry and desperate. More and more people were arrested. Or disappeared.

On the day of their liberation, Louise and a classmate, Ginette, joined throngs of strangers on Paris's streets. There was no reason—"no way," Louise clarified—to contain their delirious joy. Flags of blue, white, and red billowed and waved. They brushed away tears. They hugged and kissed strangers.

Ginette's father was Jewish. He never registered at the town hall like he was supposed to, so for the duration of the war he remained sequestered inside their apartment. On that afternoon, he stepped outside for the first time in years.

That evening, Louise and Ginette walked to Hôtel de Ville. Music and dancing filled the expansive plaza in front of the building. When Louise looked up, her heart swelled to see her beloved French flag back in its proper place atop the building. "People were drunk with joy; it was magic," she said of the day. Louise's eyes lit up as she described the American soldiers; it was as if she suddenly became her eighteen-year-old self again. "Every single one of them was handsome like a movie star," she said dreamily. "We had never seen teeth so perfect!"

Throughout the afternoon, Louise and I alternated between fits of breath-stealing giggles and moments when tears pooled in our eyes. Our waitress remarked how delightful it was to see grandmother and granddaughter having so much fun together.

"Oh, we're not related," we said in perfect unison. The waitress's jaw dropped when we told her it was the first time we had ever met.

Hours later, as we strolled out of the restaurant, Louise asked when I planned to send the next letter. I promised I would email the scan as soon as I returned home. I assured her she did not need to translate the letters so quickly—it had only been a week and she had already translated seven. But Louise seemed to be as obsessed with Marcel's words as I was.

Marienfelde, Germany
September 10 (1943)

Two thirty

My little darling,

As you see I'm writing in pencil, my pen is empty and my ink bottle perished in the fire.

    I got some letters Monday, but nothing since then, but the morale is good, and today is a day to mark with a white stone "let's hope tonight it will not be all dark" because the news is good, amazing even; nobody was expecting Italy would fall so rapidly. I imagine you at news time, you must look happy like in the beautiful old days. Here everything is jolly, but on one side only, because the others are rather sad. Well, it's taking a turn for the best, and I hope that it will not stop here. Because every time something happens crazy lies are running and always from an official source. At the camp we now have sentinels because of the Italians.

    Today was pay day. Everyone was happy because for the last three weeks all we got was down payments. Let's hope that next week pay day will be back to normal because they already owe me 65 marks. At camp we see our new barracks grow from where we are; this time they're made of brick, but in spite of that they most likely will not resist [illegible]. For the time being I'm in good health, I manage and I eat a lot of apples. Each one of our gentlemen just received a pound of honey; it might be the honey meant for the prisoners. With all that, time still goes slowly, even though I've been here eight months already. And we still have to wait to go on leave, and with what's going on these days, we can't hope to leave soon. My poor darling, we still need a lot of patience and courage, and just think that after all that we'll be able to catch up during the beautiful days that we'll have to stay together. Same old song, I'm anxious to hear from you; one letter reads so fast. I'm going to return to work, so I'm leaving you for today, my little treasure. Kiss my little dolls for me and Mom too. Say hello to everybody for me in Berchères, and also in Montreuil if you still go there. And for you, my little treasure, your big guy who loves you more than ever sends you his most tender kisses.

Marcel

Chapter Twenty-Eight

White Bear Lake, Minnesota

September 2012

Two months before Marcel wrote that letter, 200,000 Allied troops descended on Sicily. Within weeks, Patton's Seventh Army secured the Sicilian capital, and Mussolini—Hitler's Fascist ally—was arrested. By mid-August, three weeks before Marcel wrote that letter, the Germans were in full retreat. And on September 8, two days before Marcel wrote his letter, the Italians surrendered.

Marcel's access to timely news surprised me. I had read that the only news many French workers in Germany had access to were propaganda newspapers, or second- and third-hand reports from Allied radio broadcasts. The misinformation—the isolation—had to have been excruciating. At one point, an especially cruel rumor swirled that Paris had been burned down and all relatives of men working in Germany had been shot.

When I sent the next scan to Louise, I told her to do her best. The card was small like a postcard, though it had neither stamps nor a mailing panel. The front was readable, but water stains on the back rendered complete words and phrases nothing more than streaks of cobalt blue. It was as if the card had been caught in the rain.

Paris, France

Wednesday, Noon

Dear all,

Some people are lucky, really; since you left, the sun has been shining. Yes, of course, I know, it still isn't very warm this morning; there's some frost in Berchères; until recently it was zero. Claude made it fine yesterday, not like me, because with the strike I had to go on foot twice. Denise and Eliane were more lucky, they took a cab yesterday morning [illegible] a customer took them back. Some news: Jacques returned with [illegible] the owner of a [illegible] that we made use of by uncorking it; the bottle of rosé that you are keeping [illegible] Mom, if you think of it, save me some eggs for Monday. I gave six of them to Figueras, and he gave me some chocolates for my little ones, a surprise from Marcel. My little [illegible] if you think of training for soccer, be very careful not to catch cold. My darling, kiss the whole little tribe for me. Lots of kisses from Daddy.

Chapter Twenty-Nine

White Bear Lake, Minnesota

September 2012

It took a few moments to realize what was *in* the letter.

I read it again, feeling blindsided by its revelation. Bile flooded my mouth.

Had the family been lying this whole time? Had everything been a lie?

I berated myself mercilessly: *You. Are. So. Fucking. Gullible.*

"There's no way these letters were confiscated by a German soldier," I explained late that night after Aaron got home from work.

All evening, I sat on the couch, processing the evidence: Marcel sent this undated letter from Paris to Berchères-la-Maingot. Even if I had that backward and the letter had been sent from Berchères to Paris, Marcel had been *inside* France. And if letters written in France were together at the flea market with letters that had been sent from Germany, the letters could not have been taken by a German soldier as the family claimed. In the fourth letter, Marcel had written, "there might be some letters that you didn't receive." But even if *some* letters had been taken by Germans or were lost in transit, it seemed as though *these* must have been the letters that made it through.

Guilt, then shame, alternately skewered me as I thought about the people I had told—friends, family, clients—that Marcel's family had never before seen his letters. That scenario now appeared impossible. But the thing that made my head and heart ache the most was the realization that if the letters had been in the family's possession, the family had to have discarded them.

"How old were the girls when the letters were written?" Aaron asked. In January 1943, Suzanne had been nine and a half, Denise had been seven and a half, Lily had just turned four.

"So they might not remember seeing them," Aaron said in a consoling tone.

"But they *had* to have seen them," I said.

"Think of Nadine and Agnès, Natacha, and Tiffanie," Aaron said. "*They* haven't seen them before. Their surprise seemed genuine." That was true; their astonishment seemed real. "What did Nadine tell you? The only things they know about Marcel's time in Germany are what they learned from these letters. So maybe Denise and Lily read them sixty-eight years ago, so what? Do you think they were touched to read the letters again?"

"Yes," I whispered, as I thought of the email from Tiffanie where she said they laughed and cried.

I yearned to find any other way the letters could have been together at a flea market, but other scenarios did not seem to exist. In the days that followed, I reluctantly came to terms with the fact that the letters had to have been with the family in Berchères-la-Maingot.

Three letters remained. I sent the next scan to Louise with conflicted feelings. I felt grounded in the truth, and pushed far, far off kilter.

Marienfelde, Germany

October 21 (1943)

My little darling,

Last night I received your letter of October 15. It came fast. I wish I could tell you when I will leave, but we don't know anything yet. Every day they tell us a different story. It is 2:20; at 3:00 we might know something. That's the way it goes. We have to go to the Foreigners' Office, and there we ask when we leave; no one gets the same answer. I believe that the reason is that they need more and more [illegible] in spite of what they say. In the end, the opposite happens; instead of going up, it goes down, because as each day goes by, it eats away a little more at our daily ration of courage. It will not bring them luck. All I can say to you, my little treasure, is that we have to make the best of it. Believe our little Lily when she tells you that Daddy will come home. As for me, I will not talk to you about it any longer. I prefer to tell you that you must not count on me. When I don't think about it anymore, maybe that's when things will be decided. Last night, when you were at the Gare de l'Est, you probably were not alone, because many among us had written to their wives to come and wait for them at the station. Last night we had quite an alarm from 8 to 10; it wasn't for us, but it rang hard. Ah, I forgot, last night also I went to get my suit. You should see it; I who like the color brown above all, it is brown, and actually I don't know what kind of brown, because I've only seen it in artificial light and it looks like it's goose shit. Besides that, the coat is not lined, so the inside pockets don't exist and the buttons have gone on leave. The main thing is that it fits me; what hurts is the price. Well, at least I will be cleaner, and now that I've been here more than ten months, maybe I'll be able to go to the movies. My recommendation to you is not to worry, take care of yourself as well as possible, and take good care of the children so that I can find all of you in good health when I come home. I hope that it will not be too much longer now, because each day makes it a little more painful. In the meantime, continue to write, because when there is no letter, the day is long. You say that I don't mention the photos; I think you look nice, but you know, I don't always think of everything; because the same thing runs constantly in my head, to leave, to leave, so there are times when I don't know exactly what I'm doing. To leave for an exceptional reason, I'd have to get a certificate signed by the Kommandantur, testifying that you or one of the children is gravely ill. Can you picture it? Death does not count any more; there are several guys whose father died, and they're still here. Nothing new in the newspaper; all the attacks are repelled everywhere. Kiss our little girls for me. Your big guy who thinks of you more than ever and who loves you above all else, kisses you very tenderly.

Marcel

Chapter Thirty

White Bear Lake, Minnesota

September 2012

I choked back a sob as I imagined Renée standing alone on the station platform. I pictured her wearing her best dress, with her hair done as it was in their wedding portrait. The cleaving heartbreak she must have felt, as the station emptied and Marcel was nowhere to be seen, was immeasurable.

Marcel's references to leaves had always confused me, but I would learn promises of furloughs after six or twelve months of satisfactory work had been dangled in front of French workers as a way to encourage compliance. Leaves had been granted for some of the earliest workers, but according to some accounts, only 5 to 10 percent of Frenchmen returned to Germany. As a result, leaves were canceled because the Germans were unwilling to lose their workers. In other cases, leaves were promised, but made logistically impossible by a "maze of regulations" and complex train schedules.

The morning after sending the translated text, Louise called. With unusual formality, she announced, "I would like to make an edit."

As my mind scrambled to identify what might have been wrong, she said, "I should not have written 'goose shit.' Will you change it to 'poop'?"

I nearly laughed aloud, but recognized the gravity in her voice. "Shit" felt like a crass way to translate Marcel's description of his brown suit, she explained. "Don't you think poop is better?"

I disagreed, though I could not bear the notion of arguing with her. "Shit" seemed to be the best possible word to describe everything about Marcel's situation.

The dates on the last two letters—May 8 and June 10, 1944—meant six and a half months had transpired since the previous letter. Marcel had spent two and a half of those months imprisoned in Spandau.

The May 1944 letter looked similar to others: butter-yellow paper, a return address of Lager D4 West, censor numbers scribbled in pencil. The blue and red stripes were accompanied by a third translucent stripe that made the blue ink it was brushed over feathered and watery. The page bore scars from folds and creases. Drops of blood stained one frayed edge. The letter was dirty. Worn down. It was as if even the paper fibers were exhausted.

Clear cellophane tape held the final letter together. One line of writing was obscured by the repair, but it seemed certain any attempt to remove the tape would have destroyed the fragile paper. I told Louise to do the best she could.

The final letter had been written four days after British and US troops landed on the beaches of Normandy. Berchères-la-Maingot would bear witness to tremendous carnage before France would be liberated. Allied planes, shot down by Germans in nearby Chartres, would plummet into the fields surrounding their cottage. Renée would confront a German soldier. The girls would have a rifle pointed at them. They would have to abandon everything and hide in the woods. But the end was finally in sight.

Marienfelde, Germany

May 8, 1944

My darling little wife,

This evening I'm writing you a letter to talk to you about the events a little bit, and to give you some news. Since the operations have started, we don't know much about how they are proceeding. The newspapers don't say much. Today we had the L'Écho de Nancy, so we have a description of the beginning of the landing. This time I think it's for good. It must be frightening for those who stayed there; it must be enough to drive you crazy.

I don't think I have any more recommendations to give to you, except be careful and don't panic. We still have very difficult moments to live through. With God's help we'll get through the great storm which is hitting our France one more time. For me, here things have been fine because we haven't had any alarms for the last two weeks; I assure you that we feel the better for it. If the mail worked better, the morale would be better too and everything would be real fine. I don't have any news from anybody.

They told us that we could take our leave in Germany. I'll wait a little while and maybe I'll go visit André or Emile. Today I managed to send you 200 marks—what can I do with those here? If they arrive that will be a good thing, because these days they find a way to take them from us. I told you in March that they had given me a suit for work, and today I have to pay for it 13 marks per week for four weeks. I still have 200 marks, so you see, with the wages coming, it will work. It is 10:15, you must go to bed at this time. During the day you must be glued to the radio to learn how the operations are going. It seems that they're on their way to Paris. And fast as they're going they'll be there in no time. It must not be fun to get food, especially since the attack is going on in a rich region. I would give a lot to be with you, you know, especially since you must wonder how it's going to end up. You remember [19]40. I am very anxious. I'd like to be two weeks older. Don't mind my writing; the thoughts are bumping together in my head, and I have a hard time writing them as fast as I'd like. I don't know if you'll receive this letter. There must be such turmoil at this time. We are all nervous, and as you can imagine, the conversations are all about that. In spite of that, write me as often as possible, one never knows; and don't be afraid to tell me the truth. My little sweetheart, I'm going to leave you because it's eleven o'clock. The little chat is finished already.

I see you sleeping with your girls. You remember when I used to watch you sleeping. Sleep well, my little treasure, and think of your big guy with confidence, he who is gathering all his courage so he can find you again with his little brood. Good night, my little girl. From your husband who loves you receive the best kisses and the sweetest caresses. Kiss my little ones and take good care of them. Your big guy who adores you says goodnight.

Marcel

June 10, 1944

My little darling,

Finally, last night I got some news and two beautiful letters with pictures in each one. My two little rascals haven't changed. I think that Suzanne has grown, and she is beautiful like the day in her beautiful white outfit. I'm proud of my little brood. You, my darling, you're beautiful too. It had been a long time since I'd seen you dressed up. Lily looks angry, or is it that her hat is too small? And you, my Denise, it looks like you're happy to be with your sister. I hope that when your turn comes, we'll all be back home. My dear precious one, you're right, there will be hard times ahead. And you'll need to keep cool. It enrages me not to be able to be with you. If sometime you see that it's getting close to home, don't panic, hide what's the most precious, do all you can not to go too far away; you know what I used to tell you when we went to the woods, think about selling [illegible]. Sometimes it's better to be afraid of the animals for a while in order to save one's skin. My sweetheart, you might think that I'm seeing things too dark, but according to the newspapers, the fighting is frightening, and the people who are there must be terribly scared, so I don't know just what to tell you to help you to hang on. By the way, now that all the countries have goats, you don't say if Grisette had babies.

I asked Maurice if his parents could go to see you, and he is going to write to them so they can contact you. He received another letter last night, and his father says that things are worse and worse. Don't worry for nothing. You already have enough problems. Ah, what's great, is I found a tailor who is going to make me a windbreaker with the rest of the suit that I paid 56 marks. That way I'll be able to use it. You tell me to buy socks; I'd like to, but try to find some! You can imagine that since the bombings, clothing has become very rare. The packages have been arriving in good shape, and you can send some more, at least while it's possible. My little darling this is the end of another little conversation, and my thoughts are going towards you, always more strong to help you in your work. Kiss my three little rascals that I'm looking at now, and also their grandma. And for you, my beloved one, I always save my most tender kisses. Your big guy, who is burning, kisses you very tenderly.

Marcel

Chapter Thirty-One

White Bear Lake, Minnesota

September 2012

After reading the last translation, I did not feel sadness like I had after reading the last of the first five letters. I felt privileged to read the poetry in Marcel's words. I felt honored to glimpse his sense of humor when he mentioned his buttons had gone on leave, or when he had joked about needing breasts to fill the darts in his shirt. And, I felt awe he could continue to muster words of optimism and love.

Marcel's family knew when Aaron and I would be flying into Paris and that meeting them was our singular priority. I told them we were available to meet any day, any time. Aaron and I would fill other days with sightseeing.

When Agnès invited us to her apartment for lunch, I inquired whether Denise and Eliane would be there too, or if I needed to arrange a separate time to meet them.

Her response was unequivocal: one big meeting was never going to happen.

Nadine and Agnès had been frank about the absence of a relationship with aunts and cousins. Before Agnès's most recent email, I assumed it was a divide caused by slowly growing apart. But it was something bigger.

A fissure in the family existed, and I would come to learn it was deep and still raw. It seemed to be a fissure beyond repair, and it raised a bigger question: who would I give Marcel's letters to?

Asking the family to come to a consensus on one caretaker was an impossibility. If I returned the letters to Denise, Eliane, or the son Marcel, Agnès and Nadine would never see them again. If I gave them to Agnès and Nadine, Denise, Eliane, and Marcel would never see them. I refused to choose sides. I refused to drive the wedge in the family even deeper.

"Rock," Aaron said, "meet hard place."

I studied the situation from every angle before determining only one solution seemed to exist: no one. It seemed the best possible caretaker would be an archive or museum in France that would protect the letters forever and make them available to everyone: all generations, all branches of Marcel's family tree.

Yet it felt unimaginably cruel to make that suggestion.

One evening on my walk with Hoover, as I tried to find a way to broach the topic, I thought back to the week in May when I established contact with Tiffanie and Natacha. Only now did I understand how serendipitous it was that within days I connected with second cousins who did not know each other and whose families had not talked in more than seven years. By establishing relationships with both branches of the family tree at essentially the same time, a type of equality existed that had been absent for years. I could not help but smile. *Had the Universe played a part in the timing? Had Marcel?*

"It is no problem for us that you keep the letters or entrust an institution of World War II," Nadine responded after I sent an email suggesting I bring copies, but not the originals. "We agree. A copy for us is enough. We are sure that you treat them with respect. Honestly, we prefer you keep. Without you, we would know nothing of these letters and Marcel's life as a prisoner. It is better they are at your home rather than astray in the family." Nadine also said giving the letters to Denise or Eliane was problematic since Denise was "very sick," and Eliane lived far away.

My head snapped back. *What did "very sick" mean?* The last thing Aaron and I wanted to do was stress Denise's health. Tiffanie confirmed her grandmother had Parkinson's disease and tired easily, but assured me as long as her grandmother could sit, a short visit would not be a problem. As far as the custody of the letters, since Tiffanie did not know Suzanne's side of the family, she also thought my suggestion was a good one.

I was relieved both sides agreed, yet I was filled with guilt. *How could a solution everyone agreed to feel so wrong?*

Days later, I received a cheery voicemail from the letterpress printer, Kent, letting me know the custom linen-wrapped case was complete. "It's perfect," I said when I picked up the case and wrote a check for his flawless work.

I could not bear to tell him it would never be used.

Chapter Thirty-Two

White Bear Lake, Minnesota

Early October 2012

I carried the seventeen just-printed pieces of paper into our living room and sat on the floor in front of the coffee table. The table held half-assembled pieces and parts for the open house: little placards for the food, still-empty wooden picture frames, freestanding reference cards, empty menu covers.

It was the first time translations of all seventeen letters were together. Previously, each translation existed only as an email from Tom or Louise, or as a print of the email covered with my notes and scribbles. Now, every translation had been carefully typeset using a classic serif font, then printed onto thick white paper.

I shuffled the translations into chronological order. The dates ranged from January 17, 1943 to June 10, 1944; the span represented five hundred and ten days of excruciating separation.

I had to guess where to place the two dateless translations within the overall order. I placed the letter written on grid paper next to the other letter written on similar grid paper. And the water-stained card from Paris was placed near the end.

For weeks, I had racked my brain for the best way to display Marcel's letters at the open house. I wanted each original to be next to its translation, yet I wanted to avoid an unruly jumble of papers. More than anything, I wanted to protect Marcel's original letters from wear or tear. When the solution finally came to me, it seemed perfect: clear plastic menu covers. Side-by-side pockets meant the original letter and the translation could be paired together, both the front and back would be visible, and the letters would be safe.

I began inserting the translations into the right-hand pockets. When I got to the March 12, 1944 translation, I let out a long sigh and stared at the words, "for the class and by the will of God." I knew what was positioned next to those words on Marcel's original letter: the swastika. It seemed undeniable that the wobbly, overlapping lines had been drawn by Marcel. Yet even after all this time, that mark, those words, confounded me.

Why did you draw that?

I had not intended it to be a question directed to Marcel, but I realized it was.

When I first saw the swastika at Belle Époque, it seemed like a powerless relic; an artifact disconnected from Marcel and his beautiful writing. The symbol now felt like an ugly asterisk, a stain that could forever be attached to Marcel's name. I feared the symbol—small in size, enormous in its ability to offend—might neutralize, or worse reverse, every positive sentiment our guests might have about Marcel.

I considered displaying the retouched version of the letter I emailed to Tom nearly fourteen months earlier—the version where I digitally erased every trace of the odd little mark. But I suspected our guests would wonder why I showed a *copy* rather than the original. I considered folding over the corner, putting a sticker over it, masking it with a blot of ink. The thought even entered my mind to rip off the corner and pretend it had always been that way, but I could not do that. Swastika or not, I could not destroy any part of these pages.

I let out another long sigh. Aaron glanced at me with raised eyebrows. I gave a shrug. I still had a day and a half to figure out what to do.

The day before, Aaron drove to a specialty cheese shop and procured wedges of a sheep-milk cheese from the French Basque region, a tangy blue from Auvergne, a double-cream from Rhône-Alpes. At another store, he bought a pork and chicken-liver pâté, along with savory *Saucisson Sec aux Cèpes*, dry sausage with mushrooms. At a third store, he stocked up on bottles of a rich Burgundy and a case of Champagne.

I typeset little placards, using the font, to set next to the delicacies. As I prepared the placards for the cheeses, I noticed all sorts of details that needed refinement: the *B* in St. Agur Blue needed to be narrower, the top curve of the *s* in Fromage d'Affinois needed to be smoother. But I refrained from opening the font file and fixing the glyphs. Too many things had to be done before Saturday afternoon, and I knew all too well there was no such thing as tweaking just a few things.

Aaron assembled a playlist of classic World War II-era songs of love and Parisian life by Josephine Baker, Yves Montand, Charles Trenet, Edith Piaf, and Maurice Chevalier. I asked Aaron to be sure to include the song Mimile sang inside the barrack, "La Chanson du Maçon." I had listened to that tune often while working on the font. As soon as the trombones began their brassy pulse, or when Chevalier began to whistle the refrain, I could not help but envision the barrack. *Did they clap when Mimile finished? Did he take a comical bow? Had anyone else sung along? Or did they listen in silence, exhausted, stacked like boards onto wooden bunks?*

I returned to my office and printed photos of Marcel and Renée, which I laid into the brown wooden picture frames. I bought the frames special for the event because Marcel had noted his favorite color was brown.

We wanted to make the open house a celebration Marcel would have been proud to attend. That was the reason Aaron went out of his way to buy French cheese and Champagne. That was the reason I purchased blue, white, and red paper napkins. That was why Aaron created a playlist with music Marcel would have known. Yet we knew our guest of honor would only be present through a couple of photos and seventeen sheets of sixty-nine-year-old paper. That was why the swastika remained a nagging problem.

Nearly everyone we invited planned to attend. Most were friends or family, design colleagues, or Type Tuesday people. A few of my clients and a handful of Aaron's co-workers planned to attend, too.

I still felt bad Kathy, Tom, and Dixie were not going to be there; the party would not be the same without them. Aaron expressed surprise I had not *un*invited Tom since I had been so angry he did not translate Kim's twelve letters. Tom was unequivocally part of this story, I explained; I wanted him to celebrate with us.

I ticked through a mental checklist of things that still needed to be done: we had to pick up white tablecloths from the rental company. I needed to retrieve Marcel's letters from the safe-deposit box. Aaron and I would pick up the chocolate *gâteau* Friday evening and fresh-baked baguettes and macarons Saturday morning. Individual bottles of Perrier and mini quiches were already in the refrigerator. Champagne glasses were cycling through the dishwasher.

Everything was coming together nicely. Everything except that swastika.

"I forgot to do the map," I whispered as I snapped my fingers. I removed a mirror that hung near our front door, unfolded a large map of France, and wrapped the paper over the mirror as if it were a present. I positioned little flags near Berchères-la-Maingot and Montreuil so our guests could easily locate the cities. As I rehung the map-wrapped mirror on the wall, the city of Amiens caught my eye and I recalled Marcel's note: "There's a guy from Amiens who has some tricks to get food."

I returned to my office to put away the scissors and tape, then slumped into my chair and opened the scan of the March 12, 1944 letter. I stared at the tiny blue handwriting that went to the edge of each page, the thick painted stripe, the odd-looking swastika. And I asked Marcel again: *Why, why, why did you draw that?*

As I stared at his crooked, overlapping lines, another question popped into my mind: *Why are you odd-looking?*

I took a deep breath before tapping eight letters into a search engine: s-w-a-s-t-i-k-a. My heart lurched as my computer monitor blossomed with a hundred thumbnail-size swastikas. I recoiled and rolled my chair backward, distancing myself from the ugly sea of red and black.

As I stared at the hate-filled symbols, the corners of my mouth slowly—involuntarily—began to curl into a smile.

It was then I heard Marcel for the first, the only, time.

"Good girl," he said.

Maybe it was not Marcel; the words were in English, after all. But the voice wasn't mine, either. The two words sounded both intimately near, as if someone had whispered directly into my ear, and like some celestial message that had carried from a million miles away.

I stepped into the living room, mouth agape. "What?" Aaron asked as he noticed my stunned grin. Hoover got up and walked to me, tail wagging. He must have sensed my revelry, too.

Marcel might have seen a swastika every morning as he walked under the arched entryway of the Marienfelde factory complex. The overlapping lines would have been emblazoned on flags, uniforms, armbands, coins, currency. For all I knew, swastikas could have been painted onto the tanks that rolled across Daimler's factory floor. Marcel might not have been able to get out from underneath the symbol's dark shadow no matter how hard he tried.

Marcel would have known with absolute clarity what a swastika looked like.

Moments earlier, when I looked at the screen filled with red and black, I realized Marcel's swastika did not face right like a Nazi swastika. His faced left. Marcel's swastika was backward, and it was impossible to believe it was backward by accident.

"Marcel wasn't saying 'for the class and by the will of God,'" I said as an astonished laugh burst out of my lungs. "He was saying the opposite." It seemed it was an anti-Nazi message hidden in plain sight. A fearless *fuck you*. I wanted to pop open one of the bottles of Champagne, throw my middle fingers in the air, and yell the thing Marcel could not: *Fuck! You! Nazis!*

Maybe, as I had for so long, the German censors had only noticed an odd, hand-drawn mark. If they had noticed it was backward, Marcel's letter might have been confiscated and destroyed. Marcel might have been beaten—or killed—for desecrating their symbol. It was astonishing to realize the risk he took by drawing that backward little mark.

For more than a year, the mere presence of that symbol had created doubts that nibbled at my certainty of Marcel's allegiance. Discovering it was backward meant he was finally—and fully—exonerated. Completely, utterly exonerated. Relief filled every cell of my body.

Saturday morning was consumed with cleaning and last-minute errands. A sign placed in front of our home directed guests to enter through the kitchen door, since three long tables spanned the combined length of our dining room and front entryway and blocked the front door from the inside. After draping the tables with the rented cloths, I set out the letters, which had been tucked into the clear plastic menu covers next to their translation. The framed photos of Marcel and Renée, along with freestanding cards with historic information about STO, the Vichy regime, and Daimler's collaboration, were set between the letters. Additional notes provided clarifying information for specific passages, such as DCA being the equivalent of anti-aircraft artillery. And I made a special sign to set next to the March 12, 1944 letter noting that the swastika was backward.

As I stepped into the kitchen, freshly showered and dressed, Aaron was carefully rearranging a tray with sliced meat so his pre-party thievery could not be detected. Part of a fresh, crusty baguette, slathered with mustard, lay nearby.

I took one last walk through the house to ensure everything was in order, then coaxed Hoover into the basement. He would be unhappy about having a houseful of visitors he could not greet, but we could not take the chance he might sneak out unnoticed as guests entered or exited. For several minutes, Hoover butted his head against the basement door in protest.

Promptly at 3:00, I watched my Uncle Allen and Aunt Barb walk up our driveway. The increased shuffle in my eighty-seven-year-old uncle's steps was alarming. He had always been the healthiest, most active person I knew, but in recent years, five full inches of height had disappeared from his hunched frame.

Sixty-nine years earlier, in the summer of 1943, Allen returned to his parents' home after completing basic training. He took one surprised look at his mother's rounded belly and blurted, "What happened?"

Allen still burst into laughter whenever he told that story. My father was *what happened.*

Allen fought in the Battle of the Bulge, was awarded a Bronze Star for clearing a minefield while under enemy fire, and walked through Buchenwald not long after the camp had been liberated. But, like so many other veterans, Allen rarely talked about what he witnessed. Barb only learned about his Bronze Star when she found his medal in their basement.

I felt a lingering worry about how Allen might react to the letters since Marcel could have built one of the tanks Allen faced. But I invited him because I thought he might relate to the random circumstances that determined one's fate, the deep yearning for faraway family, and the friendships that provided sustenance during the darkest days. And I hoped Allen might be touched for another reason: after the war he had three daughters.

Aaron and I greeted Allen and Barb with hugs, and I smiled as my happy-go-lucky uncle said "helllllooooooo" in a familiar, drawn-out way that lasted three full seconds. Within minutes, other guests arrived. Before long, our home was full.

One friend did not even make it through the first table of letters before she began to weep. Another admitted she had to stop reading halfway through. A few hopscotched from letter to letter. Most guests, though, read every single word. Several people remarked on Marcel's expressiveness, and how they could feel the depth of his love.

Guests were astonished to learn men like Marcel had been forced to go to Germany. They asked questions about the camp, about STO, about Daimler's collaboration. Others barraged me with questions about our forthcoming meetings with the family. Graphic design and Type Tuesday friends asked to see the font, so I showed test pages printed with the lyrics of "La Marseillaise." But I was careful not to give the font much attention. I wanted Marcel to be the star.

I was chatting with a friend from college when Louise quietly walked in. Her diminutive size—contrasted by several of our taller-than-average friends—made her look as though she was a lost child wandering through a forest.

"I have something for you," I said as I gave her a gentle hug.

"You do?" she asked, her voice lilting. "For me?"

I nodded and pointed behind her. "It's in the kitchen."

As we walked around the kitchen island, a pyramid of brightly colored meringues caught her eye. "You have macarons!"

"And French wine," Aaron added as he introduced himself and gave Louise a hug.

I reached into the refrigerator and retrieved a white rose corsage embellished with loops of blue, white, and red ribbon. "The colors of the French flag. Just for you," I said. A close-lipped smile spread across her face. Her eyes twinkled. She seemed to grow a half-inch taller. "For everything you did to give Marcel a voice."

"It was my honor," she whispered. Louise had told me several times that translating Marcel's letters was one of the most meaningful—most important—things she had ever done.

I walked with Louise to the three long tables and pointed out the original five letters; she had not seen those since they were the ones Tom had translated. She began reading them, but people were eager to meet her, and before long she was enveloped in their attention.

Hours later, after the last guest left, after we tossed or packed away what little food remained, after we corralled a counter's worth of stray Champagne and wine glasses, Aaron lay on the couch and I collapsed into the living room chair. My legs were tired. My jaw was tired. Every ounce of energy was depleted.

Since Aaron and I had been in different rooms most of the afternoon and evening—he had been in the kitchen while I mingled in the living room, then I manned the kitchen while he made the rounds—we compared notes about conversations we had and comments we overheard. I told him about the moment I found Louise and Allen sitting close, his body curved into hers so he could hear her with the ear that was not ruined by the war. As I watched them, I could not help but envision them as younger versions of themselves: Louise dancing after Paris had been liberated, my happy-go-lucky uncle standing straight and tall in army fatigues.

Throughout the afternoon, people remarked how much love they felt—not only in Marcel's letters, but in our home. Most seemed to understand how—why—Marcel's letters had consumed more than a year of my time. It filled my heart to spend the day surrounded by our closest friends, and they seemed to revel in being part of the celebration.

I attempted to force myself out of the chair to finish cleaning the kitchen, but it was impossible to move. The Champagne glasses and the serving platters would have to wait until the morning to be washed and put away.

"I'll take the tablecloths back Monday morning when the rental place reopens," I said to Aaron. Work was slower than it had been in months, and I looked forward to two quiet weeks. I could take time to pack, maybe buy some new clothes. I could refine the font and figure out how to present it to the family. I could catch up on much-needed sleep.

Unfortunately, none of those things would happen.

A Monday morning phone call would change everything.

Chapter Thirty-Three

White Bear Lake, Minnesota

October 2012

Two days after the open house, twelve days before our flight to Paris, I was quietly working in my office when our home phone rang. I rarely answered our home phone during business hours, but my ears perked up when a man with a British accent began to leave a message on the answering machine. I could not make sense of his first words, but as my brain processed the next phrase—a question about Marcel's letters—I launched out of my chair, ran to the kitchen, and ripped the phone out of its cradle.

The man, Henry, asked whether I heard his message. A jumble of words fell out of my mouth that included "yes" and "no" and "*whodidyou-sayyouareagain?*"

Henry, a Paris-based UK reporter, stated he had questions about the article that ran in that day's newspaper.

"What article?" I stammered. "What paper?"

A newspaper in Brittany had run an article about Marcel's letters, Henry explained. I tried to make sense of that information. Brittany was in the northwest of France, two hundred miles from any location connected to Marcel. *How would a newspaper in Brittany even know about these letters?*

Henry began asking questions, but I stopped him. I wanted to know what was in the original article. It was an interview with the son Marcel, Henry said. My brain scrambled to make sense of that, too, since I had not had any direct communication with Marcel.

Henry began by confirming basic facts: my age, where I lived, where I acquired the letters, how Marcel's family had been found. When Henry asked what Marcel had written, I apologized and explained the legal issues that prevented me from sharing his words. I was suddenly grateful I had sought legal advice.

In reality, I was bursting to tell Henry everything: Wolfgang found handwritten records of his two entries into camp! Marcel had been sent to Spandau! The swastika was backward! But I did not. I could not tell Henry those things either; the family deserved to learn those things from me first. *Privately.*

Henry did not ask *why* I purchased Marcel's letters, and I did not tell him about the font. It seemed too complicated to explain why anyone would design a font based on handwriting they could not read, or how anyone could work on a font for a decade but still not be done. Henry ultimately labeled me a "letter collector," which was true enough, technically.

As the call drew to a close, Henry asked whether it was true I was about to travel to Paris to meet the family. My mouth went dry. The only people who knew we would be away were clients, and friends and family who had come to the open house. *Now everyone knew we were going to Paris?* It felt as if the announcement was an invitation for burglars to empty our home while we were away.

After I hung up the phone, I cradled my forehead in my hands. *Did I disclose anything I should not have? Did my answers make sense? Why did the article have to come out now?*

Henry emailed a link to the article. It was, of course, in French. I recognized a smattering of words: Daimler, Berlin, STO, Stillwater, Minnesota, my name. A photo accompanying the article showed Marcel proudly holding a photocopy of one of his father's letters. For a few minutes, I stared at Marcel's features. He seemed to have his mother's smile, his mother's nose. Straight hair swept over his head from left to right, the same way his father had worn his hair. Copies of Marcel's other letters lay on a table beside him. It was disorienting to see the familiar cursive in an entirely unfamiliar setting. It was as if time had bent to allow the letters to be both here and there.

I paged Aaron at work, then sent frantic emails to Tom and Louise, asking if one of them could translate the newspaper article. Tom called immediately and provided an on-the-fly translation. Within hours, Louise provided a more formal written transcript.

"Letters sent from the United States 70 years later," the headline proclaimed. "Marcel Heuzé, prisoner of STO, in 1944, wondered why some of his letters were not arriving where they were meant to . . . Amazing thing, however, they were found and bought in a second hand store by an American woman, in the United States. And they arrived to the Heuzé children, in Carnoët . . ."

Carnoët. My mind raced to identify the gauzy familiarity in that word.

"'We were flabbergasted,' admits Marcel, the son, born in 1949. This former private detective, tired of the Paris suburbs and who came to the Carnoët countryside in order to live a peaceful retirement, has yet to get over it."

That was it! I laughed and scolded myself for the missed opportunity: Carnoët had been one of the five cities listed for Marcel Heuzé in the French phone book.

"I started to see him as an old friend," the article quoted me as saying. "This led me to wonder how his letters ended up in a small antique store halfway around the world." It felt surreal and bewildering to read quotes attributed to me since I had not talked to the reporter. It took a moment to realize why the words sounded familiar: they had been taken from the letter I had written Denise.

"Marcel, the son, has a little idea of his own about this mystery," the article continued. "'I think those mails were censored by the Germans (one of them is marked with a swastika). The Americans must have got-

ten them after they entered Berlin. A soldier must have taken them and
sold them after he returned home.'"

"No, no," I whispered.

The core facts in the article were correct: Marcel sent the letters from
Marienfelde, I bought the letters in Stillwater, I contacted the family. But
the speculation that a soldier brought the letters to the States made my
heart lurch, and I berated myself for not disclosing everything I knew in
my initial letter to Denise. In an effort to be kind, it seemed, I had made
a mess of everything.

I sent messages to Natacha and Tiffanie asking if they knew about
the article. Natacha did not. Tiffanie had only learned about it hours earlier. Anger began to smolder. *Why did the article have to run now?* There
were so many things to discuss when I met with the family—including if,
how, and when to go public with our story. *We'll be there in less than two
weeks, for Chrissakes!*

The next day, Tiffanie sent an email informing me the biggest television channel in France wanted to film our meeting. She sounded excited
about the possibility. It made me want to throw up. *What if Denise wanted
to share private details of Marcel's time in Germany but wasn't willing to do so
on camera? How could I summarize the last year into a tidy, ten-second sound
bite? How could we talk about the swastika, or discuss how the letters might
have ended up at the flea market, with a camera crew in the room? What if the
producer demanded to know why I was not returning the originals? How could
I answer that without exposing the rift in the family? What about Denise's
health? Or the language barrier? How could we laugh or cry—or let whatever
emotion was going to happen, happen—without it looking orchestrated?*

"Please, please," I begged Tiffanie, "I am not comfortable with that."

On Tuesday evening, Kathy and Dixie came to our home for a private viewing of Marcel's letters. We could have done it after our trip,
but Aaron and I wanted them to partake in some sliver of the pre-trip
celebration. As Kathy and Dixie savored each letter, they commented
on Marcel's descriptions of food or housing, sighed at tender phrases to
Renée, or chuckled at his insatiable desire for tobacco.

Kathy asked about our trip: Was I going to show the font? Which family members were we going to meet? Who would translate? I told her I planned to bring both my laptop and printed samples showing the font. Tiffanie would translate when we met at Denise's apartment. Tiffanie's mother, Valentine, and her uncle, Philippe, would be there; she believed Eliane and Marcel would be there, too.

And we planned to meet Suzanne's daughters, Agnès and Nadine, for lunch at Agnès's apartment. They had arranged for a neighbor to translate. Natacha would be there to translate, too.

"You're going to their apartment?" Kathy's eyebrows shot up.

I nodded hesitantly, sensing some bigger issue hiding inside Kathy's question. She stared blankly for a moment. "Do you have *any* idea what that means?"

"No. Why?" I was horrified I had committed some grave faux pas.

"People in France *never* invite strangers into their home," Kathy said as surprise curled into a giddy smile. I smiled, too. Fundamentally, we were strangers. But we were strangers already deeply, inextricably bound.

Henry emailed a draft of his article and requested I make any revisions immediately. Facts and details taken from the original article had been supplemented with quotes from me and Tiffanie.

"[Tiffanie], Heuzé's great-granddaughter, said she first [thought] the letters were a hoax when she opened them at her grandmother Denise's home. 'Then when we realised it was true, it was like a magnificent film. It gave my grandmother so much joy but also sadness that her parents were not there to see them.'"

Henry's article repeated the claim a German censor drew the swastika and Marcel's speculation soldiers brought his father's letters to the US. The inaccuracies made my stomach churn, but there was no way I was going to point out Marcel had drawn the swastika. *What happened if someone shaved down my statement to include the fact Marcel drew it—but not also include the note it was backward?* And I did not know how to tell Henry the soldier-took-them supposition was untrue without also telling him I knew Marcel's letters had been at a flea market. I didn't want that information to be public until I could talk with the family.

Henry's article ran in the UK on Friday morning, accompanied by a photo of me. He had requested an image, so I took a photo with a self-timer after securing permission from Denise and Eliane to show an image of one letter. In the photo, I sat in our living room, smiling, holding the letter with the beautiful swash *M*.

By Friday afternoon, a sliced and diced variation of Henry's story made it into the US. The article included one new embellishment: I was labeled a die-hard romantic.

I sent Aaron a text at work, and as soon as he could, he read the newest article. The inaccuracies remained a painful flaw, but he reminded me all core facts were correct. I informed Kathy, Tom, Dixie, Kim, and Louise about developments, but I did not promote the story or post anything on social media. Nevertheless, I knew the story was making the rounds when a friend from college made a three-word post on my Facebook page: "die-hard romantic."

"I've been called worse," I typed with a chuckle.

Little could I guess how true my statement would turn out to be.

That evening, I navigated to the comment section at the end of the article. I hoped to see that Marcel's story touched readers, that the article provided a few moments of feel-good happiness. Instead, readers accused me of being a liar. They believed the entire story had to have been invented. They claimed prisoners could not mail letters from camps, that the letters had to be fake. They berated me for wasting years of time and speculated I was scheming to turn the story into a book or movie. They commented that it was unconscionable not to return the original letters, and that the photo of me smiling, holding one of Marcel's letters, was wholly inappropriate. A few felt my blonde hair and blue eyes were damning. They described me wearing a Nazi uniform.

I knew I should snap my laptop shut and look away, but I could not. I read every single grisly comment, and there were hundreds. I wanted to hurl every insult back with the force and fury of a tornado, but I did not. Any response would have fueled their entertainment. Deep down, I knew it should not have mattered what people called me. I knew they had written the debasing comments for a laugh, yet I was blindsided by the vitriol. I did not understand how anyone would feel anything other than soaring joy to learn Marcel had made it home.

Other websites—history and lifestyle websites, blogs—reposted the article. Before long, I found my stupid smiling face staring back at me from a neo-Nazi website. I stood up, walked to the bathroom, stood over the toilet, and threw up as the reader comments swirled inside my head: *Liar. Fake. Opportunist. Nazi.*

Eventually, I shifted to my left and stared into the mirror above the sink. Mascara had relocated to my eyelids and cheeks. A black smudge streaked across my forehead. I wanted to crawl into bed and pretend I had not brought this on. But no matter how I dissected it, my actions caused this: I could not let go. I kept digging. I wrote Denise. I supplied the photo to Henry.

So I had to allow the comments, the accusations, the insults.

Sticks and fucking stones.

I wet a washcloth in the sink, then held the cool fabric over my face. A song began playing inside my head. First, I heard violins, then a trumpet's blare, then a slow and steady drumming build. Then Edith Piaf began singing. Her raging, crumbling, defiant voice began belting the first words of "Non, je ne regrette rien."

I imagined the moment Denise first opened my letter and saw her father's writing. I envisioned the photo from the French newspaper of Marcel smiling and proudly holding his father's letter. *Call me whatever you want*, I thought. I would do it again. I would do everything again. *No, I regret nothing.*

Sleep eluded me. All night, I sat on the couch. Hoover sat vigilant by my side, as if he were protecting me from some invisible assailant he did not quite understand. On our morning walk, a neighbor bolted out of her house, hands flapping in the air. She was bursting with excitement that someone from our sleepy street made the news. As she told me how much she loved the story, I nearly wept with gratitude. Each kind word seemed to chip away at the moat of hate that had surrounded me the night before.

"Finding those letters was no coincidence," she said. "Those letters found you, you know."

"Do you know the letters are in the news?" I had not talked with my brother and sister-in-law since the open house.

"Oh yeah, I know," I replied.

Strangers had emailed me, asking if I would help with their genealogy research. A client had emailed a friendly accusation: "You've been leading a secret double life, I see." Interview requests began coming in, so I reached out to a friend who had experience with media. After discussing the legal issues that prevented me from disclosing the letters' contents, my hesitance to talk about the font, and the complicated relationships within the Heuzé family, he recommended I decline additional interview requests.

Despite my silence, new articles appeared. Some included surprising embellishments. One described how lines of writing had been covered with thick black censor marks. Another claimed I had returned the letters to France months earlier. Another described the meeting I had with Denise and Marcel, which had, according to the article, already taken place.

A second French television producer attempted to secure an on-camera interview and pressed for details on when I would arrive, where I planned to stay, when I planned to meet the family. I began swallowing Tums by the fistful.

Aaron had been on high alert since reading the online comments. His anger finally erupted. "If one reporter in France knocks on our door, if one producer touches you, if we sense someone is getting to the family, we're leaving. We're heading to the airport with the clothes we have on and we're buying new tickets home."

"That would be so expensive," I mumbled.

"I don't care," he stated.

"What about the meetings with the family?"

"Right now," he said, "I *really* don't care about them."

"Die-hard romantic" apparently translated into something slanderous in French. Natacha told me to "go to the police and make a handrail!" I should have laughed at the situation—and at whatever Natacha thought a handrail was—but I could not find humor in anything.

Agnès sent an email wanting to be sure I understood her branch of the family was deeply upset the story had gone public. Angry phone calls had gone back and forth between various family members. Media coverage had turned into a "spectacle," she explained, and Marcel and Renée would have been displeased with the circus it had become. I would later learn one family member had been the target of the same type of comments that had pained me.

The weight of everyone's anger and disappointment made my knees buckle. Perhaps it had been a naïve belief, but I hoped these letters would stitch Marcel's family back together. The opposite seemed to be happening, and I could not see how this enormous black cloud was not going to cast a dark shadow over our time in Paris.

For an hour, Agnès and I messaged back and forth; my emails were translated into crude French, hers into rough English. Three of her four children would join us for lunch, she wrote. She attached a photo. Arms draped over shoulders like teammates in a rugby scrum, and it looked as if they had forced themselves to stop laughing long enough to snap the photo. Their youngest, Eugénie, was fifteen; their oldest, Jean-Noël, was thirty-five.

"Because of you, we know a page of our history and can tell it to our children," Agnès wrote. "That part of our grandfather's life is, for me, very personal because Marcel barely talked about it. I think he kept his fears, his hunger, and the feeling of missing his family private because he wanted us to keep the memory of a happy man and not of a hard worker. I think he suffered and tried to protect us. Our grandfather was a man of peace."

On Friday morning, Aaron left for one last, grueling shift. My day disappeared in a flurry of last-minute client requests.

Five complete sets of Marcel's letters had been printed onto the highest-quality photographic paper, collated, and placed inside envelopes. The prints captured every tiny wrinkle, crease, fold, stain, and subtle change in color. Despite the quality, I knew copies could never compare to holding the paper Marcel had written on, paper he might have held to his heart or lips, paper that, at one time, held traces of his DNA.

By late afternoon, the guilt of not returning the originals smoldered like kindling about to erupt in fire. The bank would be open another hour, which left enough time to retrieve the originals from the safe-deposit box, which is where I had returned them after Kathy and Dixie's private viewing.

"Don't do it," Aaron responded after I paged him at the hospital. He reminded me I could always send the original letters after the trip if I identified an ideal long-term caretaker. But if I had the originals with me, he feared I would hand the letters to the first person who asked for them.

Aaron then reminded me of a different scenario we had discussed. Since we did not know how the letters ended up at the flea market, we had to consider the possibility they had been stolen. If that was true, I would be entering France possessing stolen World War II memorabilia. The thought of the original letters being confiscated as I passed through customs, of being interrogated in French, or ending up in some legal quagmire made me feel like retching.

"Promise me you won't get them," Aaron said with an exasperated sigh.

"I promise." My head knew not bringing the original letters was the right thing to do. But my heart still believed it was wrong.

By 9:30 Friday evening, my to-do list had been scratched clean. My suitcase and carry-on sat near the front door. Hoover seemed to understand I was leaving; he would not let me out of his sight.

I nestled into the couch with the translations of Marcel's seventeen letters. I had glanced at them while preparing for the open house, but I had not taken the time to read the translations in weeks. As I read each letter, I tried to let Marcel's words of love be a salve to the anger, to the misinformation, to the words of hate. Despite everything that happened during the previous twelve days, despite the unknowns that lay ahead of us, I tried to release everything except the one truth that had always made this project important.

The one truth that made *everything* important: love.

Chapter Thirty-Four

Paris, France

October 2012

Our little apartment was unavailable our first night in Paris. We knew about the scheduling limitation from the outset, so for one night, we reserved a bare-bones hotel room near the apartment. We arrived hours before we could check in, but the hotel's front desk attendant said we were welcome to leave our luggage until our room was ready.

We stepped outside and strolled toward the Eiffel Tower. Aaron had never seen it before, and I enjoyed watching him smile as he gazed skyward, spellbound by its majesty. I had visited Paris briefly in 1992, eight months after I graduated from college. But I had forgotten how intricate the ironwork was, and that in bright sunlight the Tower glowed the color of milk chocolate.

We did not have anything on the afternoon's agenda, so after wandering around the base of the Tower, we claimed a street-side table at a nearby café. Aaron had only studied French for two weeks compared to my three-month study, yet he had a gift for pronunciation that completely eluded me. "*Deux sandwiches de poulet et de l'eau minérale gazeuse, s'il vous plaît*" rolled off his tongue after our waitress asked for our order. I stared at him in astonishment.

After checking in to our room, washing up, and changing out of travel clothes, I turned my laptop on so I could send Agnès an email. She made me promise I would let her know we had arrived safe and sound. Her email had ended with "keesses." The misspelling made her note even sweeter.

Eventually, Aaron and I went back outside and meandered through neighborhood streets. Paris's charm seemed to infuse every cobble, every bentwood café chair, every perfectly twisted neck scarf. The intricate wrought iron adorning the city's elegant white stone buildings reminded me of calligraphy; it was as if some master penman had dipped a steel-point pen into a jar of black ink and decorated every gate and window guard with swirling, scrolling ornamentation.

After watching the Eiffel Tower's evening light show, Aaron and I wandered again until we came across a restaurant with an available outdoor table and a sidewalk menu board that caught both of our fancies. Aaron was drawn to the dishes advertised; I was charmed by the curlicue chalk script.

When our waiter came to take our order, I felt emboldened to put my yet-untested skills to work and order in French.

"*Je voudrais que le—*"

"No, no, Madame," the waiter said as he threw a flat hand in the air. "Order in English. I will have *some* chance of understanding you that way."

Aaron could barely contain his laughter; I wanted to crawl under the table. As the waiter walked away, I decided I would not let his boorishness ruin this moment. Accordion music wafted from the restaurant's interior, the Eiffel Tower's lights twinkled in the distance, and Aaron sat across from me. The evening was perfect.

Je voudrais graver ce moment dans ma mémoire pour toujours.
I would like to remember this moment forever.

For the first three hours I lay in bed, wide-eyed, marking time as the Eiffel Tower's hourly light show reflected off a nearby building: 11:00 p.m. Midnight. 1:00 a.m. When Aaron's snoring grew so loud it hurt my ears, I retrieved a spare blanket from the closet, propped my legs on the luggage rack, and tried to sleep in the desk chair. At 4:00 a.m., I abandoned the thought of sleep entirely, flipped on the desk light, and read the only English-language magazine in the room.

Aaron awoke sometime around 5:00 and mumbled, "Why are you awake?"

I told him his snoring made any attempt to sleep futile, but the truth was more complicated. A brew of excitement and anxiety had made it impossible to calm my mind. Every unknown about meeting Marcel's family—every worry about what might go right or wrong—had caught up with me.

Aaron urged me to sleep, and promised not to make any more noise. He moved to the desk chair, and I slid into the warm bed. As I tumbled into a deep sleep, I calculated how the morning's itinerary could be adjusted. We did not *have* to be anywhere until 11:30.

Fifteen minutes later, I woke to a crunch so loud it was as if someone had crumpled cellophane next my ear. "You have got to be fucking kidding me," I snapped.

"What?" Aaron asked through a mouthful of half-eaten peanuts.

I was wide awake again.

After showering and packing our bags, we checked out of our room and turned our suitcases over to a sleepy bellman.

We ambled past the darkened Tower, crossed over the Seine's ink-black water, climbed the curved steps of the Trocadéro, and sat on the marble steps of the Esplanade. From our elevated vantage point, it appeared as though the enormous Tower stood guard over the city, sprawling and still asleep.

As the sky slowly lightened to baby blue, then as a strip of fiery orange erupted along the horizon, church spires were the first structures to appear from the shadow of night. The city reminded me of a vast classroom, and those spires seemed to be hands volunteering to greet the morning. And as light finally took hold, the frustrations of the sleepless night faded away.

Promptly at 8:30, a crew of rail-thin men hawking miniature Eiffel Towers appeared, followed by busloads of chattering, camera-wielding tourists. Though we knew it had not been true, for nearly two hours it felt as if Aaron and I had had the Eiffel Tower—the entire city of Paris—all to ourselves.

We stopped along the nearby Place du Trocadéro—a semi-circular road ringed with restaurants—for a warm breakfast before meandering to the Arc de Triomphe, then down the Champs-Élysées. All the while, we kept a close eye on the time.

"Where should we wait?" Aaron asked.

I shrugged. It was 11:30. We had returned to the Eiffel Tower and were standing underneath its soaring arches.

"What does she look like?"

"I don't know," I said as I shot Aaron a look letting him know it was pointless to ask additional questions. The previous weekend, when she suggested we meet underneath the Tower, I agreed without asking for more specific information. *Could there be a more perfect place to meet?* I provided a physical description of Aaron and myself, and I assumed she had seen the photo of me that ran with Henry's article.

I scanned the crowd for any woman walking or standing alone. I checked my watch. I took deep breaths to calm my racing heart.

Military police strolled by with rifles held at a low, ready position. Clusters of tourists stared skyward, or stood with noses buried in maps and guidebooks. Others trailed behind tour guides like ducklings following their mother.

I checked my watch again. I took more deep breaths.

Just then, I noticed a woman walking toward us. She had a gentle smile. Her long, shiny hair had a hint of auburn she inherited from her grandmother.

I do not recall if we even formally introduced ourselves, but as Natacha—Nadine's daughter, Suzanne's granddaughter, Marcel's great-granddaughter—walked up to us, I knew we had found each other. She greeted us with kisses and a broad smile. As she inquired about our flight and what sights we had seen that morning, I had the compulsion to reach forward and touch her arm, as if my sleep-addled brain needed confirmation this moment was really happening.

"For you," she said as she held out a mint green bag embellished with a gold Ladurée logo. "A gift from my family. You know Ladurée?"

"No," I apologized.

"The best macarons," she said as she rolled her eyes in delight. Ladurée's world-famous macarons, I would learn, were as much of a cultural icon as the Eiffel Tower itself.

Natacha suggested we head to Place du Trocadéro for lunch, so for the second time in less than six hours, we crossed the Seine, then climbed the steps of the Trocadéro. We claimed a small outdoor table. After ordering lunch, Natacha pulled a large, thick-framed photo out of her shoulder bag. It was Marcel and Renée's wedding portrait, and I imagined Natacha plucking it off her living room wall as she walked out the door to meet us.

The only images of Marcel and Renée I had seen so far were low-resolution scans. This image was large and clear, and I stared at every magnificent detail: Marcel's straight, thin nose, a smile that curled ever-so-slightly more to the left than to the right, straight eyebrows, the arch of a widow's peak.

Natacha's eyes lit up as she told stories about Marcel and Renée, but especially about Marcel. Natacha had been ten when he died, but the warm, familiar way she talked about him made it seem he had always been present. *No; it was if he were still present.* "You have given us so much joy, you must know that," Natacha had written in an email the week before. "Thanks to you, I learned so many things about my family."

She showed additional photos of her grandmother. In each, Suzanne seemed to burst with life. "She was so beautiful," Natacha remarked with pride.

Natacha showed photos of her two boys: Ethan, three, a ginger-haired firebrand, and Nathan, two, an inquisitive prankster with big brown eyes. She passed a snapshot of her fiancé across the table. There were many things to love about him, she said with a dreamy smile; the thing she loved the most were his hairy arms.

Sitting with Natacha was a surreal delight, and an ease existed that made it feel we had known her for years, but I desperately needed one thing: sleep. I attempted to calculate how long I had been awake, but even simple math seemed impossible.

I asked Natacha if she was her family's "advance scout." It took her a moment to process the word "scout," but then she sat ramrod straight, smiled, and with a single confident nod, proclaimed "*Oui!*" without any trace of shame. "They are sitting by the phone, waiting for a full report." I assumed that would be the case, but I had not expected her to be so fiercely honest. I immediately adored her.

The three of us strolled to a *crêperie* on the Esplanade. We stood in almost the exact same spot where we had watched the city wake up as we enjoyed the hot, sweet treats. After taking a handful of photos to remember our precious first meeting, we walked back to the Eiffel Tower and said our goodbyes. As Natacha headed in the opposite direction, my heart began to ache. I missed her already.

Aaron and I walked to the hotel, retrieved our luggage, and checked in to our apartment. Space for the building's elevator had been carved from the center of a seventeenth-century staircase. Without bags, Aaron and I could both squeeze into the coffin-size elevator car. With a suitcase in tow, we had to go up one at a time.

The apartment's living room had a wingback chair and a couch adorned with red gingham pillows. A tray on the coffee table held a handwritten note of welcome and a bottle of white wine. Double doors in the bedroom opened to a small balcony that overlooked a courtyard. The coziness created a delightful space to call home for the next eight days, and the private, secure building provided a shell of invisibility I yearned for.

Aaron sat down and opened the box from Natacha. He peeled back the tissue paper, revealing rainbow rows of flawless Ladurée macarons. I kissed his forehead, then stepped into the bedroom. I was asleep in seconds.

The next morning Aaron and I walked along the Seine, heading to the Cathedral of Notre Dame. Along the way, we passed flower markets, grand statues, elegant buildings, and striped-awning *boulangeries* with rows and rows of glossy pastries. Even lampposts were beautiful, with wrought iron crowns, acanthus leaves, or fat-lipped fish swirling around the base.

Notre Dame's stained glass windows were rich with pattern and seemed to glow with an impossible luminescence. I imagined spending an entire day walking laps around the sanctuary, watching as morning light shifted to afternoon light, allowing each window to glimmer in new and astonishing ways.

The cathedral's *trésors*—gilded platters, jewel-encrusted headpieces, and hand-lettered manuscripts—were housed in a maze of rooms off the nave. On some manuscripts, words had been foiled with gold. On others, lines of intricate Blackletter were decorated with fields of flowers or woven into vines. One particular "Amen" caught my eye because it had been lettered in an astonishing six colors of ink.

After exiting the cathedral, we walked across the plaza in front of Hôtel du Ville—the grand building where Louise watched the Nazi flag raised and where she danced with American soldiers. We walked past the Louvre's glass pyramid, then strolled the length of Jardin des Tuileries.

When we returned to the comfort of our little apartment, we tended to electronics and checked email before going to dinner at a restaurant owned by a chef Aaron had long admired. He would gush about the chef's squid-wrapped ham for weeks.

Our first destination on Wednesday was the Musée d'Orsay, where prints by Toulouse-Lautrec made me recall the afternoon playing hooky at the Milwaukee Art Museum. It seemed impossible TypeCon had only been eleven weeks earlier. After a picnic lunch in Jardin des Tuileries, we viewed room-size Monet landscapes at Musée de l'Orangerie, then walked past a thousand Renaissance paintings at the Louvre.

That evening, back in our apartment, I turned on my laptop and noticed a Facebook message from a member of our Type Tuesday group. My head jerked in surprise; I had never before received a direct message from this type designer.

"I think I found out how those letters got to Minnesota," he wrote. "My friend (along with a friend of hers) picked up those letters on a buying trip in France and brought them back here to sell in their antique shops."

I had not seen or talked with this type designer in the four months since I gave my presentation, so he wouldn't have known I had established contact with Kim, or that she had sent me twelve more letters. But when I read his entire message again I gasped so loud Aaron asked what happened. He wasn't talking about Kim—he was talking about Kim's former business partner.

The woman's most recent Facebook post included a link to Henry's article and announced, "Amazing story: Kim and I bought all these old letters when we were on a buying trip in Paris." Neither she nor Kim knew what the letters said, but they found the penmanship alluring. She claimed to have sold several of Marcel's letters when she had space at Antiques Riverwalk, a now-closed antique mall in Minneapolis. "Somewhere in a box in our garage, I know I have more. Can't wait to find them and send them to their rightful owners."

My jaw dropped. "There are more letters," I whispered in astonishment. It felt as if every cell in my body was about to crackle and explode.

"Will you please ask her if she would consider selling the letters to me?" The type designer suggested she and I connect directly.

Within minutes, the woman and I were messaging back and forth. She lived in Roseville, a city ten or so miles from White Bear Lake. I told her I had been in touch with Kim, and acknowledged I knew the letters had been purchased at a flea market, not, as Henry's article repeated, that they had been brought into the US by a soldier.

She and Kim had bought the letters at the Clignancourt market, she clarified. Clignancourt was the largest and most famous of Paris's flea markets. Once they returned to the states, she and Kim divided Marcel's letters. Kim sold hers at Belle Époque in Stillwater; she sold hers in Minneapolis. As messages flew back and forth, I read each one to Aaron. He seemed as dumbfounded as I was. Once again, it felt as if the Universe was conspiring in the most astonishing way.

When I asked if I could buy the letters from her, she typed back immediately: "Oh geez I wouldn't ask money for them."

The woman had to get back to work and logged off of Facebook. I slumped into the couch. For twenty minutes, I sat in wondrous disbelief. *How many letters did she have? When had they been written? What would they reveal?*

I had not yet checked email—only Facebook—and had promised family I would check email once per day. An email titled "Heuzé Letters" from Agnes waited. Once I opened the email, I realized it was not from Suzanne's daughter, Agnès. It was a different Agnes. This Agnes was a television producer.

"I just got off the phone with Tiffanie who seems open to the idea of being interviewed on camera but she told me you are reluctant to do so. . . . You are the link between the past and the present. This story would be impossible to tell without you."

I told Agnes my expectation was that our meeting would remain private, but in a follow-up email, it sounded as though Agnes was going to try to move forward regardless of my hesitation.

"If there is a single reporter or a single camera-person waiting when we get there, we're turning around and leaving." Aaron's words were firm and forceful. His anger was palpable. I had no doubt he would carry through on that threat.

At dinner, thoughts ping-ponged between Agnes trying to film our meeting and the amazing claim from the woman in Roseville. The divergent thoughts were too much to process, and at one point I caught myself staring far into the distance, oblivious to the restaurant's rattle and hustle. I looked at Aaron and apologized. During the previous days, I had made a conscious effort to be present *with* Aaron. I had been careful not to mention Marcel each time I wondered if he had seen the same sight, or if he had strolled the same street.

Aaron reached out and held my hand.

That night, sleep was as elusive as it had been the first night. For hours, I sat on the couch and churned through the new information: *Could it be true? Could the woman in Roseville really have more letters? What if a news crew waited outside Denise's apartment? What if Aaron tried to drag me away?*

Aaron and I spent Thursday at Versailles touring the palace, then the gardens. On Friday we explored Montmartre, first visiting the massive Basilica, then strolling through Place du Tertre, the bustling square famous for its artists. We meandered the neighborhood, walking past quirky buildings, charming cafés, and an apartment Picasso once rented. Our path led to stairs that descended into Cimetière de Montmartre, one of Paris's famous park-like cemeteries. A cobblestone path decorated with fresh-fallen yellow leaves led past crypts with ornate stained glass windows, scrolled wrought iron, arches, and carved columns. Some family names were incised into stone in ornate Blackletter; others were gilded in gold. Fresh flowers adorned some crypts, while others were covered with moss and ivy and appeared untouched for a century. One crypt included a life-size copper sculpture of a mourner doubled over in grief; the green patina running down the stone seemed to be stains of perpetual tears.

It was late by the time we returned to our little apartment. I logged into email and scanned new messages. Every day, emails from clients arrived, but I did not read them. I did not want to know about the projects that awaited. The only email I opened was from Tiffanie. I read her short message and let out a deflated sigh.

"Marcel isn't coming tomorrow."

In my mind, I began listing all the reasons why his change of plan had to be my fault.

"You can only change the things you have control over," Aaron repeated. It had become his mantra during the previous weeks.

I tried to force a conciliatory smile, but my expression remained as stony as the statues in the Cimetière. I had hoped the family would be as eager to meet me as I was them—but now that Marcel was not going to be there, I had to face the sharp reality that that was untrue.

Aaron retreated to the bedroom and in a few minutes' time, his resonant snore filled our apartment. Seeing Paris's sights had been amazing, yet everything—paintings, palaces, stained glass, gardens, cathedrals, flower markets, monuments—had been viewed through a filter distorted by a thousand unknowns. At times, the week felt as if it were flying by. Other times, each minute felt like an hour. From the elation of learning about the additional letters, to the worry Agnes was still going to try to film our meeting, to the joy of meeting Natacha, to the lingering anxiety about all the still-unanswered questions, the whiplash between the week's emotional highs and lows had been exhausting.

I crawled into bed next to Aaron, curling in tight so I could feel his chest rise and fall. He wrapped his arm around me. He was asleep, so he had no way to know how much I needed that embrace, or how the weight of his arm felt like a tether holding me to his safe ground.

Chapter Thirty-Five

Le Plessis-Robinson, France

October 27, 2012

"You stay," Aaron said in a tone he would use with Hoover. I wanted to go to the outdoor market with him, but he gave me no choice. After eating breakfast, he grabbed his backpack and left so quickly I barely had time to say goodbye.

Ultimately, he was right. I needed time alone to gather my thoughts. I slumped into the apartment's couch and took long, deep breaths. *Who would be there? How bad will the language barrier be? What will I learn?*

I tried to envision the first moments, and practiced a short list of phrases: *Enchantée*. Nice to meet you. *Je m'appelle Carolyn*. My name is Carolyn. *C'est mon mari, Aaron*. This is my husband, Aaron. Yet, as much as I tried to conjure any image of what came next, everything that followed seemed to be hidden behind a thick, mysterious fog.

I ironed my suit, showered, and fixed my hair. I carefully applied makeup and took more deep breaths. As I packed my laptop, envelopes with copies of the letters, and printed samples of the font into my shoulder bag, I could not shake a feeling I was missing something critical while also knowing precisely what that *something* was: Marcel's original letters.

Aaron returned to the apartment at 11:30 with a content smile. It had been a glorious blue-sky morning, he said, and the market had been filled with colorful produce, fragrant cheeses, and fish so fresh they still smelled like the ocean. He unzipped his backpack and extracted oranges, savory lunch pastries, a raspberry pastry for the next morning's breakfast, and bottles of Burgundy—gifts for Denise and Agnès.

At 2:00 Aaron and I caught the Métro and headed to St-Michel Notre-Dame, where we transferred to the RER, a commuter train that ran to Paris's far-flung suburbs. We climbed aboard and claimed seats across from each other, knees nearly touching. As the train lurched forward, I began to feel a tremor. I thought the vibration was coming from the train—then realized the quaking was coming from inside of me. A year's worth of adrenaline, hope, and worry was pulsing through my veins.

To occupy my mind I practiced my phrases: *Enchantée. Je m'appelle Carolyn. C'est mon mari, Aaron.*

As our train crawled through the Port-Royal station, then Denfert-Rochereau, Cité Universitaire, then Gentilly, each stop seemed to take longer than the last. Every acceleration seemed more labored. I cradled my shoulder bag tighter. Aaron leaned forward and squeezed my knee.

How would I ask in French, I wondered, *what the fuck is about to happen?*

Will they show us photos? What will they think of the font? Will Agnes make a last-minute attempt to film our meeting? Please, please, I silently begged as I looked at Aaron, *don't let a producer be there.* I took more deep breaths as the train inched to Laplace, then Arcueil-Cachan. *Five stops to go.*

Drops of rain appeared on the window. First in ones and twos, then they joined to form rivers that zigzagged down the glass. I watched in helpless disbelief. *It had been a cloudless morning!*

As the train headed for the last stop—Robinson—Aaron leaned even farther forward and grasped one of my hands. "Ready?"

As promised, Tiffanie waited near one of the station exits with Louna, her golden retriever, in tow. Tiffanie greeted us with kisses. Louna greeted us with kisses, too. Without delay, we began walking to Denise's apartment. It was only a third of a mile or so, but between the rain and my pointy-toe heels, it felt like miles.

Tiffanie's long blond hair was pulled into a side ponytail. Parisian chic seemed to infuse even a simple combination of jeans, high-heeled boots, and a trench coat with a flipped-up collar. She typed a code into a security box. After a buzz and a click, we stepped inside the lobby of Denise's building. Fifteen minutes earlier, our trip seemed to be taking forever. Now everything was moving too fast. I wanted to stop, take a deep breath, and compose myself, but before I knew it, we were stepping inside Denise's apartment.

Tiffanie's mom, Valentine, and her uncle, Philippe, greeted us with kisses. "*Enchantée,*" I said directly to each of them, self-conscious about my pronunciation.

"May I take your coat?" Philippe said. In perfect English. Aaron and I peeled off our jackets. My wet trousers stuck to my thighs.

"Come in here," Valentine said. She took a couple of steps down the entry hall and gestured for us to enter Denise's living room. "Have a seat."

Valentine offered apologies that neither Eliane nor Marcel would be joining us. I speculated the reasons Valentine provided for their absence were untrue, but I appreciated the gentle way she delivered the news.

Watercolor cityscapes hung on the living room wall. A patterned rug lay over a parquet floor. A collection of ceramic owls sat above the fireplace. A wooden cabinet held books, knickknacks, and what appeared to be an urn. Butter-colored leather chairs and a matching couch were positioned around a long coffee table.

I sat at one end of the couch, Aaron sat in the chair nearest me. I dried my glasses and tried to discreetly determine if anything could be done to rescue my hair; the rain had turned the hairspray to glue. Aaron must have sensed my skyrocketing self-consciousness because he leaned forward and touched my knee.

Half-packed cardboard boxes ringed the room's perimeter. The disarray seemed incongruous with the space's orderliness; it was like a designer dress with an unfinished hem. Aaron and I would soon learn

Philippe was in town to help pack Denise's apartment. Her declining health meant she needed more care—in two months' time, she would move across France to be near Philippe. I was filled with gratitude that Dixie had found Denise when she did; in eight weeks, Denise would be nearly untraceable.

Just then, we noticed Denise herself. She was tiny, silent as a feather, and she had already taken a few steps into the room. Aaron and I jumped to our feet. Denise's alert brown eyes darted between the two of us. Wispy brown hair with auburn highlights ended at the nape of her neck. She reminded me of a bird: a house sparrow, perhaps a finch.

I stepped to Denise and kissed her cheeks. *Enchantée* was not a full enough reflection of the emotions that filled my heart. I regretted not asking Louise to prepare a statement that would have expressed more than "nice to meet you." I wanted to tell Denise it was an immeasurable honor to meet one of Marcel's "little darlings."

"*Enchantée, Madame,*" Denise said. She enunciated every syllable in a way that made the words sound regal. I suddenly no longer cared about my rain-wet pants or my sticky hair. In that moment, nothing else in the world seemed to matter.

"*C'est mon mari,* Aaron," I said as I stepped aside.

Aaron leaned down to kiss her. He touched her carefully, as if she had been made of glass. Later that night, Aaron speculated her petite size might have been a result of malnutrition during the war years.

Valentine gestured for us to sit. Philippe sat on the couch to my left. Tiffanie sat on an ottoman on the far side of the coffee table. Denise sat in the chair at the opposite end of the table. Despite proper posture and a smile that seemed to reveal a younger, stronger version of herself, Denise looked fragile. A camera crew invading this space would have been unimaginable. I was glad I had stood my ground.

Valentine stood next to Denise, arms folded tight over her chest. Valentine was fifty-three years old, five years older than her brother. She was a school administrator, and had spent years as headmistress at a French school in Shanghai. She radiated authority, and despite seeming to welcome us warmly, she was standing guard. As it dawned on me who Valentine was protecting Denise from—*me*—I sat a little straighter and folded my hands in my lap. I suspected Valentine questioned the motives for our visit.

Aaron thanked them for their hospitality and handed Valentine one of the bottles of Burgundy. Aaron explained his nursing background and acknowledged we knew about Denise's Parkinson's. He asked Valentine and Philippe to please tell us if our visit became too much for her. "We'll leave immediately," he promised.

Valentine asked where we were staying, so we told her about our little apartment with the coffin-size elevator. She asked about our week, so we listed the sights we visited. I did not want to spend this precious time talking about Paris, but I understood we needed to pass this interview before we would talk about anything else.

I wanted our meeting to begin on a positive note, so I shared the news about the woman who claimed to have more of Marcel's letters. When Philippe translated the announcement, Denise smiled and her eyes lit up. They wanted to know how it could be true, so I explained how she fit into the winding story.

"Thank you for letting us come here to meet you," I said when the time felt right. I explained I had spent so much time looking at Marcel's letters, but knew little about him other than what I had seen by peeking through a tiny keyhole of time. I told them I would be grateful to hear any story or look at any photo they would be willing to share.

Valentine and Tiffanie retrieved two boxes from the edge of the room and lifted them onto the coffee table. Photo albums filled one box; the other was half full with loose photos and papers. I wanted to dig through the photos in the same way Hoover burrowed through piles of dirt, but I remained still. They looked at images first, then handed over photos they thought we should see. A black-and-white photo of Marcel shucking oysters followed a color Polaroid of him surrounded by grandchildren. A photo of Marcel and Renée on a beach followed a photo of Denise as a young woman embracing her brother. As the minutes passed, Denise, Valentine, Philippe, and Tiffanie began to laugh and smile. Old snapshots began to elicit stories about what had been happening when the photo was taken.

Philippe handed me a black-and-white photo of Marcel holding a bird and a shotgun.

"Is this Berchères?" I pulled the photo close to take in every detail: the stucco wall, the windows flanked by shutters.

Other photos from Berchères-la-Maingot showed the narrow, vertical pieces of glass in the entryway, the steep pitch of the cottage's roof, the brick and stone barn, the tall stone wall along the road. I lingered over each image before passing the photos to Aaron.

They showed us wedding portraits of Suzanne and Claude, Denise and Jacques, Eliane and André. Dresses billowed with tulle. Baskets overflowed with flowers.

"How do you say 'beautiful'?" I asked as I held Denise's wedding portrait.

"*Belle*," Philippe said gently. The word got Denise's attention. A photo album spanned Denise's lap; before looking up, she laid her hand flat across the page as if she wanted to stop time. Jacques had died of a heart attack three years earlier; they had been married fifty-three years.

Philippe showed me a photo from Eliane and André's wedding. A dozen or so people stood on the steps of the city hall. Marcel and Eliane were front and center; one of her gloved hands wrapped through the bend of her father's elbow. Extended family gathered behind them, and Valentine identified who was who. Renée's brother, also named André, stood near the back. He had been sent to work in Germany during the war, too, I would learn. He refused to ever speak of it.

"That is Jacqueline Gommier," Valentine said as she pointed to a woman with short dark hair. "You know her, yes?" I smiled, amazed to be matching a face to another name.

Valentine's face erupted into a smile as she looked at a photo of herself as a young girl with Marcel. They had the same color ice-blue eyes, she said. Marcel had called her "*ma petite fille aux yeux bleus.*"

An hour or so into our visit, I felt Philippe and Valentine—especially Valentine—relax. Perhaps she realized my interest in Marcel was sincere. Perhaps she saw me study the detail in each old photo. Perhaps she finally understood I did not seek anything other than information. Whatever the reason, the change was palpable. She now sat on the floor and warmly handed photos across the coffee table.

Valentine's father, Jacques, and Marcel had a very compatible friend-ship. Their families—Marcel and Renée; Denise, Jacques, Valentine, and Philippe—often vacationed together. "Within fifteen minutes of arriving somewhere new, Marcel would have made friends," Valentine said with quiet wonder. "He'd learn which restaurants to go to, or who to call if he needed something." People in the country did not usually receive Pari-sians warmly, but Marcel's affable nature immediately put people at ease. "People were drawn to him. Know what I mean?"

Yes, I wanted to say. *I know precisely what you mean.*

"Those qualities might have helped in camp," Aaron said. "The ability to get along. To figure out who had connections for supplies or food." Valentine and Philippe nodded. I looked at Aaron, surprised at his insight.

Marcel always stayed current on world news and politics, Valentine added. He felt it was important to be able to talk to *anyone* about *something*.

Their families routinely ate Sunday dinner together. "Anytime Mar-cel learned someone was alone on a Sunday, he invited them to join us," she said before adding a firm, "family or not." I wondered if his need to make sure no one was alone had roots from his time in camp, too.

"He was a nice dresser," I said as I cradled a scallop-edged photo of Marcel in a tailored suit and a fedora.

"Always," Valentine said, full of pride.

Photos of Renée confirmed her elegant beauty. "She was always fash-ionable," Tiffanie stated in admiration. Before the war, she worked in Paris's flagship department store Galeries Lafayette.

I asked what Marcel and Renée were like together. They comple-mented each other, I was told. In public, Marcel was a bright light, and Renée was proud to let him shine. In private, Renée was the center of his world.

"He's so serious," I said as I examined a photo of Marcel seated at a small table, a kitchen table perhaps, surrounded by friends. He scowled at the camera.

"Oh yes." Valentine threw her head back in a laugh. "He took his cards seriously!" I imagined Marcel offering the exaggerated scowl for the camera, then erupting in laughter after the grimace had been committed to film.

The scowl made me realize something: in almost every other photo—which at that point had numbered a hundred or more—Marcel had been smiling. My heart could barely contain the swell of joy. I did not know what scars Marcel might have silently carried from his time in Berlin, but after the war, life had been full. He had laughed. He had been happy. He had been surrounded by love.

Philippe stepped to the bookcase along the far wall and retrieved a small painted case. As he walked back to the couch, he removed the lid and dumped three metal discs into his hand, then passed one to me. I did not know what it was, so I held it flat in my outstretched palm. It was the size of a quarter, though thicker and heavier. It had holes and sharp, precise ridges.

"Marcel made that," Philippe said as Denise, Valentine, Tiffanie, and Aaron looked on.

I looked down, still unsure of what it was. The guess that came to mind was some kind of gear from inside a clock. I swung my hand to show Aaron.

"Oh!" he said. "A threading die."

"Yes," confirmed Philippe with a smile and a nod.

I looked at Philippe, then Aaron. "What does that mean?"

"You take a smooth metal rod; a pipe or something," Aaron said as he pointed to the silver disc, "and you use that to cut grooves to make a threaded rod." I looked close, trying to understand the mechanics of that process.

"Marcel made this at work?" I asked. Philippe nodded.

"After the war?" Philippe nodded again.

"Did he work for a car manufacturer?"

"No," Valentine answered. "A tool and die shop."

"As a turner?"

"Yes, but more than that," she said. "They did custom metal work. Companies would go to them when they needed a specialty replacement part or a one-of-a-kind die. They were the best in the business."

"Moutardier was his boss." Valentine nodded to confirm I understood who she was talking about. Moutardier had been referenced in several letters: the father of four, the friend he picked cigarette butts with, the man who worried about Marcel when he had not heard from him.

"How long did he work there?"

"His entire career," Valentine said, adding the sobering caveat, "except when he was in Germany."

In the weeks before our trip, I had tried to figure out how to ask about the timing of Marcel's departure. The timelines and details of the various labor requisition laws were tangled inside my head, but I did not think the STO law from September 1942—the one that applied to any man between the age of eighteen and fifty—took effect until mid-March 1943. I had never been able to figure out why Marcel had been in Berlin in January. *Unless he had volunteered.* I had considered different turns of phrases, different ways to pose my question, but nothing sounded right. Every question seemed too sharp, too knife-like. Even in the second before I asked whether Marcel might have volunteered, I was unsure which words were going to come out of my mouth.

Valentine's response was immediate and unequivocal. "No. He never would have left Renée and the girls."

That was what I hoped to hear. More than *hoped*—her confidence validated everything I believed. *No matter how hard things might have been in Berchères, Marcel could have provided the fundamental thing he could not provide from far away: protection.*

But the question lingered. *Why had he been there in January?*

Months later, the question of timing still nagged at me. I dug for answers until I came across this paragraph: "Almost half of the 650,000 workers formally required to go to Germany went before the institution of STO in February, 1943 . . . Those compelled to go under the law of September 1942 before February 1943 were mainly workers (the Germans were particularly interested in skilled metallurgists)."

That was what Marcel had been—a skilled metallurgist! And the Germans wanted him sooner rather than later.

His profession, I realized, might have been a blessing and a curse. It was the reason he had been selected to go to Germany, but it also could have been the reason he was sent to Spandau for violating food rules rather than being shipped to an extermination camp. The Germans ultimately might have needed him alive more than they wanted him dead.

The skill that got him sent to Germany, it seemed, might have also saved his life.

I reached into my shoulder bag and took out three thick envelopes that held prints of Marcel's letters. One set was for Denise; the other sets were ultimately for Eliane and Marcel. For nearly twenty minutes they devoured Marcel's words. They occasionally laughed. Sometimes they read passages to each other in French. They, too, observed how often Marcel wrote about his beloved tobacco. I made sure they knew the swastika was backward.

I explained how the twelve additional letters came into my possession, and summarized what I had been told about the letters being at Clignancourt. I asked if they knew how the letters might have ended up in Clignancourt. After a pause, Tiffanie offered one suggestion: she had once heard that undeliverable "dead letters" would sometimes be discarded in bulk by the French postal service.

Valentine, Philippe, and Tiffanie eventually set the letters aside, though Denise continued to read. Her left elbow was propped on the arm of her chair. Her hand cupped the side of her neck, and a gentle smile warmed her face. It was as if the handwritten pages had transported her to a different time and place. I asked Philippe if he would ask Denise whether she recalled seeing any of these letters before. Philippe translated my question. Denise slowly turned to me and shook her head.

We turned our attention back to the last of the photos and papers in the cardboard box. Valentine reached forward with the single known photo taken of Marcel in Germany. In a somber black-and-white portrait, Marcel sat ramrod straight in front of a plain background, shoulder to shoulder next to another man. *Had Marcel resigned himself to the fact he might not make it home? Did he want Renée to have one last photo?* I turned it over, hoping to see a familiar name—Mimile, Bernard, or one of the other men he had mentioned—but the back was blank. I asked whether Marcel kept in touch with other workers after the war. Neither Valentine nor Philippe knew.

Valentine reached forward with a small tan envelope. My head jerked in surprise as I looked at the name and address scrawled across the front: Marcel Heuzé, Lager D4 West S1-21/3, Berlin, Marienfelde. The letter had been written *to* Marcel.

The smudged cancellation stamp showed an eagle clutching a swastika tight in its talons. The year was impossible to decipher. *Did it read February 1945? 1943?* A single piece of paper was folded inside. Valentine nodded permission to take it out. A brief message had been typed in German.

"Do you know what it says?"

Philippe and Valentine glanced at each other, then shrugged. I passed it to Aaron. He carefully set it on the coffee table, not wanting to hold the fragile sheet more than necessary. He puzzled over it, then shrugged, too.

If this letter had been written in February 1945, could it have told Marcel he could go home? It crossed my mind to snap a photo and have the letter translated. But I did not. It felt inappropriate to ask. Yet this mystery letter revealed one thing with absolute certainty: if the family kept this piece of paper for nearly seventy years—a letter no one could read, a letter that might or might not even be important—there was *no way* they would have knowingly let Marcel's precious letters go.

"Lager D4 West was one of the two barracks that housed French workers," I said as I refolded the paper and tucked it inside the envelope. "D4 South was for Russians."

"I remember him mentioning Russians," Valentine said slowly, as if Marcel's remark had been a cobweb in a dusty corner of her memory. "He always felt sorry for them. He said they suffered more than anyone."

The few things the family knew about Marcel's wartime experience were like worn puzzle pieces that could never be reassembled. But, relative silence was unsurprising, particularly for STO workers. Silence could have been the best—perhaps the *only*—way to rejoin a society that regarded deported workers as complicated others: men and women who were neither hero nor victim.

Some French citizens understood STO workers had been pawns sacrificed by their own government. Others considered STO workers willing collaborators whose labor contributed to the war's brutal continuation. Yet others believed they could have, or should have, worked harder to avoid deportation. The absence of any clear or definitive label, it seemed, made it easy for STO workers to become footnotes in the war's history.

In the late 1980s, as Daimler prepared to celebrate its 100th anniversary, their use of wartime forced labor received media attention. After months of skewering press, Daimler donated twenty million deutschemarks to the Jewish Claims Conference for the care of aging concentration camp workers. The donation came with a stipulation: it did not constitute recognition of legal liability. And the donation did not provide for any other category of forced laborers.

In 2000, after years of legal wrangling, a foundation was established to take broad "political and moral responsibility . . . for the wrongs committed in the name of National Socialism." The German government, along with companies including Bayer, DaimlerChrysler, Deutsche Bank, and Volkswagen, donated 4.4 billion euros to pay reparations to *any* surviving forced laborer. For their participation, corporations received immunity from any future legal action.

Wolfgang, I would learn, worked to help many former Daimler-Benz forced laborers find evidence to support their claims.

It was impossible not to feel cynical about the delays, the legal protections, the tax-deductible donations. By the time the foundation was funded, the youngest forced laborers—those who had been teenagers during the war—would have been in their late eighties or nineties. Most, like Marcel, had already died.

I told Valentine, Philippe, and Tiffanie I had been in touch with an archivist at Daimler. When I mentioned Daimler had requested copies of Marcel's letters, Valentine bristled as visibly as if I had raked a wire brush over her arm. Marcel carried feelings of guilt his entire life about his time at Daimler, she said. The notion anyone might have been harmed by anything he did was a burden he had never been able to shed.

"For the rest of his life," she added, "he did not trust Germans."

I had promised Wolfgang I would let him know whether the family would give Daimler copies of Marcel's letters. With this new information, I knew what my email to him would have to say.

"How did they end up with the cottage in Berchères-la-Maingot?" I asked after a few moments of silence. "Was family in the area?"

"No," Valentine said. No one knew how Berchères, specifically, had been chosen, though the location was considered one of the best in the country. The rich farmland provided the possibility of growing food. Food meant the possibility of survival.

Once war was imminent, Renée's aunt Valentine, who lived in New York, sent money so they could buy the cottage. Valentine had been named in honor of that aunt.

"When they arrived in Berchères, they called Renée 'The Parisian,'" Tiffanie said, though I could not determine if the name had been a term of endearment or a label that identified her as an outsider. Renée was the first woman in Berchères to wear pants. At first, I envisioned billowing, high-waist silk trousers immortalized by Katherine Hepburn and Lauren Bacall. But I corrected myself. Renée probably wore pants because of the practical requirements of her dire new responsibilities: growing food, tending animals, procuring supplies, protecting the girls. "She taught sewing lessons to the women in Berchères. In return, they taught her how to care for the animals and tend the garden," Tiffanie said.

Suzanne, Denise, and Eliane, 1939

Renée had to be vigilant about every resource. Cooking oil, which had an official price of fifty francs per liter, sold for twenty times that—1,000 francs—on the black market. That amount equaled a month's salary. When Renée noted the slow disappearance of her cooking oil, she tried to determine where it was going. Or, more accurately, who was stealing it. Late one night she discovered the culprit: a rat. It dipped its tail into the oil, then licked its tail like the outside of a straw. Valentine laughed as she told us the story, but an oil-siphoning rat was the least of Renée's worries.

Once, when food was precariously low, Renée snuck out under the cover of night and stole beans from a neighbor's field. Stealing from a neighbor seemed particularly risky. Being labeled a thief could have made her an outcast, and being an outcast in a small community could have been a death sentence. The morning after her thievery, Renée watched the neighbor's wife march up to her cottage. Her crime, it seemed, had been discovered. Instead, the neighbor's wife invited Renée to help with the upcoming harvest. She would be paid for her labor, the woman said. She would be paid in beans.

At times, Renée and the girls subsisted on nothing more than ruta-bagas and goat milk, two foods, we would learn, Suzanne refused to eat once she was an adult.

One morning, Renée discovered a German soldier inside her barn. She marched out to confront him, interrupting him mid-shave. The thought of Renée confronting the soldier made my heart lurch, but I speculated she did it because confronting him in the barn was a better option than risking a confrontation inside the cottage, in front of the girls. I hoped, for Renée's sake, that facing an enemy with whorls of soap across his face made him appear slightly less terrifying. He had deserted, he apparently explained. He intended to walk back to his family.

On another occasion, Renée and the girls encountered a German soldier while walking through the village. He ordered them to stop. They complied. Lily called him a "dirty Boche." The insult had been said quietly. But he heard it. And he couldn't unhear it.

He lifted his rifle and aimed it at them.

Throughout the afternoon, I wished there had been a way for Denise to participate more easily in our conversation. Valentine or Philippe translated questions about photos, clarified details of stories, or asked about dates or places, but when they told us about the German soldier raising his rifle, I was grateful we were not speaking the same language. I did not want Denise to relive that moment.

Lily was much too young to understand the gravity of her insult, and I imagined Renée pushing Lily behind her body, staring at the German with an expression that combined a resolve to protect her girls while also pleading for their lives. When the soldier realized the insult came from a tiny waif of a girl he lowered his rifle and allowed them to continue on their way. I nearly cried in relief.

The late summer of 1944 was particularly treacherous as the Allies and Germans fought for control of the area. Soldiers from either side could have raided Renée's garden, stolen their goat, kicked down the cottage door. Any night, bombs could have rained down from the sky.

At some point, mid-August I guessed, Germans overran Berchères. Renée and the girls abandoned the cottage and hid in the woods. I was unsurprised to learn that had happened; Marcel had even written, "If sometime you see that it's getting close to home, don't panic, hide what's the most precious, do all you can not to go too far away; you know what I used to tell you when we went to the woods . . . Sometimes it's better to be afraid of the animals for a while in order to save one's skin."

As I pictured Renée huddling with the girls, trying to keep them calm while keeping alert for any sight or sound of danger, I felt immeasurable admiration for her bravery and tenacity.

In one of Tiffanie's earliest emails, she mentioned she believed Denise had—or once had—some of Marcel's letters, so I asked whether she had found any. She shook her head and said they still hoped to find them while they packed up Denise's apartment. I asked whether the letters they thought Denise had might, in fact, be the same ones I had. She did not think so. No one remembered the painted blue and red stripes.

I asked if I could show them the font. As the computer booted up, I handed them pages printed with the lyrics of "La Marseillaise" and explained how Marcel's beautiful swash *M* had inspired the entire project.

It was unclear how much, if anything, they knew about fonts, so I opened the Preview Panel, rotated the laptop so it faced them, and typed in each of their names. As they watched letters combined into words, smiles indicated they finally understood what my "police" project was. As I typed Denise's name, I hoped she could still see her father in these glyphs—despite the thousand tweaks and revisions.

They commented on individual letters, and asked questions about what I intended to do with the font. When I told them I hoped to name the font "Marcel," they were quick to provide their blessing. In fact, they said they would be proud to see it bear his name.

"Did Tiffanie talk with you about custody of the letters?" I asked as I looked at Valentine and Philippe. It was the topic I fretted bringing up the most. But I could not leave without addressing it.

They nodded and concurred that choosing one person in the family to be the designated caretaker was a problem. I expressed my hope that someday Marcel's letters would find a home at some museum or archive in France.

Philippe remarked he could not imagine anyone else going through the trouble of tracking the family down. He knew I had protected Marcel's letters for a decade and assured me copies were enough. Then, in a moment that nearly brought me to tears, Valentine said she *felt* my deep connection to the letters. It was more than that, she clarified; she believed Marcel's letters had found me.

"The letters," Valentine quietly said, "they are yours."

For a few moments—as the enormity of Valentine's statement sank in—I was too stunned to move.

I extracted photos of Kathy, Tom, Dixie, Kim, and Louise from my shoulder bag. I passed the photos around and explained how each person fit into the story. Valentine, in particular, seemed touched to learn an entire team of people cared about Marcel.

"You're meeting with Suzanne's daughters tomorrow, yes?"

I looked at Valentine and nodded. The depth and location of emotional land mines were still unclear, so I did not offer more information.

"When do you fly home?" she inquired.

"Tuesday. The flight is what? 11:30?" Aaron nodded and shrugged, confirming my answer was close enough.

"Do you have plans for Monday?"

"We're going to Les Invalides." My shoulders sank; I was certain I had butchered the pronunciation. Aaron had hoped to see the Army

Museum's vast collection of military artifacts earlier in the week, but we ran out of time. He was delighted when he learned the museum would be open Monday.

"I was going to offer to take you to Berchères on Monday," Valentine said. "If you would be interested," she added.

Had I had heard that correctly? My heart seemed to stop beating as I processed her words: *Berchères . . . Monday . . . Interested?*

"We could drive out Monday morning. It's an hour away, near Chartres." She made sure we understood the cottage was no longer there, and cautioned there might not be much to see.

Images of the land, the forest, the pond, and the cherry trees flashed in my mind.

In Minnesota, it is polite to decline three times when somebody offers to do a favor; everyone knows the steps to this ridiculous, passive-aggressive polka. On this trip, I failed with the language and stumbled with simple things like cheek kisses, so I did not know the appropriate way to answer Valentine. *Should I say "No" to be polite? What if saying "No" once closed the door on her offer?* I could not take that chance. Before I could stop the words from flying out of my mouth I blurted, "Yes, yes, that would be amazing."

"Okay, we'll go on Monday," Valentine said with a nod.

I swiveled and locked eyes with Aaron. I had not consulted whether it would be okay with him, but if need be, I decided I would buy him a plane ticket back to Paris just to tour Les Invalides.

Valentine and Aaron discussed logistics for Monday morning as I listened in disbelief.

We were going to Berchères-la-Maingot.

"We should leave," Aaron whispered to Valentine.

Denise had a gentle smile on her face, but she looked tired. I looked back at Aaron, and offered a nod, grateful for his vigilance. We had been there three and a half hours.

By the time I got my things in order, Denise stood to say goodbye. We kissed cheeks, and for a couple of seconds we locked eyes. "*Merci beaucoup, Madame,"* she said, clear and slow as I clenched my jaw to hold back tears. I wished I had words to express the mountain of gratitude I felt. Seeing photos, hearing stories, and securing confirmation that Marcel and Renée had been deeply loved was beyond what I could express. But as Denise and I looked at each other, I believe she knew.

"À bientôt" was the only thing I knew how to say. I will see you again. Deep down, though, I understood it was probably untrue.

Valentine, Philippe, Tiffanie, and Louna walked us out. Aaron and I said a temporary goodbye to Valentine and Tiffanie, then Philippe drove us to the train station. Philippe would not join us on Monday, but I knew we would remain in touch.

After slumping into facing seats aboard the RER, Aaron and I let out long, simultaneous exhales.

"That . . ." Aaron said, followed by a long pause, "was amazing."

As the train rattled back to the center of Paris, I looked out the window at the bright blue, cloudless sky and realized the day's biggest surprise. It was not hearing stories about Marcel. It was not even seeing photos of him. It was learning about Renée. She was no longer someone who fulfilled Marcel's requests for cigarettes and passed along hugs to his daughters. She was remarkable in her own right: tiny, beautiful, fierce, fearless. Without getting to know and understand who she had been, I realized I would have only ever known half of Marcel.

Chapter Thirty-Six

Villemomble, France
October 28, 2012

We did not have to be anywhere for hours, so for the first time since Aaron and I watched the sunrise from the Esplanade, the two of us were still. "I could get used to this," I said as I wriggled even lower into the apartment's couch. Mugs of coffee and a plate of golden pastries sat on the table between us.

I still felt buoyed from the previous day's visit. In my mind's eye, I could still see photos of Marcel, Renée, and the girls. My ears still echoed with Denise's slow and deliberate enunciation of "*Enchantée, Madame.*" And I could feel the weight of the threading die as if it still lay in my palm.

"Thank you," I said.

"For what?"

"For everything. For your patience." Aaron seemed surprised, so I added, "You've spent a lot of time listening to me talk about another man's love letters."

He squinted and offered a mock scowl. "Yeah, an older man."

By 11:30, we were dressed and ready to leave. The forecast was clear, but I was unwilling to take chances. On the way out the door, I grabbed the apartment's umbrella.

Agnès did not live near a Métro station, so I had prearranged a taxi to drive us to Villemomble, one of Paris's eastern suburbs. A half hour later, as we exited the taxi outside Agnès's tall apartment building, Agnès's son Jean-Noël and his longtime girlfriend, Mereym, claimed us at the curb.

Inside the building, we were directed down a hall where Agnès and Nadine waited. After kisses and introductions, they gestured for us to step into Agnès's living room. A long dining table had been carefully set with wine glasses and scarlet-red stoneware plates. Bowls placed along the table's spine overflowed with sliced peppers, olives, crispy vegetables, and cornichons.

Everyone shuttled through a line to greet us, and I tried to make sense of who was who: Agnès's husband, Michel; Agnès's daughter, Eugénie; Agnès's twenty-two-year-old son, Louis, and his friend, Alexandra; Jean-Noël and Mereym, the two who had claimed us at the curb. Natacha and her boys would arrive later, we were told; they had an obligation with her fiancé's family. Agnès's son Sébastien and Nadine's son Guillaume were absent, too. One worked in St. Tropez, the other in Australia.

Lastly, we met the translator, Sébastien. For some reason, I expected Sébastien to be an old man. But he was a twenty-year-old computer-programming student wearing thick hipster glasses. Sébastien had studied at Iowa State University and spent months in the Minneapolis/St. Paul area. Throughout the afternoon, Aaron and I chuckled whenever Sébastien said something in English with the comically long vowels characteristic of a Midwestern accent.

Agnès held her hands up flat to indicate we should remain precisely where we stood.

"They want to show you something," Sébastien said as Agnès retrieved a thick roll of wallpaper from a desk in the corner of the room. Wide stripes of pink, purple, and blue covered the roll. My mind raced to find any reason Agnès would want to show me pastel wallpaper. I looked to Sébastien. He shrugged.

With Nadine and Michel's assistance, Agnès began to carefully unroll the paper. The treasure it held revealed itself like a sacred scroll.

"*Notre famille*," she said. Our family. The paper's smooth, white back side held hundreds of names and dates. Every name and number had been written by hand in careful, vertical cursive. Ruler-straight lines extended from one generation to the next; the handwritten loops and lines entwined like rows of intricate lace.

By the time the paper was fully unrolled, it extended diagonally across the entire room. The amount of work the scroll represented was astonishing, and they beamed with pride. *This*, I realized, *is what allowed Dixie to find the family.*

Agnès and Nadine had documented six generations of ancestors for Marcel and Renée, which meant eleven generations were mapped on that roll of paper. This was not a family tree. This was an entire forest.

I asked if I could take a photo. When I pointed the camera in Agnès's direction, she stood tall and held one end of the wallpaper roll high in front of her. Agnès was fifty-six, the oldest of Suzanne's four children. Warm brown eyes shone behind wire-rim glasses. Her short hair was strawberry blond.

When I inquired which was the oldest record, Nadine pointed to an Humbert Chevalier who had been born in 1662.

Nadine was three years younger than Agnès. She also wore wire-rim glasses and had short hair, though hers was a rich auburn. Months later, I would receive a giddy email from Nadine punctuated with a dozen exclamation points. She had just found four more generations of relatives, which meant she was able to trace her family back more than 450 years.

As Agnès rerolled the wallpaper, Nadine gestured for us to sit down. A couch had been shoved along one wall to accommodate the long dining table. An armoire, which I presumed held a television, sat along the other wall. A sliding glass door opened to a patio where Agnès carefully tended potted flowers and fresh herbs.

A pewter figurine sat next to my plate. It was a fox, with pointy ears and a cowl of fur that curled around its neck. Its elongated body, designed to be a knife rest, ended in a bushy tail. One leg on Aaron's knife rest was broken. Other animals—a cat, rabbit, deer, dog—had missing parts, too. It appeared Agnès and Nadine set the table with their best and finest, even though their best and finest was chipped and had broken parts. It made me even more honored to be welcomed into their home.

Jean-Noël poured a dash of Crème de Cassis, a blackcurrant liqueur, into glasses followed by white wine. The traditional apéritif was called *Kir*. We lifted our glasses. Aaron and I did not understand the toast, but their broad smiles left no doubt this was a celebration.

Agnès emerged from her galley kitchen with bowls of sauces for the vegetables. As she passed the dishes around the table, Nadine seemed to chide Agnès for the shirt she had on. It was a short-sleeve, off-white knit shirt with thin horizontal stripes. Later, we would learn Agnès had intended to change out of it before we arrived. Agnès looked at Nadine and tugged at a seam as if to say, *this old thing?*

"*C'est Chanel,*" Agnès said. "*Non, non, Yves Saint Laurent,*" she added as she burst into laughter. Agnès twisted her torso, raised her chin, replaced the laugher with a stone-face pose, and pulled her shoulders back as if she had on a couture ball gown. "*C'est Givenchy,*" she proclaimed before bursting into laughter again. I swiveled to look at Nadine. Her whole body jiggled as she tried to hold in laughter. I adored the familiar ease between the sisters.

Despite the language barrier, I was surprised how easy it was to communicate. Like the day I first heard Edith Piaf sing, emotion—love, laughter, joy—transcended language. Charades filled in some of the remaining holes; Sébastien filled in everything else.

As we nibbled on the vegetables, they asked questions: Had we enjoyed Paris? What sights had we seen? Agnès inquired whether we met Denise, Eliane, and Marcel. I confirmed we met Denise. I told them it had been a nice visit. I wanted to exclaim the visit had been amazing, but I was cautious not to say more than necessary.

Through Sébastien, Agnès asked if we had seen many photos. I nodded, but assured her I would be thrilled to see more. She grabbed a thick stack of photos from an end table. She pushed plates aside and began setting them down one by one in rapid fashion: *Mon frère.* My brother. *Ma tante.* My aunt. *Mon oncle.* My uncle. *Ma cousine.* My cousin.

Decades-old images of Agnès or Nadine in Berchères followed images of family gatherings in Paris. Photos of Suzanne, Denise, or Eliane as young girls followed images of them as adults. New and old mingled together as if it were impossible to untangle past from present.

My breath caught when Agnès set down a tiny photo of Suzanne and Denise on a beach. They appeared to be in their late teens, and the smiling duo had their arms wrapped around each other so tight it seemed impossible to rip one from the other. It made the fact their grandchildren had barely heard of each other feel like an even bigger loss.

In another image, taken sometime in the 1970s, Suzanne stood in a kitchen, her mouth open mid-laugh. Her hair was clipped to one side in the style she had worn since she was a girl. Unlike other images, this one was in color. Perhaps it was how the photo developing chemicals discolored over the decades, but Suzanne's hair was not the auburn Natacha described. In this image, her hair was vibrant red. The bright color seemed to match her *joie de vivre*.

The previous day, Valentine said Suzanne died after a "brain attack." During the privacy of dinner, I asked Aaron what that meant. *Was that a stroke? An aneurysm?* He was unsure, but whatever happened happened suddenly, and it devastated the family. Valentine even acknowledged Marcel was never the same after losing Suzanne.

One photo included Marcel's younger brother, Pierre. Pierre had been sent to work in Germany, too. My heart ached at the enormity of that revelation. Three men in their family had been gone during the war: Marcel, Pierre, and Renée's brother, André. Remarkably, all three returned.

After I returned home, I reread Marcel's letters and realized he had mentioned both Pierre and André. In February 1943, Marcel had written he was "waiting for news from Pierre," then, nine months later, he noted he was "looking for permission to go see Pierre." And in May 1944, Marcel had written, "They told us that we could take our leave in Germany. I'll wait a little while and maybe I'll go visit André." But whether Marcel was able to visit his brother or brother-in-law, along with information about where Pierre or André had been, seemed to be lost to history.

Anytime a photo showed the property in Berchères-la-Maingot—even if it only showed a corner of the barn, part of the plum tree, a section of rock wall, or a vine that meandered up the cottage's stucco wall—Agnès pointed to be sure I noticed.

Agnès placed another photo on the table. She set it down carefully, as though she knew it was special. Indeed, it took my breath away. It was as if everyone left the room and the only thing that existed was this precious little black-and-white photo from Berchères-la-Maingot. Suzanne, Marcel, Denise, and the son Marcel were piled together onto one wooden lounge chair on the grassy yard in front of the cottage. Suzanne reclined in the back, her head rested on the lounge chair's long back. She was seventeen or eighteen and wore a short-sleeved, patterned dress. She looked directly at the camera with an expression that combined a smile with a hint of surprise, as if the person who snapped the photo had just called her name. Marcel sat in front of Suzanne, leaning back onto her. He wore a white T-shirt, dark shorts, knee-high socks, and sandals. The tendon on the underside of his knee stood out from his long, thin legs like a bracket. Marcel looked straight ahead. Smooth dark hair swept over the top of his head. One wayward lock fell onto his forehead. Denise, who was fifteen or sixteen, sat in front of Marcel and leaned back so her head rested on his chest. Denise looked at the camera with a smile that revealed utter contentment. Marcel the son, who appeared to be two or so years old, sat on top of the pile, looking down at his sister. His blond hair ruffled in the wind. I marveled at the way their bodies draped together into a jumble of knees and elbows. It seemed impossible one small wooden chair could bear the weight of all that love.

Suzanne in front of cottage in Berchères-la-Maingot, sometime between 1950–1954

As I slowly handed the photo back to Agnès, I couldn't help but wonder: *When Marcel huddled inside a bomb shelter, when his stomach growled with emptiness, when the Daimler factory floor rumbled with machines of war, could he imagine he would live to experience this moment of simple, all-consuming joy?*

I corrected myself. *Maybe I had that backward. Maybe it was precisely the thought of a moment like this that fueled his strength to live.*

Agnès brought out platters with the second course: cured meats, sausages, pâté, and shaved ham rolled into perfect, pencil-like cylinders.

Aaron and I asked questions: What did Eugénie want to do once she was done with school? *Study law, maybe become a doctor.* What were Louis and Alexandra studying? *Bio-chemistry.* The pride Agnès and Michel had for their children was palpable, and they struck me as the kind of parents who would do anything to help their children succeed. But more than anything, it seemed they wanted their children to be happy. Throughout the afternoon, the room filled with laughter as they joked with each other. As they joked with *us*.

The third course was chicken with mustard sauce, fish with lemon sauce, green beans, and French fries. Agnès had told us she would make lunch, but I had not expected a feast. I felt overwhelmed at both the abundance—and the effort—that had gone into preparing this meal.

"Would you like to see the letters?" I asked after dishes had been cleared. Sébastien translated.

"*Oui!* Yes!" Nadine said as she practically bounced out of her chair.

I handed one thick envelope to Nadine, another to Agnès. They slid the prints out of the envelope, wide-eyed and transfixed. The room was silent as everyone watched them leaf through the pages. I had Sébastien explain the envelope held copies of the five letters they had already seen, plus the twelve more that had been in California.

Nadine said she would keep them forever with her genealogy records.

A few moments later, both Nadine and Agnès slipped the pages back into the envelopes, then set the envelopes aside. I looked at the discarded envelopes, then at them, bewildered. *Weren't they thrilled to see these letters? Didn't they want to read what Marcel had written?* I did not want to be rude, so I did not say anything. But, their disinterest was crushing and confusing, especially because when I had Sébastien tell them about the woman in Roseville, they seemed overjoyed to learn about the additional letters.

Weeks later, Agnès would send an emotional email letting me know she finally read Marcel's letters. She had waited until she could read them in private because she did not want her husband or children to see her cry. As soon as I read the email, I understood why she and Nadine set the letters aside. Reading Marcel's words was far more emotional than I could have anticipated. Agnès explained it made her angry to learn how much her grandfather suffered. I choked back tears as I read that she wished she could rewind time; she regretted not asking Marcel to talk about his time in Germany while he was alive.

I inquired whether Eugénie, Louis, and Jean-Noël had learned about STO in history class. Sébastien translated the question, and after a pause, they slowly shook their heads. Eugénie and Louis still did not seem to understand why Marcel had been in Germany, and for a few more minutes they talked among themselves. Sébastien whispered to Aaron and me that he had never heard of STO before either.

Agnès stood up, and a moment later a dinner-plate-size rock landed on the table in front of me. The deep *whump* made me jump. "Berchères," Agnès said. The rock was an off-white of bleached bone with mottled spots of amber, rust, and gray. Faceted planes and razor-sharp edges made it look as though it had just been chipped from a quarry wall.

I looked up. "Berchères," she said again as she gestured to the rock.

We simultaneously turned to Sébastien. They talked, then he explained: "That came from a wall in Berchères." Agnès said something else to Sébastien, and he added, "after the cottage came down." The rock, it turned out, had been part of the wall that extended between the cottage and the garden.

After the war, Marcel, Renée, and the girls had moved back to Montreuil. Marcel returned to work at the tool-making shop; the girls resumed school in the city. But they returned to Berchères on weekends and during summers. As the girls grew, they brought their husbands, then their children, then their grandchildren.

The sale of the land was one of the core issues that created the rift in the family, I had learned before our trip. Not everyone wanted to sell. Yet dividing, or sharing, between multiple generations scattered across the country seemed impossible. Selling seemed an inevitable heartbreak. This chunk of rock—an astonishing artifact to see in this Parisian apartment—seemed to provide a tangible connection to all that had been lost.

"We are going there tomorrow," I announced with restraint. "Valentine is driving." I felt it was only fair to disclose our plans. Agnès bristled as Sébastien translated our announcement. Aaron moved his leg against mine, as if to remind me not to say anything more.

In clipped words, Agnès said something to Sébastien, who translated. "The cottage isn't there. There isn't anything to see." At Agnès's insistence, Sébastien explained one of the things that still hurt: Marcel had planted a tree for each of his grandchildren, and those trees had been chopped down.

I wanted to redirect the conversation to something positive, so I asked if they wanted to see the font. They agreed, though it was still unclear if they knew what they were about to see. While my laptop was booting up, Natacha and her boys burst through the front door. In unison, everyone seemed to warn us her boys were chaos.

A fresh round of greetings went through the room, and within moments, Nathan crawled into Nadine's lap. He clutched a pewter knife-rest figurine in each hand. The animals began to battle. I smiled. *Perhaps Nathan was the reason for the broken legs and missing ears.*

I opened FontLab's Preview Panel and began typing names: Nadine, Agnès, Ethan, Nathan. Natacha pointed out favorite glyphs as I typed. When I said I hoped to name the font "Marcel," she shared the news with her mom and aunt. "They are happy to hear that," Natacha affirmed. Months later, Natacha would send me an email letting me know that between the font and everything her family learned about Marcel from his letters, it was as if I had brought Marcel back to life.

I handed out pages printed with the lyrics of "La Marseillaise." I wanted them to see the swooping *M*, the *ll*, and line after line of the font in use. Nadine drew the sheet of paper near to take a closer look.

The hair on my arms stood on end as I heard her sing the first note. Others joined. By the next line, everyone was singing "La Marseillaise." The chorus filled my ears, filled my heart. I swiveled and looked at Aaron as my hand moved to cover my mouth. I thought of the countless nights those lyrics filled my computer screen, the hours spent detailing individual letters, the rounds and rounds of laser prints still stacked in my office, marked with a red pen where spaces or curves needed yet more attention.

Never had I imagined I would hear Marcel's family sing that anthem. Never had I imagined those words would bring me to tears.

Aux armes, citoyens! To arms, citizens!

Formez vos bataillons! Form your battalions!

Marchons! Marchons! March! March!

Qu'un sang impur Let impure blood

Abreuve nos sillons! Water our furrows!

At the anthem's conclusion, I leaned to my left and gave Nadine a hug. She had no way to know the enormity of that moment.

Agnès retreated to the kitchen and brought out plates piled with cheeses—Camembert, chèvre, Roquefort, Comté—accompanied by bowls of green salads and bread. I had Sébastien inform Agnès that from now on, Aaron and I were going to come over every single Sunday. She seemed confused, then burst into laughter and swung her arms wide as if to say: *you are welcome any time.*

After another hour joking and laughing about tattoos, travel, food, and culture, Agnès emerged from the kitchen with desserts. Not one: four, including an ice cream cake that had eight enormous hubcap-like meringues around the edge. I would have thought it impossible, but within a half hour, our group of fifteen devoured all four.

Nadine began to sing again. Ethan was curled in her lap, and she seemed to be singing just to him. Unlike the boisterous chorus of "La Marseillaise," this lullaby had tender phrasing and a sweet melody. Before long, the room filled again with song. As I looked around, others sat with bodies and arms draped together. The affection in the room was palpable, and as I watched and listened, I tried to commit the scene to memory.

I wanted to stay here forever. But it was time to leave. Aaron and I had been there five and a half hours.

Aaron and I thanked Agnès, Michel, and Nadine for their remarkable generosity. As we kissed and hugged goodbye, I did not know when or if I might see them again, but I had no doubt we would be lifelong friends. And even though I had not heard many stories about Marcel and Renée, the closeness, the joy, and the family's laughter provided as much insight into their legacy as any story they could have shared.

Chapter Thirty-Seven

Berchères-la-Maingot, France

October 29, 2012

Valentine rolled her car to the curb outside the Robinson RER station and offered a friendly wave. Aaron crawled into the passenger seat; I hopped in the back with Tiffanie. As I relaxed into the seat, my heart filled with wonder and gratitude. *This was really happening! We were really going to Berchères-la-Maingot.*

After twists and turns through Robinson, Valentine merged onto the motorway heading southwest. As the trappings of Paris's suburbs gave way to vast open land, Valentine inquired about our visit with Agnès and Nadine. I told her we had a lovely time. I did not disclose that my cheeks still ached from laughing, that Agnès spoiled us with a five-course meal, or that hearing Nadine lead a chorus of "La Marseillaise" had brought me to tears. I did, however, mention that Agnès and Nadine had inquired about Denise's health, and that they were pleased to hear she was well.

The drive to Berchères-la-Maingot was only an hour. At first, we filled time with small talk about culture and travel, but as each mile rolled past, I felt the urgent need to hear more stories about Marcel.

Valentine had been on a ski trip in the Alps when she received a message from Renée imploring her to return home, she quietly stated. That had been twenty years earlier: January 1992. Valentine's eyes remained glued to the motorway, but as she began to tell us about Marcel's death, her voice began to tremble.

Valentine brought a small bag of Marcel's favorite honey-flavored candy to the hospital, she told us. But his body had already started to shut down. An oxygen mask made it impossible for him to enjoy the candy, and Valentine's gift remained unopened on his bedside table.

Marcel died Saturday, January 4, 1992. I nearly remarked that it made my heart happy to hear that in his final hours Marcel had been as comfortable as possible, surrounded by people who loved him. For so long, that ending seemed impossible—and it was an ending fate cruelly withheld from too many. I glanced up at the rearview mirror and noticed tears had started to dribble down Valentine's cheeks; I was glad I had kept the thought to myself.

January 4, 1992 was three weeks before Marcel's eightieth birthday. Five days earlier, he and Renée had marked their fifty-ninth wedding anniversary. The word that came to mind was *lucky*, and I smiled. Marcel, indeed, had been an extraordinarily lucky man.

January 4, 1992 was also nearly thirteen years to the day before Renée's death. Her body would join his in Montreuil's old city cemetery. I did not know if or when I might return to Paris, but I made a silent promise to place flowers on their graves someday.

Two days after Marcel's death—January 6, 1992—I purchased a guidebook to Paris. I know this only because the purchase was scribbled in the margin of a journal I kept back then. One month later, I stood in front of the Eiffel Tower, gazing skyward at its majesty.

It did not occur to me to look for that decades-old journal until long after our return. On the day I read the ink-filled pages, and saw the note about buying the guidebook, I wondered if even then—ten years to the day before I bought Marcel's letters, twenty years before his family would hear about the font based on his writing—some cosmic string was already pulling me toward Marcel.

Valentine exited the A11 northeast of Chartres, driving ever-narrowing roads with familiar ease. As we passed a sign displaying the name of the tiny commune of Saint-Prest, my body jerked and twisted and I tried to steal a second look. *That was it—Saint-Prest!* I smiled, knowing with certainty what I would see when I returned home and looked at Marcel's postcard. He had not addressed the postcard to "Route de *Sr.* Prest." It read "Route de *St.* Prest." The card did not have an address so much as a description of the location: the cottage had been on the road that ran from Berchères-la-Maingot to Saint-Prest.

Valentine wanted to start our visit in the village of Jouy. Jouy had the closest train station to Berchères-la-Maingot, and she wanted us to understand how far the family had to walk or bicycle each time they traveled to and from Paris in the decades before anyone in the family had a car. The best way to appreciate the four-mile distance, she explained, was to retrace their path.

A few hundred feet beyond the train station, Valentine brought the car to a gentle stop. "Sometimes Marcel kept a bicycle in the back," she said as she pointed to a cozy *brasserie.*

I imagined Marcel sweeping his hair over the crown of his head as he stepped inside, greeting friends with a familiar pat on the back. After having a drink, catching up on local news, and smoking a few of his favorite cigarettes—Gauloises unfiltered—I envisioned a jovial goodbye before pedaling away. It was as if the photographic paper that swished back and forth in developing chemicals a year and a quarter earlier had finally come into clear, beautiful view.

After a few quick turns, we were out of Jouy and surrounded by vast open farmland. I had studied satellite images of the area, so I knew what to expect, but the landscape was familiar in a surprising way: these fields, fringed with groves of thick trees, looked remarkably similar to the land that surrounded my childhood home. This landscape, it seemed, was already deep in my bones.

As we crawled through an intersection, I saw a sign: Berchères-la-Maingot, 4.5 km ahead. My heart soared. We passed acre after acre of vibrant green plants, lush and low to the ground. We passed another sign: Berchères-la-Maingot, 3 km ahead.

Back in the 1940s, I guessed, the road had been gravel. Maybe it wasn't even that; perhaps it was dirt. The walk could have been miserable, especially if the road was mud-slicked, or if ruts were frozen hard as cement. Or if the girls were tired and wanted to be carried. Or if Renée and Marcel lugged bags filled with supplies.

Or if darkness was descending.

Or if Germans lurked nearby.

Another sign: this one marked the boundary of Berchères-la-Maingot. I took a deep breath and smiled.

Valentine rolled to a stop next to a large pond. "This is where we used to fish for frogs." I could not help but smile an even bigger smile as I realized this was the pond in the picture postcard where the woman sat along the water's edge. It was also the pond Marcel wanted to return to so he could "tease the little fish a bit in the ferns" with Renée.

As Valentine drove Berchères's narrow lanes, I found the village even more enchanting than I had imagined. Entire buildings were overgrown with thick quilts of ivy. Shutters were painted candy-apple red or rich caramel brown. Ghosts of old painted signs adorned walls and buildings. Tall privacy walls were made of stacked stone or brick. In other walls, round stones protruded beyond a stucco surface that made it appear as if the wall had been made of enormous sheets of plastic bubble wrap.

I smiled as Valentine drove past a building with diamond- and herringbone-patterned brickwork and rows of dark and light brick that looked like Morse code. It was the building pictured on the postcard where villagers stood in the street and stared as if it was the first time they had seen a camera. Shutters no longer framed the windows, and brickwork needed repair, but it was, without a doubt, the same building.

We drove past a grassy wedge of land that was Berchères's central square. Trees framed one end, a henge of boulders framed the other. "Whenever there was a community gathering, it would happen here,"

Valentine explained. My mind filled with images of picnics, kids playing tag, and spirited debates about the price of sheep. I also imagined German soldiers in long, gray-green wool jackets, sucking on cigarettes as they watched the citizens of this quiet little village.

Valentine pulled the car to a stop in front of a large metal gate flanked with stout brick pillars and tall stone walls. "I'll be right back," she said. She unlatched the metal gate with an ease that revealed she had opened it a hundred times before, then walked to a single-level house on the far side of a courtyard. An elderly man slowly pushed open the door, then gave her a long embrace. The man had been friends with Denise since childhood, Tiffanie told us.

Valentine waved for us to come over. They spoke only in French, but I could tell she introduced us as the Americans who had found Marcel's letters. *How many people here still remembered Marcel?* I wondered. *How had the news of the letters reverberated through this little village?* Before we departed, Valentine had Tiffanie take a photo. Valentine told us it would bring Denise immense joy to see a photo of her dear old friend.

"This is where they bought milk," Valentine said as we drove past a farm. I caught a brief glimpse of cows inside a courtyard—the same courtyard, I believed, as the postcard that showed the thick pinwheel of sheep, and the wagons with wheels as tall as a man.

Valentine rolled to a stop in front of burgundy metal gates. "This is where the Gommier family lives. Do you want to meet them?" My breath caught. Mrs. Gommier, I had learned, had been like a second mother—a second grandmother—to the family. She taught Agnès and Nadine how to crochet, and each year they gathered to watch Bastille Day parades on the Gommier family television. I told Valentine I did not want to intrude, and she continued down the road.

A handful of seconds later, Valentine brought the car to an abrupt halt. Between the time she applied the brake and the moment she and Tiffanie jumped out of the car, the two spoke tersely to each other in French. As they walked down the road, Aaron and I tried to figure out what was happening. More accurately, what might be wrong.

"Should we get out?"

"Not yet," Aaron warned.

A moment later, Valentine signaled for us to join them.

"This is new," Tiffanie said as she gestured to a modern house in the final stage of construction.

"This is . . . *it?*" I stammered. Tiffanie nodded.

Unlike the ivy-covered stucco and brick buildings throughout the village, this was a modern, two-story rectangle covered with stained-wood siding. The side of the house that faced the road was devoid of windows. The roof was flat. It was as if an enormous shipping container had been delivered to the edge of this picturesque village and someone decided to move in.

As the shock of seeing the modern house dissipated, Valentine's expression softened, and a gentle smile washed over her face. "When Marcel was here, when he was *in residence*, he would hang a white towel over the wall," she said as she gestured to a stone wall that flanked the road. "It is like when a flag flies over Buckingham Palace indicating the Queen is in residence. It was a sign Marcel was here. Anyone was welcome to stop by." Back then, the wall had been more than eight feet tall and "Berchères-la-Maingot" had been painted across the stones in large white-on-black block letters. If someone arrived from the southeast—from Saint-Prest—this would have been the first property they would have seen.

In one of our first emails, Tiffanie noted Marcel had been the "star of the village." Initially, the statement seemed to reflect an idyllic vision of a great-grandfather she barely knew. But after learning how deeply he had been loved, I now believed her claim with my whole heart. I smiled as I envisioned Marcel flipping a towel over the wall, welcoming anyone for a laugh, a glass of wine, a game of Belotte.

The four of us walked up the driveway. An empty wheelbarrow sat at the ready and construction remnants were scattered around. As Valentine knocked on the front door to see if anyone was home, I asked Tiffanie whether she had heard the towel story before; she had not.

I asked Tiffanie and Valentine to show me where on the property the cottage had been. In unison they pointed to the property's northern corner. The new house had been built in what had been the courtyard between the cottage and the barn.

Months later, Nadine drew a map of the property for me. The day it arrived, I pored over every detail until I could have redrawn it from memory. She marked the locations of the peach and apple trees, the plum tree whose branches held a swing, red and white gooseberry shrubs, mulberry and hawthorn hedges. She noted the location of the outhouse, and a wall that had been overgrown with artichoke flowers and white roses. She identified which part of the barn housed the rabbits and sketched out the locations of Renée's vegetable and herb gardens. Nadine even marked the tree her uncle André, Eliane's husband, preferred to nap under—naps he took at his own risk since Agnès and Nadine were known to ambush him with a water sprinkler.

I did not yet have the map as I stood on the property, but it wouldn't have mattered; the cottage, barn, and gardens had long ago returned to dust. A tangle of trees and waist-high sections of two stone walls were all that remained.

Marcel and Renée's cottage had had two rooms. The main room— which functioned as the kitchen, living, and dining space—held a table with chairs, a wardrobe, a folding bed, and a buffet. A stove and a washbasin sat along one wall. Tile covered the floor. A crucifix hung on the wall.

The second room held a wardrobe, a dresser, and three beds covered with feather-filled comforters.

The cottage did not have running water or electricity until the 1960s.

I was grateful Marcel and Renée had three years to make this plot of land feel like home before Marcel was sent to Germany. It explained his references to the work completed early on: "And what about the little plum trees that we put in at the beginning, will I maybe have the honor of eating some plums this year?"

I asked Nadine once what smells came to mind when she thought of the property. "Grass, hay, mushrooms," she wrote, "and ripe plums."

Most of the ground around the new house had been churned during construction. But as we walked around the far end of the property, Aaron touched my elbow and nodded for me to look down. Atop a small, undisturbed patch of clover sat two dinner-plate-size rocks the color of bleached bone with mottled spots of amber, rust, and gray.

Along with the detailed drawing of the property, Nadine and Agnès sent a handful of additional photos. One idyllic black-and-white photo showed the family gathered around a long table next to the barn. Fresh-cut daisies billowed from a milk pitcher set atop a tablecloth. Marcel and Renée sat next to each other at one end. Denise crouched at the opposite end, near her brother, who had his arms wrapped around an infant Valentine. Agnès, who would have been four, knelt on a wooden chair. Other family members, even some neighbors—including the father of the elderly man we had met minutes earlier—gathered around. I imagined the sound of laughter echoing between the cottage and the barn before carrying over the fields to the far-off woods.

During the previous days, the phrase I repeatedly heard was that the cottage "came down." As I attempted to parse what that meant, I imagined the roof and walls collapsing in a sob of grief after Marcel died, or crumbling after Renée moved to a nursing home in Châtillon. In my mind, it was as if the cottage could not bear to exist without them.

The truth, I learned, was more benign.

Several fierce windstorms blew through France in late 1999. Ten thousand trees were uprooted at Versailles. Windows broke at Notre Dame. Cranes toppled. Roofs were destroyed. And one old two-room cottage in Berchères-la-Maingot *came down.*

I walked to the edge of the property, gazing east and west at fields where Renée stole beans, where planes plummeted to the ground, where parachute silks had been abandoned. I gazed beyond the fields to thick groves of trees and tried to decide which one would have provided the best hiding place for Renée and the girls. I looked south to where the road—now called Rue Albert—bent into the distance. If we walked down the road a short distance, the horizon would reveal the spires of Chartres's famous cathedral.

I took long, deep breaths, filling my lungs with air that seemed both sweet and musty, before swiveling to look at Valentine. She had her arm wrapped tight around Tiffanie's shoulder. She might have been offering warmth, but the embrace reminded me of a graveside hug, a gesture of consolation, like when someone simultaneously celebrates a life, mourns a loss, and says a final goodbye. I understood why losing this land felt like losing a family member. This land sustained them. After the war, it provided a place to heal. A lifetime of memories had been worn into these roads, grew on these trees, echoed off these stones.

I turned and looked at the new house again. Criticizing its modernity had been unfair, I decided. Maybe the foundation incorporated stones from the barn. Maybe traces of laughter still infused the dirt. Maybe the land still yearned to provide and protect. Maybe another family was on the cusp of creating four generations of memories.

As I finished walking the property's perimeter, then as we walked down the drive, I thought of a black-and-white photo I had seen months earlier. It had been taken mid-1945 in Fribourg, Germany. Five uniformed German soldiers stood in a row, feet spread wide, hands clasped above their heads. They were powerless. Leaderless. Defeated.

In the foreground, liberated STO workers walked past the soldiers as if the soldiers were invisible. The man in the lead carried a ragged suitcase. His smile seemed to reveal astonishment he was free. A man following close behind had a hand raised in a wave. An insuppressible smile filled his face.

Some men did not get home for months due to the near-complete annihilation of Germany's infrastructure. Some did not get home until 1946. Once back in France, workers were processed in reception centers where they received a health check, a repatriation card, one thousand francs, and some tobacco.

Did Marcel return before the war's end, as Valentine and Tiffanie believed? Did Daimler release him after the Marienfelde factory was destroyed? Or did Germans hold him as a prisoner as Natacha once suggested? When frustration surged at the still-unanswered questions, I reminded myself those details did not matter. He made it home. *Marcel made it home.*

The only thing about his return we knew for sure was that it was here—on this very piece of land—where they were reunited.

A friend picked Marcel up at the train station, sparing him the long walk to Berchères-la-Maingot. I imagined Renée pacing the courtyard as she waited, listening for any distant engine rumble, looking for any billow of car-blown dust. I imagined the girls perched on the tall stone wall, hair brushed shiny, wearing worn-but-clean dresses, scanning the horizon for the first glimpse of their father.

I imagined honking horns, waving arms, tears of joy. And after Marcel stepped out of his friend's vehicle, I imagined him folding his girls into his long, thin arms, promising to never let go.

But I did not need to close my eyes to imagine it.

They were here.

Marcel and Renée and their precious girls would always, forever, be right here.

Chapter Thirty-Eight

White Bear Lake, Minnesota

January 30, 2014

In the days after our return to White Bear Lake, an exhaustion bigger than what could be blamed on jet lag inhabited my body. My legs and arms felt heavy. I slept twelve hours at a time. Short-term memory was absent. Yet, I understood precisely what was happening. My body had returned to Minnesota; my heart and mind were still in Le Plessis-Robinson, in Villemomble, in Berchères-la-Maingot.

Friends and family were eager to hear about our trip, but other than emailing updates to Kathy, Tom, Dixie, Kim, and Louise, our time in France felt simultaneously too enormous—and too intimate—to share. I needed time to process all I had learned.

One of the few people I wanted to share our experience with was the woman in Roseville. I hoped we might meet so I could welcome her into the circle of people inextricably part of Marcel's story. And so she could give me the letters from her garage.

She told me she would be in touch.

A month later, I reached out to her again. She noted she had been busy and had not found the letters yet. She assured me "they are there."

After 2012 rolled into 2013, I sent another message, hoping that now that the holidays were over she might have time to look for the letters. She responded weeks later, promising she was going to try to find them, but noting again how busy she was.

People in France were eager to know when I expected to hear from her. They were bewildered by her inaction. Louise seemed more impatient than anyone.

Months later, I reached out to her again to let her know Agnès was interested in writing her a letter, a personalized plea. She did not respond, so I asked Kim and our mutual Type Tuesday friend for help and advice. After they mentioned the letters to her, she erupted in anger.

"I am crazy busy," she wrote. "I'm not dodging finding them. For the Heuzé family this is not life and death but a really cool thing for them—kinda like having the luxury of time to play around on Ancestry.com." She seemed incapable of believing the family was heartbroken. ". . . anticipatory? Yes! Eager? Yes! But 'heartbroken'?!" she wrote.

Three days later, a breezy Facebook post said, "Great day in MN to put on your bikini, spray down with some coconut scented Tropicana oil and listen to this!" with a link to a Stan Getz album.

Agnès's letter was returned to France with dates scribbled across the envelope by the post office—dates the woman refused to accept the letter. Meanwhile, Facebook posts showed her at a music festival, a hiking outing, a running club event, and at the White Bear Lake Yacht Club. Anger burned through me, especially when she posted about her interest in genealogy. "I could spend hours on Ancestry.com," she wrote.

A year later—after Valentine informed me Denise's health had declined precipitously, after Louise spent days in intensive care, after Kathy was diagnosed with cancer and in her indomitably cheerful way announced a surgeon had sliced her head open and scooped out part of her brain—I reminded the woman in Roseville time was not unlimited. A tick box indicated she read the message.

After even more time went by, she posted smiling photos from a multi-week vacation to France and Spain.

Perhaps she found the letters right away and decided she did not want to part with them. Perhaps she looked for the letters but could not find them. Perhaps she never looked. Perhaps she never had them. Perhaps she once dreamed of searching for Marcel's family and felt *she* should have been the one to find them. Perhaps she got angry when I reminded her of her promises. *Perhaps, perhaps, perhaps.* I do not know why she lied. But I regretted ever mentioning her name and her promises to the family. I introduced false hope, and I knew too well how cruel hope could be.

As I struggled to salvage something from the situation, I clung to this fact: *if* she told the truth when she claimed she sold some of Marcel's letters at the antique mall in Minneapolis, more letters are out there. *Somewhere.* So I continue to look. Every time I visit an antique store, I ask the clerk if they have handwritten World War II letters. Often they offer an empty shrug. Sometimes they escort me to display cases stacked with military memorabilia: canteens, patches, moth-eaten jackets. Occasionally, they point me to shoeboxes filled with musty cards or letters.

I realize chances are slim I will find them.

But it is impossible to abandon the hope that more of Marcel's letters will someday be found.

In the months after our return, countless emails, messages, and letters went back and forth between me and various family members in France. I provided updates on the font. Sometimes they shared newly dislodged memories about Marcel or Renée. Sometimes one of us wrote just to say hello.

Natacha shared photos of her boys when they lost their front teeth, then when they climbed the Eiffel Tower. Later, she sent a photo of her swollen belly, and a list of names she and her fiancé were considering for their baby boy.

Agnès always ended her emails with "*Mille baisers*." A thousand kisses. The words always made me smile.

In one email, Agnès casually noted she had a nice phone conversation with Eliane. She mentioned it as if it had been as routine as a trip to the grocery store. She did not offer more information, and I did not ask, but

I knew it had been their first conversation in more than seven years, and my heart swelled with joy. I could not recall ever being so happy to read that something had been *nice*.

Soon after, I received a brief email from Eliane. She wanted to be clear that she and Denise believed the letters had been received in Berchères-la-Maingot, and that in "no case were they blocked in Germany." The evidence, she outlined, was the undated, water-stained card that mentioned Claude, Jacques, and a strike. She guessed the card had been written in 1957 or so; she recalled transportation strikes then. Timing made further sense since Suzanne and Claude married in 1955, Denise and Jacques in 1956. And it was the only letter where Marcel called her Eliane rather than by her childhood nickname.

Eliane's conclusion did not surprise me; it was the only scenario that made sense. And I respected her desire to be forthcoming about what she knew about the letters' long journey.

Eliane recalled her mother kept a small stack of letters inside a dresser drawer in Berchères-la-Maingot. But Eliane never read them. "They weren't ours to read," she noted, apparently unaware sections had been written to her and her sisters. "The mystery is how they found their way to the flea market," she added.

"That is the mystery, indeed," I whispered.

One possible scenario was that the letters had been scavenged from the ruins of the cottage after it came down in 1999. Or perhaps the letters had been inside something that had been carted from the rubble, only to be discovered later once the source was no longer known. Timing made it plausible; within three years of the storm, five of Marcel's letters were in my possession.

Another scenario was that the letters had been taken from the cottage years earlier, a possibility Agnès suggested after she remembered hearing the cottage had once been occupied by squatters.

Or maybe the letters were indeed the same ones Denise once had in her possession—the letters Tiffanie looked for but had not found.

But the scenario that seemed most likely was that at some point the letters made their way from Berchères-la-Maingot to Marcel and Renée's home in Montreuil. Perhaps household belongings were purged when Renée moved to a nursing home. Perhaps the letters were still out of sight and weightless in the back of some dresser drawer. Perhaps they had been moved to a hatbox or an old tea tin. Or perhaps Marcel's letters had been pressed flat inside the cover of some book, similar to the home they had for years inside the sketchbook in my closet. Geographic proximity made it plausible; the Clignancourt flea market was less than ten miles from Montreuil. Timing made sense, too. From what I had been able to sort out, Renée had moved to the nursing home less than a year before Kim bought the letters.

But after seeing how the family treasured old photos and other artifacts—the rock, the threading dies, the letter in German no one could read—there was one thing I believed with my whole heart: I did not—*I do not*—believe Marcel's letters had been willfully discarded.

I eventually arrived at a point—and it was a surprising place to end up—where I did not need to know how the letters came to be at the flea market. The fact that his words found their way back to his family was the only thing that mattered. After hearing people say time and time again they believed Marcel's letters found me, I began to wonder if it might—if it *could*—be true. *Could the letters have found me because they needed help finding their way back home?*

I sent formal letters to two venerable institutions in Paris inquiring whether they would like Marcel's letters for their archives. Aaron and I wanted the originals to be in France so anyone in the family could hold them. We also wanted the letters to be protected for reasons even bigger than Marcel: his testimony deserved to be preserved on behalf of all French citizens impacted by forced labor.

I did not hear back from either institution. So for now, Marcel's letters remain in my safe-deposit box. Whenever I go to the bank to drop off my backup hard drive, I slide his letters from their protective sleeve and glance at the familiar loops and lines.

I thank Marcel for the people—for the wonder—he has brought to my life.

And I offer silent assurance to the Marcel Heuzé who died in Ravensbrück; I tell him he has not been forgotten.

One warm evening, eight months after our return, I walked to White Bear Lake, hoping to recall which driveway had had the name "Marcel" written in chalk. I fretted I would be unable to identify the property since the only image I could conjure was of the driveway—and most driveways looked the same. But once I neared the house, I knew it was the one. The homeowner happened to be outside, so I introduced myself and asked if, one year earlier, "Marcel" had been written across her driveway. Her eyes narrowed. My stomach lurched. For a few long seconds I feared I had truly imagined the entire thing.

"Marcel is my son. Do you know him?" I smiled and told her I did not, but over the next half hour, I told her the story of Marcel Heuzé. She listened in wonder, and her eyes filled with tears when I told her he returned home.

Her daughter had written Marcel's name in chalk on the day of his high school graduation party, she explained. She thought other words had been written across the driveway, too. "Class of 2012," or perhaps "Congratulations!"

I believed her, though to this day my mind's eye is blind to anything other than the single word: Marcel.

The following Monday, Hoover's back legs began twisting in an odd way. He avoided the stairs, and Aaron and I guessed he had pinched a nerve. Our veterinarian prescribed an anti-inflammatory medication, but his condition continued to deteriorate. Within days, twisting progressed to buckling. Before long, Hoover was unable to stand. Then he was unable to sit. For the first time in his life, he avoided eye contact. Instead, his brown eyes stared far into the distance. It was as if he knew the sobering prognosis the veterinarian would soon confirm: there was no hope for our precious thirteen-year-old boy.

In Hoover's last hours, Aaron and I lay on the floor next to him, alternately stroking his silken ears and wiping away our own tears. Shortly before the veterinarian arrived, Aaron filled a bowl with vanilla ice cream, then gently held Hoover's head so he could lap up his favorite treat.

The veterinarian shaved his leg, then told us to say our final goodbye. I kissed Hoover's blocky forehead and thanked him for being part of our family. After the veterinarian carried his blanket-covered body to her car, I wanted to crawl into bed, pull the covers over my head, and pretend it wasn't true. But I could not do that. I showered, put on dress clothes, and drove to Laura and Adam's wedding.

Aaron did not go. He *could* not go. He sobbed uncontrollably for hours.

I held my sadness in strict check. I refused to spoil the soaring joy of Laura and Adam's day by telling them what had happened or providing a reason for Aaron's absence. But on the drive home, tears dribbled down my cheeks and my head began to pound. It seemed impossible to process a day filled with loss and love in equal, immeasurable quantities.

In the days and weeks that followed, Aaron and I were like buckets of grief that leaked from a hundred pin-size holes. Our house felt unbearably empty. Every morning, every noon, every evening my heart ached that Hoover was not waiting for our walk.

I begged Aaron to get another dog. He said he was not ready.

It would be another year before we adopted a nine-pound ball of black fuzz with massive retriever paws, and eyes that would turn the color of caramel. It was no coincidence he reminded us of Hoover—our new puppy was Hoover's grandnephew.

Hoover was not replaced—he could never be replaced—but our hearts were refilled. And we were as giddy as any two parents bringing home their second baby.

A year after we returned from Paris, an employee of Seine-et-Marne, a regional department east of Paris, emailed a black-and-white scan of Marcel's birth record. Seine-et-Marne had, in some earlier decade, taken custody of Boissy-le-Châtel's civil archives.

I called Louise, who provided an on-the-fly translation of the record's eighteen lines of swirling script. "In the year nineteen twelve, January 27, before Géas Bienaimé, mayor and civil registrar of the commune Bois-sy-le-Châtel, is . . . Heuzé Marcellus Lucien, age twenty-six . . . to present his new child, male sex, born the previous evening at eleven p.m., through legitimate marriage . . .

"Oh, the French." Louise burst into a fit of giggles. "'Legitimate marriage': that's ridiculous, don't you think?

". . . through legitimate marriage with Rousseau Suzanne Marcelline, age nineteen years . . . declares us to give the first names of Marcel Georges Eugine . . ." The enormous *M* in Marcel's name had loops on each side that swirled like an old-fashioned eye clasp. Official signatures decorated the bottom of the page. Each name included some bold embellishment: a moat-like circle, a curlicue over parallel lines, a smokestack-like plume of loops. I admired the record's regal formality; it was as if the impeccable writing and ceremonial language ennobled the twelve-hour-old Marcel to rise to every grand possibility life presented.

The left margin held two annotations: a record of Marcel and Renée's marriage in 1932, and a record of Marcel's death. Handwritten scribbles of "Montreuil" and "January 4, 1992" followed the rubber-stamp imprint of "*décéde(é) à, le.*" It stung to see Marcel's death had been given no more deference than registering a car or obtaining a dog license. In fact, it seemed downright backward that the beginning of life was recorded with calligraphic fanfare, and the end of a long, love-filled life was no more than a rubber-stamped administrative annotation.

Louise and I chatted for another hour. She had grown even dearer to me, and we met often. Sometimes we talked about long-ago history, other times she was eager to chat about thoroughly modern topics: eyebrow tattoos, purple or blue streaks in hair, the allure of bad boys. Near the end of our call, she made the sound of a kiss and said, "Love you."

I told Louise I loved her, too.

Freely expressing emotion still felt unnatural, but I was making an effort to be more open—more abundant—with affection. Marcel's letters made me want to try.

After our call ended, I stared at Marcel's birth record. For months, I would have given anything for the answer scribbled in this margin. But

I suddenly realized the search itself had made my world rich with unexpected blessings. If I hadn't had to puzzle the pieces together, I wouldn't have met Dixie or Louise. I wouldn't have read the twelve additional letters from Kim. I wouldn't have learned about STO or gotten in touch with Wolfgang. I wouldn't have seen Marcel's photo or learned about Renée's bravery. Aaron and I wouldn't have gone to Paris. I wouldn't have met Natacha under the Eiffel Tower. I wouldn't have had the honor of embracing Denise, meeting four generations of Marcel's family, or walking on the land in Berchères-la-Maingot.

I doubled down on my commitment to finish the font. Weeks, then months, disappeared refining lines and curves. I listened to Edith Piaf and Maurice Chevalier while I designed alternate glyphs and swashes. I tested each glyph, then tweaked it again. I tackled kerning head-on, refusing to let it win our multi-year standoff.

I wanted to add some kind of ornament that would be a testament to Marcel and Renée. After doodling pages of calligraphic loops, one particular swirl caught my eye because the pen strokes overlapped to create a heart shape. I tweaked and refined the swirl until it looked *just so*.

"How are you and Marcel coming along?" people would ask. The question always made me smile because it felt as though they were inquiring about a person—alive and vibrant—not a font defined by thousands of coordinates and lines of computer code.

"Almost done," I promised every time.

A year after returning from Paris, I entered a distribution agreement with P22, a type foundry known for representing high-quality fonts based on art, design, and history. Their curated collection included other fonts based on handwriting, including that of Paul Cézanne, Frank Lloyd Wright, and Timothy Matlack, the man whose lettering adorned the Declaration of Independence. It was a tremendous honor that P22 Type Foundry wanted Marcel to be part of their collection.

On the morning of January 30, 2014, the font's launch was still two weeks away, though only a handful of people knew that. P22's owner scheduled the launch to coincide with Valentine's Day; there seemed no better time to release a font based on words of love.

An email arrived, and as I read it, I drew in a stuttered breath. I blinked and read the short message two more times, as if I needed be sure my brain was not playing some cruel trick. After the third time, I burst into tears. I was alone in my office, but I snapped my hands over my eyes, embarrassed by the flood of emotion the email unleashed.

When I eventually moved my hands, I glanced at a glossy black-and-white photo taped to the top edge of my computer monitor. The small image had been there nearly a year. It had been a sentinel of sorts while I finished the font—a reminder to never give up, to surround myself with love, to believe anything was possible. The photo of Marcel piled on a wooden lounge chair with Suzanne, Denise, and his infant son Marcel took my breath away when I first saw it at Agnès's apartment, and it took my breath away a second time, months later, when a copy arrived in my mailbox. Moments after opening the envelope from Agnès, I taped the photo to my monitor. It had been there ever since.

I wanted to race to our bedroom, shake Aaron awake, and tell him about the email. But he had recently gotten home from a long shift at the hospital and I knew he wanted nothing more than sleep.

I walked to the kitchen and started a fresh pot of coffee. It was the only thing I could think to do. Perhaps I hoped the coffee's bright aroma might allow me to reclaim composure. But as I waited for the coffee to brew, sobs began to flow out of me. Not in ones or twos, in tens and twenties. I folded my arms in front of me and bent forward as waves of tears rolled out.

Fifteen months had passed since the day I stood on the land in Berchères-la-Maingot. During that time, I had experienced frustration, grief, happiness. But none of that had dislodged this degree of emotion. It was as if everything I held in check since the day I learned Marcel lived flowed out in one unstoppable, uncontrollable rush.

"What's going on?" Aaron asked as he pulled on a T-shirt, his eyes adjusting to the bright kitchen light.

I stood up from my folded-over position, wiped away the tears, and shared the news. The email had been from the New York Type Director's Club—an international organization whose sole purpose was to support excellence in typography. The email announced that of the nearly two hundred submissions from twenty-nine countries, P22 Marcel Script had been one of twenty-four winners in their annual type design competition. It was the world's premier type design competition. Fourteen winners were from abroad; ten were from the United States. That was why I had to read the email multiple times before I was certain I was seeing *my* name—*Marcel's* name—on the list.

Judging had been blind. Entries could not reveal the name of the font, the name of the designer, or the font's story. Winners had been chosen solely on artistry and craftsmanship. I did not know how entries were typically formatted, but I wanted to highlight Marcel's beautiful swash *M*, the *p* with the high lead-in stroke, his unusual *ss*. The entry featured the large words "Mighty Mississippi," accompanied by a poem about a long, meandering river.

All those nights and weekends.

All those hours fretting over the tiniest nicks and curves.

All those times I tossed work and started over.

All those years second-guessing and testing.

All that work had been validated in that single email.

I shared the news first with the family in France. Then I told Kathy, Tom, Dixie, and Louise. Then I shared the news with my college Letterform instructor, Professor DeHoff.

In six months' time, an awards ceremony and exhibition opening would take place in New York. Aaron and I would go. It would be his first visit to New York City. We would stay at a hotel one block off of Times Square; I would finally get to see the bustling landmark.

At the awards ceremony and exhibition opening, luminaries in the world of typography—men and women whose work I had admired for years—drank wine and mingled. One person I was delighted to run into was Roger Black, one of the three judges who had critiqued the font nearly two years earlier in Milwaukee. He offered hearty congratulations when he saw the font displayed on the gallery wall.

On the wall, the *l* in Marcel's name entwined with the calligraphic swirl whose pen strokes overlapped to create a heart. I showcased letters *a* through *z*, numerals *1* through *9*, and a phrase from one of Marcel's letters, written first in French, then in English: "*Et toi, mon aimée, c'est toujours mes plus tendres baisers, que cela réserve.*" And for you, my beloved one, I always save my most tender kisses.

Et toi, mon aimée,
c'est toujours mes plus tendres
baisers que cela réserve.

— June 1944 —

And for you,
my beloved one, I always save
my most tender kisses.

No one attending the awards ceremony and exhibition opening could have guessed the emotions that surged through me that evening. Some of what I felt was pride in the award, but most of it was for much larger reasons. An exhibition of winning entries would travel to Canada, England, France, Germany, Hong Kong, Japan, Russia, Spain, South Korea, Taiwan, and Vietnam. In each country, people would learn Marcel's name. They would see his writing. They would read his words of love.

The trip to New York was still months away, though. In that moment—as I stood in the kitchen, wiping the still-streaming tears from my eyes—I chastised myself for getting so emotional about the announcement. It was unlike me. It did not make sense that an award would open a floodgate of tears, and it took months before I fully understood why it happened.

The font had become so much more than a collection of curves, loops, and lines.

It had become a way to immortalize Marcel's love.

It had become a way to honor his life.

It had become a way to keep the middle-of-the-night promise I made that he would not be lost to history.

Marcel's family had been generous to share stories and photos with me, but I understood he was unequivocally only theirs: their father, their grandfather, their great-grandfather.

But this—the font—would forever be *my* Marcel.

About This Book

On the day I decided to have the first letter translated, I could not have guessed the search for answers would become a book. If I had, I would have kept meticulous research notes. Absent that documentation, I have endeavored to faithfully recreate the timeline of events. To do that, I relied on calendar entries, credit card receipts, emails, FedEx delivery slips, letters, phone bills, photographs, project time logs, screen grabs, and social media posts. Events in Paris were recorded in a travel journal.

The first five of Marcel's letters have been printed in their entirety, though minor spelling, capitalization, and punctuation changes have been made. The twelve subsequent letters have been lightly edited to eliminate redundant or unclear passages. A few paragraph breaks have been added to aid readability.

Professor DeHoff's critique comments were taken from actual Letterform class assignments completed in the spring of 1989.

A video recording was made available of one of the 2012 Type Crit sessions.

A few original emails and letters cited incorrect dates or ages; corrections have been made to eliminate confusion. Minor grammar and spelling errors have been corrected.

Where possible, I have asked others to review dialogue to ensure conversations were accurately recounted.

Within the Heuzé family, accounts sometimes differ about Marcel and Renée's wartime experiences. I have attempted to respectfully navigate these differing recollections; any errors made while reconciling these accounts are, of course, mine.

Should any additional information be unearthed about Marcel's time in Germany, about the letters' journey to Clignancourt, or if additional letters are found, I will share that information on my website: www.carolyn-porter.com.

This book is typeset in Adobe Caslon, which was designed by Carol Twombly in 1990, and is based on the letterforms of William Caslon (1693–1766). The cover includes the font Tryst, which was designed by Kosal Sen, and inspired by letterforms of John Baskerville (1706–1775). The book's title, along with the dates at the beginning of each chapter, are typeset in P22 Marcel Script Pro.

Acknowledgments

First and foremost, I want to express my deep gratitude to the Heuzé family. Thank you for sharing Marcel and Renée with me; thank you for trusting me to tell their story. I hope this book honors them by telling a remarkable love story that lasted sixty years, and transcended war and separation.

French privacy laws prohibit the publication of Marcel's letters without explicit approval from Denise and Eliane. My profound gratitude goes to Valentine and Tiffanie for helping facilitate those approvals. And to Agnès, Nadine, and Natacha for answering endless questions, mapping out the Heuzé family tree, sending photos of the cottage and property in Berchères, and for cooking the best five-course meal I ever had.

I am grateful to Aaron, for everything, over and over again.

To Kathy Horton, for being a tireless cheerleader and remarkable friend. *Kathy passed away from glioblastoma sixteen days before the manuscript was submitted to the publisher. She was one of the first people to read draft chapters, and she always asked for updates on the book. Her spirit is irreplaceable, and I know she continues to cheer from beyond.*

To Louise Dillery and Tom Hazen, for giving Marcel a voice.

To Dixie Hansen, for giving Marcel life.

To Kim Salmela, for bringing Marcel's letters to the US and for generously sharing the twelve additional letters in her possession.

To Wolfgang Rabus, for providing information in Daimler's archives and for unwavering diplomacy with my many questions.

To Richard Kegler, Carima El-Behairy and the team at P22 Type Foundry, for helping usher P22 Marcel Script into the world.

L–R: Kathy Horton, Carolyn, Louise Dillery, Dixie Hansen, Tom Hazen

I am also grateful to Jill Swenson and her team at Swenson Book Development, for guidance and advocacy.

To Maxim Brown, my editor at Skyhorse Publishing.

To Katherine Kiger, copyeditor extraordinaire.

To Sharlene Martin of Martin Literary Management.

To Franklin Ennik, for sharing his expertise in chemical censoring.

To Robin Nussbaum, for providing insight on how to talk about the swastika.

To Timothy Eaton, John DuFresne, Susan Hunt, and particularly to Bill DeHoff, professors at UW-Stout for fostering a love of design and typography.

To Craig Eliason and the Twin Cities type community for continual inspiration.

To Mark Simonson for helping with some particularly complicated lines of OpenType code in P22 Marcel Script.

To the friends who sustain me. A special thanks to Jennifer Colletti, who, at the point in time when it looked like I was not going to receive permission to write the book, told me I needed to write this story even if I could never show it to anyone. Thanks to Garnett and Mike Duenow, Laura Davies, and Karen Kendall; and to Michele Tegen and Shari Sterba for never letting me take myself too seriously.

To Kenneth Mouré, PhD, Professor of History at University of Alberta, for pointing out some important edits.

To the Twin Cities Creatives Group for their enthusiastic support of the font; a particular thanks to Amy Kirkpatrick for baking a delicious chocolate *genoise* to celebrate the font's completion.

To Jeannine Ouellette and my beautiful, brilliant, inspiring sisters at the 2014 Elephant Rock Writing Retreat. *Ready, set, jump!*

To classmates and teachers at The Loft Literary Center in Minneapolis.

To Ken Kunkle and Frank Martinez, for legal guidance.

To Hope Dellon, whose initial interest in this story allowed me to broach the topic of a book with the Heuzé family.

To friends and colleagues who were brave enough to read early drafts of the book or of the book proposal: Ally Bishop, Carol Hunter, Kerstin March, Greg Muellerleile. And to others who listened as I figured out how to talk about Marcel's letters.

To my clients, for their patience with my decreased availability during the final months of editing.

And to my parents, for buying the Ken Brown Method Calligraphy Kit.

Endnotes

vii Epigraph: Testimony of Stepan Saika. Billstein, Reinhold; Fings, Karola; Kugler, Anita and Levis, Nicholas. *Working for the Enemy: Ford, General Motors and Forced Labor in Germany during the Second World War.* New York: Berghahn Books, 2000, 171. Reproduced by permission of Berghahn Books, Inc.

CHAPTER ONE

2 *Sprache Französische*: Marcel wrote something that looked more like "Sprache Französiche," which is a slight misspelling of what I believe he intended to write. This phrase also appears on other letters.

CHAPTER TWO

10 *Marienfelde's history as the site of a refugee center*: Marienfelde Refugee Camp Museum, http://www.notaufnahmelager-berlin.de/en/

CHAPTER THREE

19 *"Manufacturing was soon expanded to include the Daimler-Benz Berlin-Marienfelde plant."*: http://en.wikipedia.org/wiki/Panther_tank

20 *L'Écho de Nancy*: http://www.kiosque-lorrain.fr/exhibits/show/echo-de-nancy/un-journal-de-propogande

21 *"Ravensbrück was only fifty miles from Berlin"*: United States Holocaust Memorial Museum, Learn More About the Holocaust, Holocaust Encyclopedia, "Ravensbrück," https://www.ushmm.org/wlc/en/article.php?ModuleId=10005199. Last accessed September 22, 2016.

21 *Ravensbrück had been the Reich's largest concentration camp for women*: United States Holocaust Memorial Museum, "Ravensbrück."

22 *A "special kind of hell"*: Saidel, Rochelle G. *The Jewish Women of Ravensbrück Concentration Camp.* Madison: Terrace Books, 2006. Title of chapter.

22 *Men gassed the women, then burned their bodies*: Saidel. *The Jewish Women of Ravensbrück Concentration Camp*, 20.

22 *I hoped he had only been there minutes, or hours, or days*: Later, I would learn more about Marcel Heuzé's journey: He was arrested March 1943 and spent three months in the Saint-Pierre jail in Marseille. After that, he spent four and a half months in the Compiègne camp in northern France. Sometime around September 1943, Marcel was transferred to Buchenwald, then to Dora, "a labor camp for political prisoners well-known for its hellish conditions." He left Dora in a cattle wagon on April 4, 1945. "First he went to Oslerode (Thuringia), then endured a nine-day trip without food or water to Ravensbrück, where he died April 26, 1945." The camp was liberated four days later. Chalamet, Christophe. From *Revivalism and Social Christianity: The Prophetic Faith of Henri Nick and André Trocmé*. Eugene: Wipf and Stock Publishers, 2013, 167.

22 *Thousands of women and children*: According to the United States Holocaust Memorial Museum, the Germans gassed between 5,000–6,000 prisoners at Ravensbrück. United States Holocaust Memorial Museum, "Ravensbrück."

23 *Many women were raped*: Helm, Sarah. *Ravensbrück: Life and Death in Hitler's Concentration Camp for Women*. New York: Nan A. Talese/Knopf Doubleday, 2014, 624.

25 *Fifty million people died in World War II*: World War II fatality statistics vary, with estimates ranging from 50 million to more than 80 million. Civilian casualties 50 to 55 million. Military casualties 21 to 25 million, including deaths in of 5 million prisoners of war. https://en.wikipedia.org/wiki/World_War_II_Casualties.

25 *Registry of Protestants persecuted for their faith*: "Huguenots of France and Elsewhere: The Site of French Protestant Genealogy." Pastors of the Reformed Church of France. http://huguenots-france.org/english/pastors/pag23.htm#33

Chapter Four

29 *One of my favorite projects from those years*: 1996 annual report for The Nature Conservancy–Minnesota Chapter. Photography by Richard Hamilton Smith. Design by Eaton & Associates Design Company.

30 *The lettering had been completed by a man in Florida*: Hand-lettering by Jack Molloy.

32 *Graphic designer Brian Willson*: http://www.3ip.com; Texas Hero: http://www.3ip.com/texas_hero

41 *The instructor, James*: James Montalbano, http://www.terminaldesign.com/about/

44 *Design professor and type designer Craig Eliason*: https://www.facebook.com/Teeline-Fonts-138571842838257/

Chapter Five

51 *The Germans' tactical superiority*: Chen, C. Peter. "Invasion of France and the Low Countries, 10 May 1940–22 June 1940." World War II database. www.Ww2db.com/battle_spec.php?battle_id=32

51 *Two French Senegalese regiments were decimated in the fields and forests surrounding Berchères-la-Maingot*: Fighting took place in the area between Chartres, Dreux, Châteauneuf-en-Thymerais, Maintenon: "Jean Moulin et le sacrifice du 26e Regiment de Tirailleurs Senegalais" from "l'Empire dans la guerre" incident des 17 et 18 Juin 1940. Collectif des Guelmois site Guelma-France. www.piednoir.net/guelma/chroniques/sacrificesenegalaiseJan07.html. For more information about the 26th Regiment de Tirailleurs Senegalais, read Echenberg, Myron.

Colonial Conscripts: The Tirailleurs Sénégalais in French West Africa, 1857–1960. Portsmouth: Heinemann, 1991, 92–96.

51 *After the armistice was signed . . . Germany exercised all rights of an occupying power*: "Armistice Agreement Between the German High Command of the Armed Forces and French Plenipotentiaries," June 22, 1940. http://avalon.law.yale.edu/wwii/frgearm.asp

51 *Horses and machines were loaded onto trains*: Hélion, Jean. *They Shall Not Have Me: The Capture, Forced Labor, and Escape of a French Prisoner in World War II.* New York: Skyhorse Publishers, 2012, 99.

51 *Thousands of pigs and cows, tons of wheat, twelve million bottles of Champagne*: "Nazi Plunder Leading France to Famine." *Aberdeen Journal.* October 31, 1940, No. 26,782, 6.

52 *"Barely enough to support life"*: Vinen, Richard. *The Unfree French: Life Under the Occupation.* New Haven: Yale University Press, 2006, 218.

52 *Cheese, chicken, soap*: Taylor, Lynne. "The Black Market in Occupied Northern France, 1940–4." *Contemporary European History, Vol. 6.* Cambridge: Cambridge University, July 1997, 154.

52 *Twenty thousand Jews had been transported from France to Germany*: Yad Vashem: The World Holocaust Remembrance Center. The Holocaust in France, "The Deportation of the Jews from France." http://www.yadvashem.org/holocaust/france/deportation from france

52 *"Hunted down" by Vichy's paramilitary force*: Hilberg, Raul. *Perpetrators, Victims, Bystanders: The Jewish Catastrophe 1933–1945.* New York: Harper Collins, 1992, 89.

52 *Only a couple of thousand would survive*: http://www.yadvashem.org/holocaust/france/deportation-from-france

52 *1.8 million French soldiers taken prisoner of war*: Christofferson, Thomas Rodney and Scott, Michael. *France During World War II: From Defeat to Liberation.* Bronx: Fordham University Press, 2006, 32.

52 *1929 Geneva Conventions*: International Committee of the Red Cross. Treaties, State Parties and Commentaries: Convention Relative to the Treatment of Prisoners of War. "Part III: Captivity, Section III: Work of Prisoners of War, Chapter 3: Prohibited Work, Article. 31." Geneva, July 27, 1929. https://ihl-databases.icrc.org/applic/ihl/ihl.nsf/INTRO/305?OpenDocument

52 *Millions of Parisians who fled*: Diamond, Hanna. *Fleeing Hitler, France 1940.* New York and Oxford: Oxford University Press, 2007, 150.

53 *Twenty million working-age men had been transferred*: Billstein, Reinhold; Fings, Karola; Kugler, Anita; Levis, Nicholas. *Working for the Enemy: Ford, General Motors and Forced Labor In Germany During the Second World War.* New York and Oxford: Berghahn Books, 2000, 4.

53 *Initially, German women filled jobs*: Gregor, Neil. *Daimler-Benz in the Third Reich.* New Haven: Yale University Press, 1998, 153.

53 *Acquire new workers "at whatever cost"*: "Fritz Sauckel (Commissioner-General of Manpower) explained the nature of his duties as follows: 'The Führer has charged me with the task of replacing, at whatever cost, the German workers who have been called to the front for the world-wide fight . . . For this purpose he was given the widest powers.'" Fried, John H. E. *The Exploitation of Foreign Labor by Germany.* Montreal: International Labor Office, Studies and Reports, Series C (Employment and Unemployment), No. 25, 1945, 25.

53 *"Deported en masse"*: Billstein, et al. *Working for the Enemy,* 6.

53 *Some were as young as ten years old*: Heer, Hans and Naumann, Klaus, editors. *War of Extermination: The German Military in World War II, 1941–1944.* New York, Berghahn Books, 2000, 139.

53 *Five million workers would be brought into Germany*: Zetterberg, Harriet; Karsten, Thomas L., Lt. USNR; Mathias, James H., Captain JAGD; Meltzer, Bernard D., Lt. (jg) USNR. "The

Slave Labor Program, The Illegal Use of Prisoners of War, and The Special Responsibility of Defendants Sauckel and Speer Therefor." Nuremberg, Germany: International Military Tribunal, 1945-11-11. Ithaca, New York: Cornell University Law Library. Volume 008, Subdivision 15/Forced Labor, 38. Another source cites the figure of seven million workers: Billstein, et al. *Working for the Enemy*, 142. Another source cites the figure of eight million workers: United States Holocaust Memorial Museum. Resources for Academics and Research. Research in Collections. Search the Collections. Bibliographies. "Forced Labor." https://www.ushmm.org/research/research-in-collections/search-the-collections/bibliography/forced-labor Last accessed September 19, 2016

53 *Fewer than 200,000 were there voluntarily*: Zetterberg, et al. "The Slave Labor Program, The Illegal Use of Prisoners of War, and The Special Responsibility of Defendants Sauckel and Speer Therefor," 38.

53 *Relève*: Vinen. *The Unfree French*, 197–199.

53 *Radio broadcasts promised favorable wages, comfortable living conditions, and assured prospective workers that the Germans respected everybody, "be he manual or intellectual worker"*: Fried. *The Exploitation of Foreign Labor by Germany*, 113.; Propaganda Radio Paris broadcast of June 24, 1942. Fried. *The Exploitation of Foreign Labor by Germany*, 201–202.

53 *The Germans agreed to release one French prisoner of war for every three volunteers*: Vinen. *The Unfree French*, 197.

54 *Many of the first French "volunteers" were from the fringes of society*: *Petty criminals*: Vinen. *The Unfree French*, 122; *"The idle"*: Vinen. *The Unfree French*, 266; *Foreigners*: Vinen. *The Unfree French*, 122; *Women who were pregnant by German soldiers*: Vinen. *The Unfree French*, 165; *Or who had no other way to support their children*: Vinen. *The Unfree French*, 164.

54 *Reports even swirled of the Vichy government deporting children on public assistance*: Vinen. *The Unfree French*, 122.

54 *The pretense of voluntary recruitment was abandoned*: Fried. *The Exploitation of Foreign Labor by Germany*, 27.

54 *The first STO provisions*: "Loi du 4 Septembre 1942 Relative à L'Utilisation et à L'Orientation de la Main-D'Oeuvre." *Journal Officiel de la République Française*. 13 Septembre 1942. A 74, N220, page 3122. www.gallica.bnf.fr/ark:/12148/bpt6k9614034k/f2.item

55 *"air of legality"*: Fried. *The Exploitation of Foreign Labor by Germany*, 244.

55 *Prohibited by international law*: Fried. *The Exploitation of Foreign Labor by Germany*, 1.

55 *In a letter Sauckel wrote to Hitler*: 556 PS-43, August 1943. Zetterberg, et al. "The Slave Labor Program, The Illegal Use of Prisoners of War, and The Special Responsibility of Defendants Sauckel and Speer Therefor," 8.

55 *Five months after the September STO law was published, after Sauckel demanded even more French workers, a second law subjected men who were in their early twenties—those who had been born in 1920, 1921, or 1922—to work in Germany for two years in lieu of fulfilling traditional military service*: Loi du 16 Février 1943.

55 *In a later letter to Hitler, Sauckel explained*: 556 PS-55, January 1944. Zetterberg, et al. "The Slave Labor Program, The Illegal Use of Prisoners of War, and The Special Responsibility of Defendants Sauckel and Speer Therefor," 9.

55 *650,000 French civilian workers would be deported*: Other figures range as high as 1,100,000; however, those figures include French prisoners of war who had their status changed (voluntarily or involuntarily) to civilian worker. www.requis-deportes-sto.com

55 *Tens of thousands would not return*: http://www.requis-deportes-sto.com

56 *Had been featured on television*: "Minnesota Original" via TPT/Twin Cities Public Television: http://www.mnoriginal.org/artist/chank-diesel/

56 *One designer's font was even the basis of Facebook's iconic f*: "Klavika" designed by Eric Olson, https://processtypefoundry.com/fonts/klavika/ Per the website "Fonts in Use" (http://fontsinuse.com/uses/9/the-social-network): "The Facebook logo is a judicious modification of Eric Olson's Klavika, with tighter spacing, some wider lettershapes, and a taming of Klavika's very distinctive 'k.'"

56 *Sixteenth-century ornamented capitals*: University of Minnesota's Bell Museum collection. Ornamented capitals, curated by Bill Moran of Hamilton Type Museum. *Bell Museum*: http://www.bellmuseum.umn.edu. *Hamilton Type Museum*: http://woodtype.org

CHAPTER SIX

60 *Some camps had functions other than extermination*: United States Holocaust Memorial Museum. Online Holocaust Encyclopedia: "Concentration Camp System in Depth." www.ushmm.org/wlc/en/article.php?ModuleId=10007387. Accessed September 29, 2016.

60 *Or were specifically for Communists, Roma, or Spanish refugees*: *Communists*: "In the earliest years of the Third Reich, various central, regional, and local authorities in Germany established concentration camps to detain political opponents of the regime, including German communists . . ." Ibid; *Roma*: News Wire. "Hollande acknowledges France's role in interning thousands of Roma during WWII." *France 24*. October 29, 2016. http://m.france24.com/en/20161029-france-hollande-acknowledges-internment-thousands-roma-during-wwii; *Spanish refugees*: Gurs Internment camp in Pyrénées-Atlantique: http://gurs.free.fr

60 *I was surprised to learn that camps in Germany had opened as early as 1933, camps existed in Norway and Finland, nearly eighty camps existed inside France, and 170 camps were located in Berlin*: *1933*: United States Holocaust Memorial Museum. Holocaust Encyclopedia. "Concentration Camps, 1933–1939." http://www.ushmm.org/wlc/en/article.php?ModuleId=10005263. Accessed September 26, 2016.; *Norway and Finland*: JewishGen. http://www.jewishgen.org/Forgotten Camps/Camps/MainCampsEng.html; *Nearly eighty camps existed inside France*: Jewish Virtual Library. http://www.jewishvirtuallibrary.org/jsource/Holocaust/cclist.html#fran; *170 camps were located in Berlin*: Wachsmann, Nikolaus. *KL: A History of the Nazi Concentration Camps*. New York: Farrar, Straus and Giroux, 2015, 36.

60 *Some were outposts with a "handful of prisoners"*: Wachsmann. *KL: A History of the Nazi Concentration Camps*, 36.

60 *More than forty thousand camps, ghettos, and detention sites existed*: United States Holocaust Memorial Museum. "Encyclopedia of Camps and Ghettos, 1933–1945." Publications. www.ushmm.org/research/publications/encyclopedia-camps-ghettos. Accessed September 1, 2016.

61 *A hierarchy existed among prisoners . . . groups considered "subhuman" by the Germans*: Billstein, et al. *Working for the Enemy*, 142–144.

61 *Western European workers received higher wages for their work, and in some cases, additional food*: *Higher wages*: Fried. *The Exploitation of Foreign Labor by Germany*, 107–134.; *Additional food*: Hopman, Barbara; Spoerer, Mark; Weitz, Birgit; Brüninghaus, Beate. *Zwangsarbeit bei Daimler-Benz (Forced Labor at Daimler-Benz)*. Stuttgart: Franz Steiner Verlag, 1994, 204.

61 *The right to unlimited correspondence*: Vinen. *The Unfree French*, 291.

61 *But I kept digging, and eventually found a description within a massive encyclopedia of camps*: Megargee, Geoffrey P., Editor. *Encyclopedia of Camps and Ghettos, 1933–1945. Volume 1: Early Camps, Youth Camps, and Concentration Camps and Subcamps Under the SS-Business Administration Main Office (WVHA)*. Bloomington: Indiana University Press, 2009, 1277–1278.

62 *"This evening I was reading about the corporations that used forced labor: Daimler, Bayer, Krupp"*: Statement on Bayer's website: History I.G. Farbenindustrie AG (1925–1945). "Production requirements grew steadily, yet more and more employees were drafted into military service. For this reason, foreign and forced laborers from the occupied countries of Europe were brought to work in Leverkusen, Dormagen, Elberfeld and Uerdingen—and throughout the German industry as a whole—to maintain output levels." http://www.bayer.com/en/1925-1945.aspx; *Krupp*: Banerjee, Subhabrata Bobby. *Corporate Social Responsibility: The Good, the Bad and the Ugly*. Cheltenham: Edward Elgar, 2007, 61.

62 *Average life span of a forced laborer was three and a half months*: Friedman, Karen. "Big Business and the Holocaust." *Dimensions: A Journal of Holocaust Studies*. Vol. 13, No. 2.

63 *It was BMW, Siemens, Volkswagen, Porsche, Audi, and Kodak*: *BMW*: Govan, Fiona. "BMW Dynasty Breaks Silence Over Nazi Past." *The Telegraph*. September 29, 2011. http://www.telegraph.co.uk/history/world-war-two/8796157/BMW-dynasty-breaks-silence-over-Nazi-past.html; *Siemens*: Statement on Siemens's website: "The National Socialist Economy and the War Years (1933–1945)." www.siemens.com/history/en/history/1933_1945_the_national_socialist_economy_and_the_war_years.htm; *Volkswagen*: Volkswagen website: Place of Remembrance of Forced Labor in the Volkswagen Factory. *Forced Labor in the Third Reich: An Introduction*. Volkswagen AG, 2013. www.volkswagenag.com/content/vwcorp/content/en/the_group/history/remembrance.html; *Porsche*: Klawitter, Nils. "Porsche's Past: The Dark Pre-History of the World's Favorite Sports Car." *Der Spiegel*. October 1, 2009. www.spiegel.de/international/germany/porsche-s-past-the-dark-pre-history-of-the-world-s-favorite-sports-car-a-652371.html; *Audi*: "Audi Comes Clean About its Nazi Past." *Deutsche Welle*. May 26, 2014. www.dw.com/p/1C7E2; *Kodak*: Friedman, John S. "Kodak's Nazi Connections." *The Nation*. March 8, 2001. www.thenation.com/article/kodaks-nazi-connections

63 *It was Hugo Boss, who used forced labor to sew German uniforms*: In 2011, Hugo Boss financed the study of the company's wartime collaboration. The result of their research is published in *Hugo Boss, 1924–1945. The History of a Clothing Factory During the Weimar Republic and Third Reich*. www.group.hugoboss.com/en/group/about-hugo-boss/history

63 *It even included Ford's German division, Fordwerke*: Billstein, et al. *Working for the Enemy*.

63 *Any justice in his execution was too late for the thousands of forced laborers who died working for I.G. Farben, or for starving Siemens workers . . . or for Daimler workers executed after they "hesitated to obey a work command"*: *I.G. Farben workers*: United States Holocaust Memorial Museum. Learn About the Holocaust. The Holocaust: A Learning Site for Students, "Forced Labor." https://www.ushmm.org/outreach/en/article.php?ModuleId=10007732; *Siemens workers*: Helm. *Ravensbrück: Life and Death in Hitler's Concentration Camp for Women*, 463; *Daimler workers*: Bellon, Bernard P. *Mercedes in Peace and War: German Automobile Workers, 1903–1945*. New York: Columbia University Press, 1990, 246.

Chapter Seven

70 *Seven hundred now called it home*: EHESS (L'École des Hautes Études en Sciences Sociales). http://cassini.ehess.fr/cassini/fr/html/fiche.php?select_resultat=34118. Figures are a combined total of Berchères-Saint-Germain and Berchères-la-Maingot.

70 *On the first, which had been mailed in 1903*: The postcard included the stamp "The Sower," issued in 1903.

72 *One baby was crucified*: Account by Raymond J. Murphy, a twenty-year-old 2d Lt, U.S.A.C., and American B-17 navigator. E&E Report No. 866 filed on August 15 after Murphy had been rescued by the French Resistance and flown to England. Harris, Shane. "The Massacre

at Oradour-sur-Glane: An American lawyer finds new evidence about one of World War II's most notorious war crimes, seven decades after D-Day." *Foreign Policy.* June 5, 2014. http://foreignpolicy.com/2014/06/05/the-massacre-at-oradour-sur-glane/

72 *Only one woman survived*: Oradour-sur-Glane Memorial Center, www.oradour.org

LETTER THREE

75 *"His house has started the process to release him as a father of four children"*: "A concession was offered to French workers when, on 16 October 1943, Fritz Sauckel informed Pierre Laval, head of the Vichy Government, that Germany would not demand further French manpower for Germany in 1943; 'from now on, certain Frenchmen working in Germany will have an opportunity of being replaced, man by man, in German factories and concerns on the principle that the total number of French workers in Germany remains the same.' Men over 45 and fathers of four children were to be 'methodically' replaced by 'younger men.'" Fried. *The Exploitation of Foreign Labor by Germany*, 198.

CHAPTER EIGHT

77 *The passages about traveling to Eisenach . . . were surprising*: The Eisenach labor camp (a subcamp of Buchenwald) was for BMW workers. As such, it was plausible that Marcel knew someone who had been sent to the Eisenach labor Camp. Eisenach is 220+ miles from Berlin, which would make sense since he noted he had to leave at 6:30 to arrive by 12:30. Ferencz, Benjamin B. *Less Than Slaves: Jewish Forced Labor and the Quest for Compensation.* Bloomington: Indiana University Press, 1979, 199.

77 *Coded messages were sometimes hidden in benign-sounding phrases*: http://www.6thcorps combatengineers.com/engforum/index.php?showtopic=3770

81 *Then, as now, Daimler-Benz built Mercedes cars*: The first Mercedes-Benz brand name vehicles were produced in 1926, following the merger of Karl Benz's and Gottlieb Daimler's companies into the Daimler-Benz company. Today, Mercedes cars are produced by Daimler AG.

81 *"No other motor company did so much for the Third Reich"*: Bellon. *Mercedes in Peace and War*, 232–233.

81 *"Would be provided with sufficient business with army contracts from the War Ministry for . . . years"*: Bellon. *Mercedes in Peace and War*, 222.

81 *At least five workers had been executed*: Bellon. *Mercedes in Peace and War*, 237–238.

82 *One thousand workers had been ordered from the Ravensbrück and Sachsenhausen camps to work at Daimler's Genshagen factory*: Bellon. *Mercedes in Peace and War*, 242.

82 *"The worst human rights violations happened in Poland"*: Bellon. *Mercedes in Peace and War*, 246–248.

82 *The Daimler representative handpicked the workers he wanted*: Bellon. *Mercedes in Peace and War*, 245–246.

82 *Text from Daimler website*: Daimler, Tradition, "Company History: Daimler-Benz in the Nazi Era (1933–1945)." https://www.daimler.com/company/tradition/company-history/1933-1945.html. Reprinted with permission.

83 *The image was of the Riedmühle labor camp, not Marienfelde*: Image on Daimler's website as of September 22, 2013.

84 *"Years ago I purchased a small collection of handwritten letters."*: The letter to Wolfgang actually said "Back in 2004 or so," which was my best recollection at the time. The change has been made to eliminate confusion. Edits have been made throughout to reduce the overall length.

Chapter Nine

88 *He attached a black-and-white image of two expressionless men standing at long machines*: The photo is labeled "Ndl. Landau Dreherei."

89 *Swastika inside a gear*: That was the symbol for the German Labor Front, the National Socialist trade union organization that replaced the various trade unions after Adolf Hitler's rise to power. Ley, Robert. *Organisationsbuch der NSDAP,* 3 Auflage. München. 1937, 229 and Plate 25.

89 *International Tracing Service*: www.its-arolsen.org

90 *Offenses committed by the men transferred to Spandau*: Strafanstalt Berlin-Spandau, Document No. 11303723#1 (1.2.2.1/0001-0189/0156/0037) International Tracing Service Archives

91 *"Punishable acts" . . . were exempt from judicial review*: Fried. *The Exploitation of Foreign Labor by Germany*, 191.

91 *"On a spree"*: I believe the use of the word "spree" in this context referred to a night of drinking. That is based on the use of "spree" in this book: Hélion, Jean. *They Shall Not Have Me: The Capture, Forced Labor, and Escape of a French Prisoner in World War II.* New York: Skyhorse Publishing, 2012, 215.

91 *Work contracts were extended by the length of the prison term*: Fried. *The Exploitation of Foreign Labor by Germany*, 89.

91 *I would read an account of one French prisoner in Sachsenhausen "battered to death for taking two carrots from a sheep pen," and another account of a Frenchman executed after a German's sandwich went missing*: Two carrots: Wachsmann. *KL: A History of the Nazi Concentration Camps*, 211; Sandwich: Wachsmann. *KL: A History of the Nazi Concentration Camps*, 486.

91 *Its bricks were ground to dust, then buried*: Goda, Norman J.W. *Tales from Spandau: Nazi Criminals and the Cold War.* New York: Cambridge University Press, 2007, 272.

91 *They pooled money to buy food and help others "get on their feet"*: Hopman, et al. *Zwangsarbeit bei Daimler-Benz (Forced Labor at Daimler-Benz)*, 200.

Chapter Ten

102 *Text of the chapter Wolfgang provided*: Hopman, et al. *Zwangsarbeit bei Daimler-Benz (Forced Labor at Daimler-Benz)*, 193–210.

102 *The part of the factory that made tanks and military vans*: Information provided by Wolfgang Rabus, Mercedes-Benz Classic, Archive, in an email dated September 28, 2015.

102 *It was also the same part of the factory, I would eventually learn, where Marcel worked*: The postcard Marcel mailed January 18, 1943, has "Werk 40" in the return address. "Werk" translates to "plant" or "workshop."

104 *Hunger haunted the barracks*: Wachsmann. *KL: A History of the Nazi Concentration Camps*, 211.

105 *Wedding rings were sometimes traded for bread*: Poulard, Elie. *A French Slave in Nazi Germany: A Testimony.* Notre Dame: Notre Dame Press, 2016, 35.

105 *"Employers are only permitted to issue these clothes when absolutely necessary"*: Fried. *The Exploitation of Foreign Labor by Germany*, 102.

106 *"For the use of the clothes, the worker must pay a fee, which is to be deducted from his wages," read an order by the Reich Director for Clothing and Related Industries*: Fried. *The Exploitation of Foreign Labor by Germany*, 101–102.

106 *For East Workers, companies like Daimler paid the SS "for the privilege of using the camp inmates"*: Ferencz. *Less Than Slaves: Jewish Forced Labor and the Quest for Compensation*, 24.

106 *Any mistake was a pretext for a fine*: Histoire d'une Période Noire; Conditions de vie Des Déportés du Travail. http://www.requis-deportes-sto.com/index.php/histoire/19431945/conditions-de-vie

106 *Deductions were made for lodging and food, and up to 30 percent of a worker's wage might be withheld*: Deductions: Fried. *The Exploitation of Foreign Labor by Germany*, 129–130; *Wages withheld*: Fried. *The Exploitation of Foreign Labor by Germany*, 118–123.

106 *East Workers were also not allowed to join French and German workers inside air-raid shelters*: Vinen. *The Unfree French*, 310.

107 *Charity could be "suicidal"*: Wachsmann. *KL: A History of the Nazi Concentration Camps*, 497.

107 *Men stood little chance of evading STO*: Vinen. *The Unfree French*, 253.

107 *German officials "would enter French factories and choose workers"*: Fried. *The Exploitation of Foreign Labor by Germany*, 35.

107 *French police ruthlessly enforced summons*: Vinen. *The Unfree French*, 253.

107 *"If he could not be found, a relative was conscripted in his place or his family was deprived of its ration cards"*: Fried. *The Exploitation of Foreign Labor by Germany*, 35.

107 *Five years in prison and a fine of up to thirty thousand francs*: "Loi du 4 Septembre 1942 Relative à L'Utilisation et à L'Orientation de la Main-D'Oeuvre." *Journal Officiel de la République Française*. 13 Septembre 1942. A 74, N220, page 3122.

107 *Radio broadcasts warned that the family members of those who evaded STO might face reprisal*: Vinen. *The Unfree French*, 275.

108 *"STO was a one-way ticket"*: Vinen. *The Unfree French*, 254.

108 *"'contracts' extended . . . for the duration of the war"*: Fried. *The Exploitation of Foreign Labor by Germany*, 88.

108 *Any foreigner leaving or entering Reich territory needed a police-issued visa*: Fried. *The Exploitation of Foreign Labor by Germany*, 145.

108 *The tattered clothes covering Marcel's back might have been painted with a red acetone X*: Pantouvaki, Sofia. "Typology and Symbolism in Prisoners' Concentration Camp Clothing during World War II." PDF report posted on Academia.edu. April, 2010.

108 *Bounties were paid for the arrest of fugitives*: Hélion. *They Shall Not Have Me*, 400.

108 *Breaches of labor contracts could be punished by "hard labor, imprisonment or fine, and even, in serious cases, by the death sentence"*: Fried. *The Exploitation of Foreign Labor by Germany*, 81.

109 *The chapter Wolfgang provided on Daimler-Marienfelde listed the results of several aerial bombing raids*: Hopman, et al. *Zwangsarbeit bei Daimler-Benz (Forced Labor at Daimler-Benz)*, 210.

110 *During the first years of the war, strategic bombing raids of Germany and occupied Europe were conducted by the Royal Air Force*: Davis, Richard G. *Bombing The European Axis Powers: A Historical Digest of the Combined Bomber Offensive, 1939–1945*. Maxwell Air Force Base: Air University Press, 2006, 49.

110 *By February 1944, Berlin had seen sixteen major raids*: Royal Air Force, www.raf.mod.uk/history/rafhistorytimeline1943.cfm

110 *The US Eighth and Fifteenth Air Forces joined the RAF in targeting aircraft factories and airfields across Germany*: Davis. *Bombing the European Axis Powers*, 274.

110 *In the first week of March, the Eighth Air Force launched three major attacks on Berlin*: Davis. *Bombing the European Axis Powers*, 274.

110 *A 125-mile-long column of 730 heavy bombers*: Davis. *Bombing the European Axis Powers*, 303.

110 *US Library of Congress Archive*: U.S. Library of Congress Prints & Photographs Reading Room. Image Reproduction Number: LC-USZ62-59134 "Aerial photo of strategic bombing

by 8th USAF, World War II – panther tank plant at Berlin-Marienfelde," http://www.loc. gov/pictures/item/2003653035/

111 *From what I had been able to sort out, eighty-three of those B-17s targeted Daimler's Marienfelde factory*: Eighth Air Force Historical Society, Mission 524. www.8thafhs.org/combat1944b. htm

111 *"Eighth [Air Force] experiences"*: Carter, Kit C. and Mueller, Robert. *U.S. Army Air Forces in World War II: Combat Chronology 1941–1945*. Washington DC: Center for Air Force History, 1991, 458. http://www.afhso.af.mil/shared/media/document/AFD-100525-035.pdf

111 *On February 3, more than one thousand B-17 bombers*: Eighth Air Force Historical Society, Mission 817. www.8thafhs.org/combat1944b.htm;

111 *Dropped more than two thousand tons of explosives*: Davis. *Bombing the European Axis Powers*, 519.

111 *Fires raged for days*: Association Berliner Schlosses EV: War Damage 1945 and Demolition 1950. http://berliner-schloss.de/en/palace-history/war-destruction-and-demolition/

112 *On March 24, 1945, one hundred and fifty B-17s*: Second Bombardment Association: http://www.2ndbombgroup.org/2ndBombGroup2.htm.

112 *Damage made it "impossible for production to resume"*: Per Daimler's website, after the aerial attack of March 24, "The Marienfelde plant is so heavily damaged by an air raid that it is impossible for production to resume." https://mercedes-benz-publicarchive.com/marsPublic/en/instance/ko/24-March-1945.xhtml?oid=4910219. Archive No. 2002DIG90, 2002DIG91, 2002DIG92

CHAPTER ELEVEN

122 *Why would a Dutchman mail a letter to Sweden emblazoned with the colors of the French flag?*: The flag of the Netherlands also includes blue and red, though I did not make that association at the time.

122 *Within minutes I found a detailed report online about chemical censoring*: Ennik, Franklin. "Secret Writing and Chemical Censoring of the Mails by the German Postal Authority." Netherlands Philatelists of California, 40 Year Anniversary Booklet, 2010.

124 *The US government monitored mail for hidden messages during the war, too*: Macrakis, Kristie. *Seduced by Secrets: Inside the Stasi's Spy-Tech World*. New York: Cambridge University Press, 2008, 218.

CHAPTER FOURTEEN

137 *I found a breadcrumb: a link to an eight-year-old magazine article*: Skjong, Ingrid. "In Person" *Mpls. St. Paul Magazine*. February 2004, page 72.

137 *Furniture and interior design company*: http://www.kimsalmela.com/

CHAPTER FIFTEEN

155 *"Dear Denise"*: The original letter included the line, "I am a graphic designer and *over the last eight years* I have been designing a font . . ." I was embarrassed to admit to Denise I had been working on the font for ten years; "eight years" has been removed to eliminate confusion. The original letter also said, "I understand [Marcel] lived to be *eighty*." His age has been corrected to seventy-nine to eliminate confusion. Edits have been made throughout to reduce the overall length.

CHAPTER TWENTY-ONE

186 *Dixie searched permutations of the name I found*: Dixie pieced together information from www.WorldVitalRecords.com, www.MyHeritage.com, and www.CopainsdAvant.linternaute.com.

CHAPTER TWENTY-FOUR

205 *Fish-shaped pencil loops ran along the bottom of the first page and continued on the top of the second*: The page order is unusual in that the letter goes from the front page to the interior right, to the interior left, then to the back. For ease of understanding, I have shown the text as it was intended to be read, not in the order it appears.

CHAPTER TWENTY-FIVE

208 *"Sully the sidewalk"*: Hélion. *They Shall Not Have Me*, 204.

208 *French workers had been ordered to bring specific items with them. . . . They had been forewarned that opportunities to acquire clothes or shoes in Germany would be limited*: Fried. *The Exploitation of Foreign Labor by Germany*, 100–101.

210 *Pens were sometimes confiscated*: Hélion. *They Shall Not Have Me*, 112. Refers to French prisoners of war.

210 *In some camps, ink was forbidden*: Hélion. *They Shall Not Have Me*, 149.

LETTER NINE

213 *"The only thing is, it's going to take at least a month before you get it"*: Wages were transferred through a central government system, which regulated exchange rates and disbursement schedules. The Germans encouraged workers to send money home as a way to limit goods consumed inside Germany (leaving more goods available for Germans). "The policy was, secondly, intended to have a favorable psychological effect, because it gave the worker the feeling that by his work and sacrifice he was able to take care of his family." Fried. *The Exploitation of Foreign Labor by Germany*, 159–166.

CHAPTER TWENTY-SIX

215 *Three times per week, "special trains" transported workers from Paris*: Fried. *The Exploitation of Foreign Labor by Germany*, 262.

215 *As the trains departed, the men often sang "La Marseillaise"*: Vinen. *The Unfree French*, 97

215 *"Strict precautions were taken to prevent them from escaping during the journey"*: Fried. *The Exploitation of Foreign Labor by Germany*, 41.

215 *Prisoners were not allowed to complain*: Hélion. *They Shall Not Have Me*, 310–312.

215 *Rotten vegetables and kitchen waste*: Wachsmann. *KL: A History of the Nazi Concentration Camps*, 211.

CHAPTER TWENTY-SEVEN

222 *Some people even pushed elderly relatives in baby carriages or wheelbarrows*: Diamond. *Fleeing Hitler: France 1940*, 6. Book uses the word "pram."

223 *Radios and bicycles were confiscated*: Poznanski, Renée. *Jews in France During World War II*. Hanover and London: University Press of New England in Association with the United States Holocaust Memorial Museum, 2001, 206–207.

223 *Jews were prohibited from using cafés, markets, theaters, libraries, and public parks*: Marrus, Michael R. and Paxton, Robert O. *Vichy France and the Jews*. New York: Schocken Books, 1983, 238.

CHAPTER TWENTY-EIGHT

228 *Two months before Marcel wrote that letter*: Birtle, Andrew J. "Sicily: The US Army Campaigns of World War II." U.S. Army Center of Military History, Publication 72–16.

228 *At one point, an especially cruel rumor swirled that Paris had been burned down and all relatives of men working in Germany had been shot*: Vinen. *The Unfree French*, 310.

CHAPTER THIRTY

234 *Promises of furloughs after six or twelve months of satisfactory work had been dangled in front of French workers as a way to encourage compliance*: Fried. *The Exploitation of Foreign Labor by Germany*, 144.

234 *5 to 10 percent of Frenchmen returned to Germany*: Vinen. *The Unfree French*, 284.

234 *Leaves were canceled because the Germans were unwilling to lose their workers*: Fried. *The Exploitation of Foreign Labor by Germany*, 148.

234 *Leaves were promised, but made logistically impossible by a "maze of regulations" and complex train schedules*: Fried. *The Exploitation of Foreign Labor by Germany*, 147–148.

LETTER SIXTEEN

236 Despite handwriting that clearly reads "8 mai 1944," one historian of France has questioned whether this letter might have been unintentionally misdated (perhaps due to distraction or fatigue). He noted, "The comments about operations and the landing and being on their way to Paris all make it sound as if this was written after the June 6 [Normandy] landings."

LETTER SEVENTEEN

237 *"She is beautiful like the day in her beautiful white outfit"*: I speculate Marcel is referring to a photo of Suzanne in a First Communion dress.

CHAPTER THIRTY-TWO

248 *Allen fought in the Battle of the Bulge, was awarded a Bronze Star for clearing a minefield while under enemy fire*: *Battle of the Bulge*: Allen arrived at the front line on December 13, 1944 as part of the 303rd Engineering Battalion of the 78th Infantry Division. The Battle of the Bulge began three days later when the German offensive began. Allen was part of the 1st Army under General Parker. They were the most northern division of the 1st. When the Bulge came, they were cut off from the 1st and for a short while he was with the 9th Army. *Bronze Star*: This was awarded for his efforts securing the Schwammenauel Dam on the Roer River.

CHAPTER THIRTY-THREE

251 *A newspaper in Brittany had run an article about Marcel's letters, Henry explained*: Chélin, Marina. "Lettres. Expédiées des États-Unis 70 ans après." *Le Télégramme*, Monday, October 8, 2012, Issue No. 20.923, page 40. http://www.letelegramme.fr/ig/generales/france-monde/france/lettres-expediees-des-etats-unis-70-ans-apres-08-10-2012-1864044.php

255 *Henry's article*: Samuel, Henry. "Wartime Letters of French Father in Nazi Labour Camp Resurface." Paris: *The Telegraph*, October 11, 2012. http://www.telegraph.co.uk/history/world-war-two/9594356/Wartime-letters-of-French-father-in-Nazi-labour-camp-resurface.html

Chapter Thirty-Five

275 *Aaron speculated her petite size might have been a result of malnutrition during the war years*: Taylor, Lynne. "The Black Market in Occupied Northern France, 1940-4." *Contemporary European History, Volume 6.* Cambridge: Cambridge University, July 1997.

280 *The timelines and details of the various labor requisition laws were tangled inside my head, but I did not think the STO law from September 1942—the one that applied to any man between the age of eighteen and fifty—took effect until mid-March 1943*: In actuality, I was confusing the request of the first law with the timing of the second law. The law of September 4, 1943, was implemented to meet Sauckel's unfilled initial demand for 250,000 workers (implemented first as the *Relève*). Sauckel's second request for workers was made in January 1944, with workers to be dispatched by mid-March; this was Law of February 16, 1943 that specifically applied to men born in 1920, 1921 and 1922.

280 *"(the Germans were particularly interested in skilled metallurgists)"*: Vinen. *The Unfree French*, 198.

283 *A society that regarded deported workers as complicated others*: Vinen. *The Unfree French*, 361–366 and Poulard. *A French Slave in Nazi Germany*, 128–132.

283 *Daimler donated twenty million deutschemarks . . . it did not constitute recognition of legal liability*: Billstein, et al. *Working for the Enemy*, 236–237.

283 *A foundation was established*: The Foundation Remembrance, Responsibility and Future, http://www.stiftung-evz.de/eng/the-foundation.html

284 *Immunity from any future legal action*: Law on the Creation of a Foundation "Remembrance, Responsibility and Future," Section 16: "Exclusion from Claims." http://www.stiftung-evz.de/eng/the-foundation/law.html

284 *Tax-deductible donations*: Deutsche Welle staff (th). "German Fund Ends Payments to Nazi-Era Forced Laborers." *Deutsche Welle.* June 11, 2007. www.dw.com/p/AqRb

284 *The location was considered one of the best in the country*: Vinen. *The Unfree French*, 348.

285 *Cooking oil, which had an official price of fifty francs per liter, sold for twenty times that—1,000 francs—on the black market*: Lambin, J.-M. *Histoire, Géographie, Initiation Économique, 3e.* Paris: Hachette Education, 1993, 99.

285 *That amount equaled a month's salary*: Lambin. *Histoire, Géographie, Initiation Économique, 3e*, 99.

287 *The late summer of 1944 . . . Allies and Germans fought for control of the area*: After heavy fighting in and around the city, Chartres was liberated on 18 August 1944, by the US 5th Infantry and the 7th Armored Divisions of the 3rd US Army.

Chapter Thirty-Seven

304 *"Sometimes Marcel kept a bicycle in the back," she said as she pointed to a cozy brasserie*: http://www.lauberge-de-la-gare.sitew.com

309 *Several fierce windstorms blew through France in late 1999*: EQE Summary Report. "The European Storms Lothar and Martin, December 26–28, 1999." Paris and London: EQE International, LTD. http://www.absconsulting.com/resources/Catastrophe_Reports/Lothar-Martin%20Report.pdf

310 *I thought of a black-and-white photo I had seen months earlier*: "Retour des Déportés à la Libération." www.requis-deportes-sto.com/index.php/images-darchives/camps/category/2-camps

310 *Some did not get home until 1946*: Vinen. *The Unfree French*, 364.

310 *Reception centers*: Histoire d'une Période Noire; La Liberation des Camps et le Retour. http://www.requis-deportes-sto.com/index.php/histoire/19431945/liberation-des-camps

CHAPTER THIRTY-EIGHT

312 *Social media posts by or direct messages from the woman in Roseville*: "*they are there*": December 4, 2012; *Less busy once the holidays were over*: January 11, 2013; *The woman did not respond*: March 15, 2013; "*kinda like having the luxury of time to play around on Ancestry.com*": June 13, 2013; "*Three days later*": June 16, 2013; *Music festival*: May 26, 2013; *Hiking*: July 11, 2013; *Running club*: June 13, 2013; *White Bear Yacht Club*: June 28, 2013; "*I could spend hours on Ancestry. com*": August 30, 2014; *Time was not unlimited*: September 2014; *Posts from France and Spain*: December 2014–January 2015.

319 *Handwritten scribbles of . . . "January 4, 1992"*: The handwritten notation was written as "4-1-92." It has been spelled out to eliminate confusion.

320 *I entered a distribution agreement with P22*: P22 Type Foundry, www.p22.com/p22

320 *Timothy Matlack, the man whose lettering adorned the Declaration of Independence*: Coelho, Chris. *Timothy Matlack, Scribe of the Declaration of Independence*. Jefferson: McFarland, 2013.

322 *P22 Marcel Script had been one of twenty-four winners in their annual type design competition*: Press announcement of New York Type Director's Club 2014 award: https://www.tdc.org/competitionwriteup/tdc-typeface-design-winners-2014/